A Treasure Hunting Text

RAM BOOKS

Ram Publications
Hal Dawson, Editor

Ghost Town Treasures: Ruins, Relics and Riches
How to find and explore ghost towns; instructions for searching abandoned buildings and other deserted locations to discover buried or hidden items of value.

Real Gold in Those Golden Years
Prescription for happier, more satisfying life for older men and women through metal detecting hobby, which is ideally suited to their lifestyle.

Let's Talk Treasure Hunting
The ultimate "how-to" book of treasure hunting — with or without a metal detector; describes all kinds of treasures and tells how to find them.

The New Successful Coin Hunting
The world's most authoritative guide to finding valuable coins, totally rewritten to include instructions for 21st Century detectors.

Treasure Recovery from Sand and Sea
Step-by-step instructions for reaching the "blanket of wealth" beneath sands nearby and under the world's waters, totally rewritten for the 90's.

Modern Metal Detectors
Comprehensive guide to all types of metal detectors; designed to increase understanding and expertise about all aspects of these electronic marvels.

Gold Panning is Easy
Excellent new field guide shows the beginner exactly how to find and pan gold; follow these instructions and perform as well as any professional.

Treasure Hunting Pays Off
A basic introduction to all facets of treasure hunting...the equipment, targets and terminology; totally revised for 21st Century detectors.

Buried Treasures You Can Find
Complete field guide for finding treasure; includes state-by-state listing of thousands of sites where treasure is believed to exist.

Treasure from British Waters
One of Great Britain's best known detector hobbyists tells how and where to find treasure in the waters of England and the Balearic Islands.

New World Shipwrecks: 1492-1825
Guidebook to treasure locates more than 4,000 authenticated shipwrecks; tells exactly how to locate a sunken vessel and what to do after it is found.

Sunken Treasure: How to Find It
One of the world's foremost underwater salvors shares a lifetime's experience in locating and recovering treasure from deep beneath the sea.

True Treasure Tales -- Gar Starrett Adventures

The Secret of John Murrell's Vault
The Missing Nez Perce Gold

Revised

Modern
Metal
Detectors

Charles L. Garrett

ISBN 0-915920-75-1
Library of Congress Catalog Card No. 91-61218
Modern Metal Detectors
Second Edition.
© Copyright 1998
Charles Garrett

Third Edition, Tenth Printing, March 2008

Book and cover design by Mel Climer

For FREE listing of treasure hunting books write

Ram Publishing Company

P.O. Box 38649   •   Dallas, TX 75238

To my wife, Eleanor, and our children...

By CHARLES GARRETT

Treasure Hunting Texts
  Modern Metal Detectors
  Treasure Recovery from Sand and Sea
  The New Successful Coin Hunting
  Treasure Hunting Pays Off
  Treasure Hunting Secrets

  With Roy Lagal
  Modern Treasure Hunting
  Modern Electronic Prospecting

True Treasure Tales
  The Secret of John Murrell's Vault
  The Missing Nez Perce Gold

Security Planning Manuals
  Effective Security Screening
  School Security Screening

Garrett Guides
  An Introduction to Metal Detectors
  You Can Find Wealth on the Beach
  You Can Find Wealth in the Surf
  Metal Detectors Can Help You Find Coins
  Find More Treasure with the Right Metal Detector
  Money Caches Are Waiting to be Found
  You Can Avoid Detector Problems
  Use the Super Sniper to Find More Treasure

Contents

III. Computerized Detectors

IV. Selecting a Detector and Accessories

V. Using a Detector

About the Author

The name of Charles Garrett ranks high on any list of those men and women who have pioneered the development and use of metal detectors...whether for discovery of treasure...for security...or, for any other reason. The Garrett name is even more directly associated with the term *Modern Metal Detectors* and the use of computerized microprocessor controls on a detector. His company was granted the first U.S. patent for use of a computer chip in a detector and his Grand Master Hunter CX (Computer Express) and Ultra GTA (Graphic Target Analyzer™) detectors have blazed an amazing trail which all other detector manufacturers are now seeking to follow.

Charles Garrett did not set out to become a leading manufacturer of metal detection equipment. He prepared himself well, however, to become one of the world's foremost treasure hunters. Since boyhood he has been enthralled with stories of hidden wealth...tales which brought excitement to his semi-rural youth in the Piney Woods of Deep East Texas. Throughout his life he has continually sought to learn all that he could about techniques and equipment for treasure hunting.

Young Charles' initial interest in outdoor adventure occurred at about the age of 12 when he discovered his first "cache"...old *National Geographic* magazines in the attic of his aunt's home. Stories such as the amazing discovery of King Tut's tomb kindled a fire that burns to this day. The young man made a wish that someday he might write about his own adventures in God's great outdoors.

After graduation from Lufkin High School and service in the U.S. Navy during the Korean conflict, he earned a degree in electrical engineering from Lamar University in Beaumont and began his business career in Dallas with Texas Instruments and Teledyne Geotech.

Scarcely more than a quarter century ago, then, Mr. Garrett was a young electrical engineer deeply engrossed in development of systems and equipment required by America's fledgling space effort. In devoting himself to his lifetime hobby of treasure hunting, however, he also designed and built metal detectors in his spare time. Because his detectors were obviously more effective than any available commercially, they became popular with fellow treasure hunters for whom he was soon making them. This avocation became a career when he founded Garrett Electronics to produce his inventions.

Today, the name Garrett stands as a synonym for the treasure hunting metal detector. Mr. Garrett himself is known as the *Grand Master Hunter,* also the name of his company's first computerized instrument, described as "the finest metal detector ever manufactured."

Along the way, Mr. Garrett has become recognized as an unofficial spokesman for the hobby of treasure hunting and the metal detecting industry through a long list of honors, personal appearances and books. He is the author of several major works which have been accepted as veritable "texts" for treasure hunting.

Mr. Garrett's metal detector expertise has also carried him into the allied fields of security screening and crime scene investigation. While learning how metal detectors could be of value in law enforcement and security, he has participated in and sponsored numerous seminars and worked with law enforcement and other governmental bodies in an effort to help them develop new metal detectors as a tool for security and crime scene management. Garrett is now the foremost manufacturer of security metal detection equipment in the world. Not only do its famed Magnascanner and Super Scanner products protect air travelers all over the world, but they have been honored as the choice to safeguard historical and cultural treasures, Olympic athletes, presidents and kings.

He is married to the former Eleanor Smith of Pennington, TX, who has played a key role in the growth of Garrett Electronics. They have two sons and a daughter.

As a graduate engineer and a businessman, Mr. Garrett introduced discipline to the manufacture of metal detectors. He has generally raised the standards of metal detecting everywhere, while the hobby has grown from a haphazard pastime to almost a science.

Garrett quality is known throughout the world. From the beginning, Charles Garrett vowed "to practice what I preach"...in other words, to test his equipment in the field...to insure it will *work* for customers regardless of ground conditions and environment. Thus, with a metal detector of his own design he has searched for and found treasure on every continent except Antarctica. He has also scanned under lakes, seas and oceans of the world.

Hal Dawson
Editor, Ram Publishing

Dallas, Texas
Summer 1991

From the Author

A Note

I am indebted to all who gave of their time to help me create this book originally, and I again extend my sincerest thanks and appreciation to each of them. *Modern Metal Detectors* is a better book because of their assistance. This completely revised edition with its emphasis on new computerized detectors for the 21st century has benefited from the kindness, understanding and efforts of many of the same people, plus countless others.

A very special "thank you" to my wife Eleanor, and my children, Charles, Jr., Deirdre Lynne, and Vaughan Lamar.

Roy Lagal, author and metal detector professional, after studying the original manuscript, suggested the title. He and I have been field "sidekicks" for more than 20 years. Much of what we have learned, that no one else would take the time to learn, will be found in this book.

Robert Podhrasky, Garrett Electronics' chief engineer, and I have spent countless laboratory and field hours for almost two decades discussing metal detection. My knowledge of detectors has been greatly strengthened because of our association.

Virgil Hutton, a trusted friend and field companion of Roy Lagal's and mine, made many valuable suggestions.

FBI Special Agents (retired) Dave Loveless and Richard Graham and I have spent much time together applying metal detection techniques to many law enforcement and security situations, including the 1984 Los Angeles Summer Olympic Games and the 1984 Republican National Convention.

Garrett distributors and dealers, too numerous to name, have made contributions singly and as a group to the success of our company and this book. These men and women work with metal detector users almost every day of the year. They are aware of the problems of detector operators and they know the questions these people want to ask.

Jim Cross of Cross International leads the way in industrial and general applications of metal detectors in underwater search and salvage.

From Ed Morris' military journalistic experience came the ability to collect, sort and present difficult material in precise, usable form. At the beginning, Ed helped sort many of my notes into an organized format.

My thanks also to Andretta Lowry, Becky Boyer, Mary Alice Penson and Georgia Montgomery for their most valuable editing and stenographic assistance.

Thanks also to many Garrett Electronics' personnel who were especially helpful, including Melvin Climer, Jack Lowry and numerous others.

The First Edition of this book took ten years to complete. At least, my earliest manuscript pages date that far back. A short while before I began to write the original of this *Author's Note,* I reviewed my early book *Successful Coin Hunting* and noticed that its First Edition printing date coincided with the earliest *Modern Metal Detectors* manuscript, 1974! Of, course that coin book has been totally revised since, and I have also written and revised *Treasure Recovery from Sand and Sea,* plus writing *Let's Talk Treasure Hunting, Real Gold in Those Golden Years* and *Ghost Town Treasures.*

There are numerous manufacturers of metal detection equipment, most of whom I know and can count as friends. I regularly test their products and compare them with those made by my company. Needless to say, I can find treasure with any of these instruments. Since any comments that I might offer concerning competitive products would be gratuitous at best, however, only Garrett metal detection equipment will be discussed and pictured in this book.

It is an extreme pleasure for me to present to those millions who use or have an interest in metal detectors this completely revised edition of *Modern Metal Detectors*. The addition of material on 21st Century computerized equipment truly enables it to live up to its title, and I am proud to present it.

Charles Garrett

Garland, Texas
Autumn 1995

Facing
Charles Garrett, who has traveled literally all over the world
to test the metal detectors that he manufactures, is shown
here scanning on the banks of the Red Sea.

Over
The Author is shown in Florida conferring with Mel Fisher,
left, who used Garrett detectors to help find the 17th-cen-
tury Spanish treasure ship *Nuestra Senora de Atocha.*

Foreword

The purpose of *Modern Metal Detectors* is simply to help you be **more successful** when using your metal detector. I sincerely hope that this book will aid you in mastering your detector, rather than letting it master you. The book is meant to be an all-encompassing, comprehensive reference and "how-to" guide to metal detectors. *Modern Metal Detectors* is adaptable to your needs, whether you are just beginning or have experience...whether you are amateur or professional.

The book is not intended to replace, but to supplement, other classic Ram Publishing Company metal detector books, each of which contains invaluable, up-to-date, "how-to" material.

Modern Metal Detectors traces the history and development of metal detection equipment from its earliest days to the present. It presents complete information about all land and underwater metal detector types...how they work, their characteristics, capabilities, applications and field uses. This book is filled with "how-to" instructions

Facing

Bob Podhrasky, Garrett Chief Engineer, confers with noted prospector Roy Lagal, kneeling, as they work together in Arizona to develop a new gold-hunting detector.

Over

Charles Garrett checks out a new detector at a ruined building in the rugged Big Bend country of West Texas as he fulfills his pledge to field test all Garrett detectors.

and explains every phase of metal detecting...electronic theory, metal detector design, electromagnetic fields, search matrix, metals and minerals, detection characteristics of metals, and many more subjects.

This revised edition is divided into five sections:
1. History and Development of Detectors
2. Detectors and their Features
3. Computerized Detectors
4. Selecting a Detector and Accessories
5. Using a Detector

Section Three, of course, is totally new. When the First Edition of *Modern Metal Detectors* was published, Garrett Electronics had already been granted its patent for the use of a microprocessor computer chip in a metal detector. The first instrument requiring this patent had not yet been manufactured.

Today, our first Grand Master Hunter computerized detector, with its acclaimed *Fast Track*™ and *Ground Track*™ features, has been followed by improved models and a simplified version, and a totally new line of Garrett computerized detectors, the Ultra GTA, has been introduced.

Although I know that computers have affected my life — certainly since I was in the U.S. Navy — I lived many years without ever using them directly. So, I'll be honest and admit that I was somewhat leery of the blasted gadgets...*until I saw how dramatically they could improve treasure hunting.*

Read Section Three carefully. You'll learn that our new computerized detectors are the easiest to operate that Garrett has ever manufactured. You'll also discover how they hunt deeper and with more sensitivity. Most important of all, you'll find out how they **find more treasure.**

Every person who has used a metal detector, or even thought that someday he would, has questions about metal detectors. Some of the first questions usually asked are: "How deep will they go?" "What are the differences among the various kinds of detectors?" and "Which instrument is best for me?" As people are become more knowledgeable about metal detectors, they ask more intelligent questions, such as: "What is discrimination...what is ground balance?" "How dependable are target classification meters...how important are they?" "Can I go deeper if I use a larger searchcoil?" and "Can I use a detector with automatic ground balance to find coins, caches and gold?"

Modern Metal Detectors answers these most frequently asked questions and hundreds of others. I have endeavored to present basic, all-encompassing, up-to-date detector knowledge, so that regardless of the problems and questions you have, you will be able to find your own answers. You'll learn to bench-test your detector and take it into the field for testing to find out what you want to know about it. If you need additional information, you'll have the background you need to ask the *right* questions and to know if you get the right answers. In short, this book contains the basic information anyone needs to understand how today's metal detectors work, what metals and minerals are detectable, and why metal detectors react the way they do to these metals and minerals.

A Glossary is included to help you build your vocabulary with a storehouse of metal detector terminology. Use these terms in your everyday thinking and conversation, and you'll find yourself quickly understanding, and becoming a part of, the fascinating field of treasure hunting with a metal detector.

Let this book become your companion. Wherever you take your metal detector, take this book. You will soon find yourself becoming more knowledgeable about metal detectors. You will begin to understand more clearly all that your metal detector has been trying to tell you. You will find those things you search for and many more treasures you never dreamed of discovering. Indeed, your success will be limited only by your imagination!

Treasure Hunting

So...you want to find treasure with a metal detector? Or, maybe you just want to learn more about the science of metal detection. Either way, this is the book for you! Read on...!

Treasure hunting is difficult to define because it means different things to different people. Basically, it is the search for and recovery of *anything* that has value to you. Coins, costume jewelry, money caches and relics are all treasure just the same as gold and jewels.

The "treasure" sought by a security guard is the metallic weapon or contraband that someone is attempting to take into or out of a secured area. A law enforcement officer seeks hidden weapons.

Some people want (or, expect) to strike it rich the very first time they turn on a detector, while others are content to find rarely more than a few coins in the local park. Some individuals hunt with a detector for the excitement of digging a treasure out of the ground, while others are fascinated by the "historical" discoveries they make. Some find joy in returning lost class rings and other valuables to their rightful owners. Others enjoy displaying in their homes the treasures they have discovered. There are some who write magazine articles and enjoy sharing their treasure hunting techniques with others. Yet, some simply enjoy getting out into God's great outdoors...any treasure they find is icing on the cake.

What we mean by "general" treasure hunting is just simply searching for ALL types of treasure — coins, relics, money caches, artifacts and other objects of monetary or historical value. For instance, you may be searching in a field and stumble over the foundation of an old building. It could pay you here to scan this area carefully, using techniques specifically required for detecting money caches. You may need to switch to a larger searchcoil and scan around this foundation thoroughly to look for any money caches.

Never fail to search extensively around all suspicious objects...even trees! There have been numerous money caches, especially those in fruit jars, recovered from the forks of trees. The tree has grown up around the cache placed there many years ago.

General treasure hunting techniques involve the study of all applications as presented in this book. We realize that approximately 95% of the people who use metal detectors search for coins and that more than two-thirds of these hobbyists search *only* for coins. There is always the opportunity, however, that even a dedicated coin hunter may encounter a good lead that requires expertise unrelated to that aspect of metal detection.

If you're good with a metal detector, you're probably an inquisitive person by nature. You want to find out what's around the next bend or under the next layer of soil. If so, great success in any field of treasure hunting can be yours with a quality metal detector. All you need now is knowledge.

First, learn all there is to know about your metal detector — its searchcoils, accessories, modes of operation and capabilities. Put your study into action with practice, practice and more practice. Then, carefully review the instructions given in this and other books. Incorporate them into your daily practice. Be ready to meet any general treasure hunting situations that might arise.

Who Hunts for Treasure?

Treasure hunting has become a family hobby...husband, wife and children all become dedicated treasure hunters. Sometimes only the man of the household enjoys the hobby, but I know of some wives who will go alone when the husband can't go. Often, children become more proficient than their parents. Hunters, fishermen, campers, vacationers and backpackers are adding metal detectors to their sports gear.

Treasure Hunting Is Healthful! Who can deny that outdoor activities are healthful? Treasure hunting certainly takes you out of doors into the fresh air and sunshine. Scanning a detector over the ground all day, stooping to dig hundreds of targets, hiking several miles over the desert, or climbing a mountain to reach a ghost town...all of this can become tiring. But, this is where an extra side benefit is realized. A "built-in" body building program is a valuable *plus* of treasure hunting. Leg muscles firm up, flab around the middle begins to diminish as excess pounds drop off, breathing improves and nights of restful

Author displays leaf silver he discovered with a metal detector near Cobalt, Ontario, Canada, in two adjacent caches buried probably 60 to 70 years ago by a miner who stole the ore from a mine.

3

sleep result. Good physical exercise that is absolutely required in successful treasure hunting can lead to a longer, healthier life.

Treasure Hunting is Profitable! It is also simple and easy. Why not consider the hobby of coin hunting? The majority of all treasure hunters begin their new hobby by hunting for coins. Countless millions of coins have been lost and await recovery by the metal detector hobbyist. More coins are being lost every day than are being found...and this has been going on for centuries!

Other Benefits

Most important to many people is the awareness and enjoyment of treasures of nature that God has placed upon the earth for all of us to find. Whether the "big money treasure" is to been found is not always the point. It is truly gratifying to see nature in its purest form all around and to be a vital part of it. This alone could well be the greatest treasure ever found.

Educational factors related to treasure hunting are equally stimulating. Relics and artifacts of bygone eras create many questions. Who were the people that once lived and prospered where faint memories of an old city or town remain? Where did they come from? Why was the area left deserted? These and many more questions can usually be answered with proper research and examination of the artifacts found.

Many persons who begin by scanning only for coins quickly extend their hobby into other areas of treasure hunting. Searching ghost towns and old houses for hidden money caches, and hunting in trash dumps for relics and rare bottles can be very rewarding. One treasure hunter found $41,000 in currency in a metal box that was cached in an old dumping ground. Another man in Idaho found a $20 gold piece estimated to be worth hundreds of thousands of dollars. Countless small fruit jar and "post hole" money caches are found each year.

Research

Many find it amazing that the successful treasure hunter appears to expend no energy at all, while the mediocre treasure hunter runs about constantly in a helter-skelter fashion, chasing some sort of will-o-the-wisp... never being really satisfied or successful.

A metal detector must be used correctly and in the right places before it will pay off. Most successful finds result from research. Of course, a lot of treasure is found by accident, and all of us dream of finding the "big one" simply by stumbling over it, but that is hardly the way to go about professional treasure hunting.

Whether you are a coin hunter, cache or relic hunter, or a prospector, research is vitally important. It is a basic tool you cannot neglect to use if you want to enjoy success.

Research is a key to successful treasure hunting. Without proper and adequate research, you are shooting in the dark. Your efficiency and likelihood of successful recovery increase proportionately as the amount of your research increases. Without research you may not be as successful as you should or could be since 95% of a successful recovery usually depends on research. Always remember that you must go where the treasure is located. Even the world's finest metal detector can only inform you about what is beneath its searchcoil.

Most of the time, in order to find where a treasure is located, you must carry out a certain amount of research. You won't find treasure where it is not! You will find treasure where it is! In order to find it, you must study, read, and follow up leads. It's wise to talk to people. In short, do your research.

It is sad, but true, that most treasure hunters do not educate themselves on the correct usage of metal detectors. They do not go to the trouble to acquire correct data on treasure sites. They just don't hunt where the treasure is located. Usually, however, these people are the first to give up, perhaps blaming their instrument for their failure.

For the professional treasure hunter, however, the greatest difficulty is deciding which of the dozens or hundreds of leads to follow. They try to avoid bum steers. They use their brains and they *think*. Common sense is a big factor in successful treasure hunting. The professional treasure hunter doesn't search for one treasure. They keep many leads on the back burner and are always looking for new leads to follow. Often in researching one story, you will run across information that applies to another. The professional will select several treasure leads to follow and collect all possible information about each of them. Then each one will be followed as far as possible, and the treasure hunter will let it lie dormant for a while, letting the subconscious work on it while waiting for new leads to develop. Maybe the professional only hits once a year, but often that is more than enough to repay the effort.

Many books have been written on the subject. Many of them have been published by Ram Publishing Company. Some of these books should be on your bookshelf and should be read often. Use the order blank at the back of this book.

The successful treasure hunter lives and breathes his hobby. It is always on his mind. Consequently, everything he or she reads and everyone they talk with are potential sources of the fresh treasure leads and data they need to help in their work.

If you are a coin hunter, for instance, you can find current coins all day long at the park, playground and along grassy strips near parking meters. If you really want to start finding old and rare, valuable coins, however, you must do your research. You must learn where the old settlers' campgrounds, carnival and fairground sites are located. These are the really valuable hot spots; here you will find treasure that makes hunting worthwhile. This same principle applies to any other kind of treasure hunting If you are looking for gold, you have to search where the precious metal has already been found. Gold and silver

6

have been mined in many locations throughout the world, and to have the greatest chances of success, you must find the best places to prospect. Relic and cache hunters must also do their research. Find the hot spots, then put your expert detector knowledge to work. It will pay off!

Patience

If you have been hunting treasure for almost any length of time, you have probably run across mention of the word "patience." Absolutely and positively...unless you possess a great amount of patience and put it into practice, you won't be as successful as you could be.

Experienced cache hunters have learned that success comes as infrequently as one in ten tries. Consequently, a person without patience to spare will surely give up long before success rolls around.

Four professional treasure hunters and friends of mine whom you will hear more about in this book are Roy Lagal, the late L.L. "Abe" Lincoln, George Mroczkowski and the late Karl von Mueller. All four of these men possessed an overabundance of patience. They know that you don't find treasure every time you run out and turn on a detector. They know and have preached on many occasions, that to be successful, patience must be in your tool kit.

These men have been successful many times. They keep perhaps a dozen or more leads going at the same time. Many of Roy's successes are described in two books which he and I co-authored for publication by Ram Publishing Company, *Modern Treasure Hunting* and *Modern Electronic Prospecting*. I know of at least one project that Roy has kept going for about 15 years. "It's there someplace," Roy has said, "they put 'er down good!" But he's determined to find it and hasn't given up in all these years, nor has his enthusiasm waned. Someday he'll find it!

These men have been written about in books and magazines many times. An article about "Abe" Lincoln explained that his successes were due in part to his patience. Abe stated that patience is a true key to making finds and that if you are going to be successful, you'd better gather and store up plenty of it for yourself to put to use when it is needed.

If you have read George Mroczkowski's book, *Professional Treasure Hunter,* now out of print, you know that George possesses an abundance of patience. Several of his treasure adventures stretched over decades, proving that George has learned the value of patience. Patience and hard work are two of George's greatest virtues and reasons for success.

Hard Work

Karl Von Mueller once wrote, "You can put on your cap of patience, and it'll serve you well, but you better also pick up the shovel of hard work if you want to experience the joys and rewards of finding treasure!"

Treasure hunting is hard work. In fact, it's one of the hardest jobs a person can undertake. You could sit on a rock all day long with patience to spare, but all you would accomplish is to keep the rock warm, for that rock will never hatch. To find treasure you must get out into the field, swing your detector from dawn to dusk and dig every signal, regardless of how weak or how strong.

Many people enjoy going to a park and scanning a searchcoil back and forth over the ground for a while with discrimination set to its maximum. Occasionally they will dig a coin or two. And, there's nothing wrong with that...if it's what a person wants. Yet, there is a far greater reward in hard work, sweat and the sound of money jingling in the pocket.

If you're willing to study...

If you're not afraid of hard work...

And, if you're even willing to sweat a little...

Success in hunting for treasure with a metal detector will be yours!

8

A Metal Detector

A metal detector is, simply, an electronic device that detects the presence of metal. While some metal detectors respond to certain minerals, the main design function is detection of metal.

Metal detectors are not mystical Ouija boards, nor are they witching sticks. They are not Geiger counters which detect energy emissions from radioactive materials...although they will detect conductive metal and ferrous minerals in association with uranium. Metal detectors are not magnetometers which measure magnetic field intensity. They are not magic wands nor direction finders. They definitely will not *point to metal,* either close at hand or far away.

A metal detector is simply an electromagnetic device that detects the presence of conductive metals and certain minerals whenever these detectable substances come within the instrument 's detection area.

Metal detectors are not difficult to use. Just about anyone, after a few minutes instruction and practice, can operate a detector to find metal...regardless of that person's age, sex or education.

New detectors are as simple to operate a pushing a touchpad. In fact, that's all that's required on any of Garrett's computerized instruments...push a touchpad and begin hunting.

On the other hand, an individual could find treasure for a lifetime without learning all there is to know about metal detectors. Becoming proficient in every phase of their operation requires years of study and field application. Detectors come in various sizes and shapes. The most common configuration, shown on Page 22, is the portable, land-use instrument. A control housing is attached to an adjustable length stem. A searchcoil, which contains the antenna, is attached to the lower end of the stem. The stem allows the overall metal detector length to be adjustable from approximately 30 inches minimum to approximately 45 inches maximum. An electrical cable connects the searchcoil antenna windings to the electronic circuits inside the control housing. The control housing, in addition to containing the circuits, also contains a meter, switches, a speaker and other components, as well as the batteries necessary for electrical power.

Electronic circuits generate current signals which power the transmitter antenna. The antenna transmits an electromagnetic field into the medium surrounding the searchcoil. The electromagnetic field will penetrate a variety of materials, including earth soils and sand, rock, wood, brick, stone, masonry, water, concrete, vegetable and some mineral substances...and, of course, air. When metals and certain minerals interact with the electromagnetic field, metal detection occurs. Metal detectors cannot, except in certain situations, detect metal through other metal. In other words, gold coins in a covered iron pot cannot be detected. The iron pot and its lid can be detected, but not the coins.

Most quality-constructed instruments are built to withstand the rigors and punishment of an unlimited number of hours of heavy-duty field use while providing unfailing operational accuracy...even though the detector may be subjected to rough, often abusive treatment. A quality instrument can be expected to operate successfully in all kinds of weather and in every conceivable environmental situation, from deserts and seashores to mountains and hostile jungles. Detectors are knocked around and carried in hot and cold automobile trunks. They are stuffed in backpacks and stored in home closets. They are dropped, banged around, abused, kicked and cursed. Yet, in spite of all this, quality instruments will continue to give years of unfailingly accurate, dependable service.

The majority of portable detectors are designed and manufactured primarily for use on land or in shallow water. Some few instruments, however, are designed for underwater operation to depths of two hundred feet. Convertible models are designed for use on both land and under water.

There are numerous other types of metal detectors including those used in law enforcement and security, construction and utility industries, medicine, traffic control, lumbering and other industries...even hotels and restaurants. The mechanical configurations and circuitry may differ, but the ultimate design purpose of each of them is the detection of metal.

A metal detector is simply a tool. It is designed to get a job done by reporting what it discovers. *It will never lie!* When used correctly...for the right job, in the right location...a modern metal detector will help its user find the metal and/or minerals for which a search is being conducted.

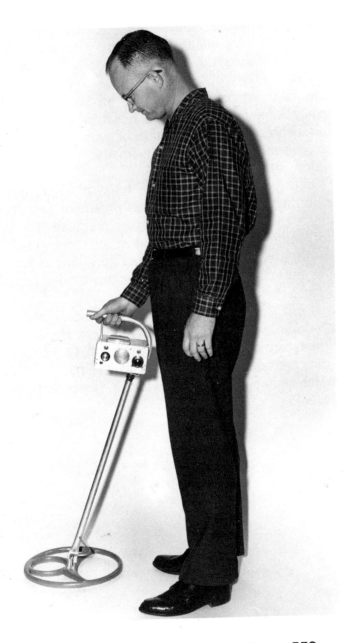

Author (above, in younger days) with first Garrett Hunter BFO.

Right, with current computerized Garrett Ultra GTA 1000.

History of Detectors

Ancient Chinese documents indicate that a metal detector was in use more than 200 years before the birth of Christ. A Chinese emperor had a doorway metal detector constructed to protect himself against assassination. His craftsman built the doorway of a magnetic mineral called magnetite with the frame possibly built something like a horseshoe magnet. Through a combination of heating and striking the magnetite with hammers, an iron metal "attractor" was created. The heating and jarring caused the molecules to align themselves in the direction of the earth's magnetic field. If a person attempted to carry iron objects such as armor, swords or other weapons through the doorway, these objects would be drawn against the doorway shown on the following page and held fast.

Alexander Graham Bell, the inventor of the telephone, was working on an electrical induction device for locating metals in 1881 when President James A. Garfield was wounded in an assassination attempt. One bullet grazed his arm and a second lodged in his back. After attempts to locate this bullet failed and the President's condition worsened, his doctors turned to Bell for help, asking him to bring his detector to the White House. Reports conflict concerning what happened next. One version relates that Bell was unable to perfect his instrument in time to locate

Hobbyists who use modern, computerized detectors are ready to hunt for coins, relics, jewelry and other treasures by just pressing a single touchpad.

15

the bullet. Another reports that he attempted to locate the bullet, but failed. Nevertheless, President Garfield died.

In 1890 tests were made to locate sulfides through the medium of conductivity, using a telegraphic receiver connected in series with a battery and a wire brush. Electrical contacts were made in the earth, and a brush was then moved over the surface. Whenever it touched sulfides, the

First known "metal detector" built to protect a Chinese emperor more than 2,000 years ago was constructed of magnetic mineral to attract iron weapons carried through the doorway.

brush would complete the circuit, indicated by a click in the receiver. Since it could be used only on exposed mineralized surfaces, the method was of limited value.

Further attempts at metal detection were made, using the Wheatstone bridge circuit for measuring resistance. Here again, conductivity was the determining factor, but the conductivity between two points on the earth's surface had to be calculated indirectly by first measuring resistance. This method also proved impractical.

Still another earth conductivity method was given considerable attention. Since electrical currents flowing through the ground cause electrical potential lines to be created, equal potential points across the ground could be measured by galvanometers and plotted. The presence of an ore body caused these lines to warp or distort. Although the method was somewhat successful, many variables were involved. In addition, water layers, areas of uneven moisture and other substances in the soil gave indications which could be misconstrued as indicating the presence of an ore body. Too, failure to indicate ore would not necessarily mean barren ground. The oxidized condition existing around sulfide ore bodies forms an almost perfect insulator that prevents accurate measurement.

Research on earth conductivity methods is occasionally conducted. Shown on the following page is a photo taken in 1963 of an experiment in which I participated. This instrument involved was a crevice detector, the brainchild of Dr. John C. Cook of Teledyne Geotech in Garland.

The closest that the early-day pioneers came to the modern metal detectors was a method designed to measure the distortion caused by magnetic fields generated by an electrical conductor of very low resistance in the earth, such as an ore body. Since this method did not require use of any electrical contact on the ore or on the earth, it avoided the problems caused by moisture and similar factors and was limited only by the short distance in which the intensity of the magnetic field was effective.

Another promising method was that of induction balance, which could detect the presence of gold as easily as sulfides or other minerals. Its prime difficulty was in obtaining the necessary depth.

The idea of locating ore bodies electromagnetically was perhaps first conceived by Dr. Daniel G. Chilson in 1904 in Goldfield, NV. Early experiments in conductivity of the earth, water and other earth substances, determined that sulfides (conductive sulfur) were the best conductors. In 1909 Chilson turned to known radio transmission/reception techniques, experimenting with short waves.

In 1925 an electrical gate checker was designed to help factories cut down on rampant thefts of tools and products. Its operation was based on the use of electromagnetic waves. Two German physicists, Dr. Geffeken and Dr. Richter of Leipzig, designed the original gate checker. Their work was continued by Gebr. Wetzel of Leipzig-

Author, second from left, monitors a crevice detector which could "detect" large subterranean cavities by measuring variations in the earth's conductivity caused by their presence.

Plaqwitz. An electromagnetic field was caused to flow across the passageway. Metal carried by persons passing through the door caused alteration of the electromagnetic field and a signal was given. The apparatus, forerunner of the modern "walk-through" detector, was adjustable to allow small objects such as watches and keys to be taken through the gate undetected while larger objects were detected. A small searching coil was used to inspect those persons who produced a signal as they passed through the doorway. This coil could be adjusted to various sensitivities, allowing small objects, such as coins in pockets, to pass undetected.

About the same time, Shirl Herr was recognized, according to reports, as the inventor of the magnetic balance, a device used for locating underground minerals and metals. In 1927 the spark gap metal detector was invented.

A report in *Popular Science Monthly,* September 1930, shows a man using a small two-coil metal detector. (See Page 71.) The man using the device was called an "amateur treasure finder." The caption said that it would find a silver dollar buried several inches underground and that it made a buzzing noise when metal was near. The metal detector, called a "radio prospector," was widely sold in kits.

From the early '30s until World War II, various companies began producing metal detector inventions based upon several of these electrical theories. During the war there was naturally a great interest in metal detectors, with resultant rapid advances in their technology.

At war's end, thousands of Army mine detectors were available as war surplus. They were eagerly bought by ex-military personnel whose training with Army mine detectors enabled them to recognize the value of such equipment in locating buried treasure.

Several companies began producing vacuum tube and transistorized detectors for the consumer during the '50s.

19

Since the development of transistors permitted construction of smaller and lighter weight detectors, vacuum tube detector production ended in the early '60s.

But, it was not until the late '60s and early '70s that a substantial interest in metal detectors arose; in the '70s great strides in metal detector development began taking place. Ultra-stable and very sensitive metal detectors that featured "Good/Bad" target identification and ground mineral rejection came into existence during this period.

The '80s ushered in target analyzer designs, and each year saw these analyzers become more accurate. The use of computerized, microprocessor-controlled circuitry represented a quantum leap in the analysis of data. Garrett's Patent #4,709,213 was the first microprocessor metal detector technology patent granted by the United States Patent Office. The company conducted ten years of design and field testing before utilizing this patent in the manufacture of a detector, an effort whose success is told in Part III's discussion of computerized detectors.

Author displays a selection of U.S. Army mine detectors, with a World War II-vintage instrument at the extreme left, typical of those that started the metal detector "boom" in 1945.

Today, modern detectors do practically everything except dig the targets. They detect it, pinpoint it, determine its size and shape, measure its depth and tell the operator whether it is worth digging for or not. Some of this target "knowledge," however, is discerned by operators who have become very efficient with their detectors by learning to interpret and analyze detector audio and indicator information. What tomorrow may bring, anyone can guess, but it will surely include new and improved detectors. It's exciting to think about!

During the very early years of metal detecting, the equipment was used mostly for prospecting for precious metals. It was not until well after World War II that metal detectors began to be used to any great extent for hunting other kinds of treasure. As the years passed, metal detector usage has greatly expanded into many fields, which include searching for coins, relics, treasure, gold and other precious metals.

Application of metal detectors to law enforcement and security situations has a surprisingly lengthy history. A number of instances have been recorded in which metal detection equipment was used by law enforcement personnel as a crime scene management and investigative tool. (As a reference see Karl von Mueller's *The Master Hunter Manual,* 1973, Ram Publishing Company, now out of print). Metal detectors of both the walk-through and hand-held type are being used to an ever greater extent today in facilities of all types where threats of terrorism and violence are increasing at an alarming rate.

Metal detector applications are constantly being expanded and now extend into many fields. New detector advances, as well as improved operating techniques and knowledge, have increased interest in the metal detector field world-wide. Metal detectors are now an essential part of daily life in perhaps every country in the world.

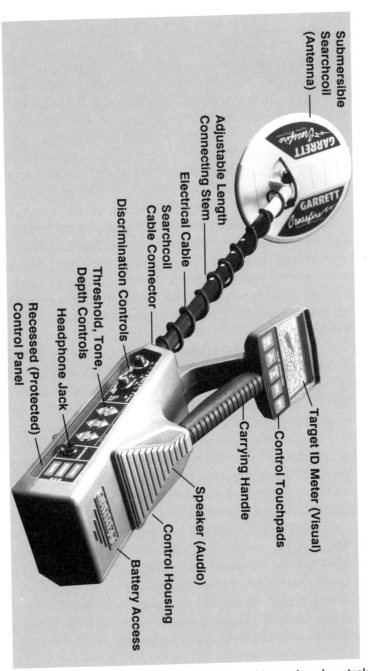

Submersible
Searchcoil
(Antenna)

Adjustable Length
Connecting Stem

Electrical Cable

Searchcoil
Cable Connector

Discrimination Controls

Threshold, Tone,
Depth Controls

Headphone Jack

Recessed (Protected)
Control Panel

Target ID Meter (Visual)

Control Touchpads

Carrying Handle

Speaker (Audio)

Control Housing

Battery Access

Grand Master Hunter CX II, modern detector with touchpad controls

22

How Detectors Work

It is not necessary to understand the scientific principles of metal detection to use a detector. You can find coins, rings, jewelry, gold nuggets, caches or whatever you are searching for without knowing how your detector works. For better comprehension of what your detector is doing, however...to recognize *why* it just made that peculiar sound...to understand *why* it reacts the way it does to metals and minerals...it is necessary to learn how a metal detector works.

Two examples illustrate this need. First, let's say you are scanning in the field and get a detector signal. You dig down a foot and find nothing. You enlarge the hole and dig another foot and still don't find anything. You might keep on digging to five or six feet before finally giving up. Yet, your signal persisted throughout all this digging!

What went wrong? Was it your fault, or that of your detector? Was a target there? Well, yes, there was a target, though it may not necessarily have been a metal one. The response could have been due to some variation in mineral content.

For the second example, let's say you are searching for a small kettle made of iron that is filled with gold coins. You know this iron kettle was left somewhere in a particular field under a large flat rock that had been placed on top of it. Unfortunately, however, there are at least one thousand large, heavy flat rocks lying in that field. The ground itself is highly mineralized and some of the large rocks themselves also contain a great amount of iron mineralization.

In these situations, knowing how your detector works, plus having an understanding of the various detectable minerals, will save you a great deal of effort. In the first instance, you will not dig at all, or perhaps no deeper than one foot, before you realize there is no metallic target in the ground. Unless you know something about iron minerals and their effect on metal detections, you will likely never find that iron kettle unless you decide to dig beneath every rock in that field.

The "answers" to both these situations are presented elsewhere in this book.

Modern Metal Detectors, seeks to present theory explanations that are simple with only very basic detector operating characteristics described. This book was intended not to be a theoretical work but a home, field and classroom textbook to help metal detector users understand basic principles of their equipment. These principles are not difficult to understand.

When you begin studying mineralization, target identification, field applications and other subjects, you will be rewarded by your study of this background material. You will understand what your detector is telling you,...why you hear certain signals. You will become better able to determine if the object you have detected is one that you want to dig. Proper and highly efficient operation of a metal detector is not difficult. It does, however, require a certain amount of study, thought and field application.

Radio Transmission and Reception

You have operated one-half of a metal detector during most of your lifetime, perhaps without knowing it...the common radio. Metal detection is achieved, basically, by the transmission and "reception" of a radio wave signal. The block diagram on the facing page illustrates the basic components of a typical metal detector. The battery is the power supply. The transmitter electronic oscillator at the extreme left of the diagram generates a signal.

24

The transmitter signal current travels from the transmitter oscillator through a wire (searchcoil cable) to the searchcoil's transmitter winding (antenna). The transmitter antenna is a few turns of electrical wire, generally wound in a circular fashion.

Electromagnetic Field Generation

As the current circulates in the transmitter antenna, an invisible electromagnetic field is generated that flows out into the air (or other surrounding medium, i.e.: air, wood, rock, earth materials, water, etc.) in all directions. If this electromagnetic field were visible, it would appear to be in the shape of a gigantic, three dimensional doughnut, with the transmitter antenna embedded in its center.

Electromagnetic field theory states that field lines cannot cross one another. Consequently, they crowd together as they pass through the circular antenna, but they are not crowded on the outside. It is fortunate this crowding takes place, because the intensity (density) of the field lines is the very phenomenon that enables metal detection in the area adjacent to the searchcoil to take place. In the drawing at the bottom of the next page note the area indicated as the two dimensional detection pattern. This is the site of maximum field crowding; it is here that metal detection occurs as a result of two major phenomena...eddy current

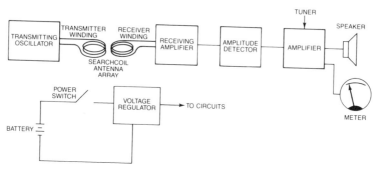

This electronic block diagram of a transmitter-receiver metal detector illustrates the basic components of a metal detector as they are pointed out in the description at left.

generation and electromagnetic field distortion. (Note the mirror-image detection pattern above the searchcoil.)

Eddy Currents

Secondary Electromagnetic Field Generation — Whenever metal comes within the detection pattern, electromagnetic field lines penetrate the metal's surface. Tiny circulating currents called "eddy currents" are caused to flow on the metal surface as illustrated in the figure on the facing page. The power, or motivating force, that causes eddy currents to flow, comes from the electromagnetic field itself. Resulting power loss by this field (the power used up in generating the eddy currents) is sensed by the detector's circuits. Also, eddy currents generate a secondary electromagnetic field that, in some cases, flows out into the surrounding medium. The portion of the secondary field that intersects the receiver winding, causes a detection signal to occur in that winding. Thus, the detector alerts the operator that metal has been detected.

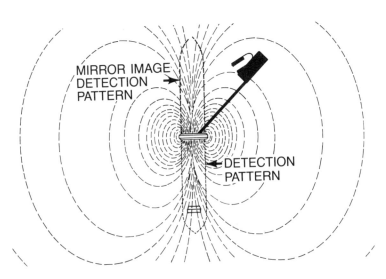

As transmitter current from the antenna generates the electromagnetic field, detection pattern (dotted lines) is the area within which metal detection occurs. Mirror-image pattern atop coil is not used.

Electromagnetic Field Distortion

The detection of non-conductive iron (ferrous) minerals takes place in a different manner. When iron mineral comes near and within the detection pattern, the electromagnetic field lines are redistributed, as shown in the figure on the following page. This redistribution upsets the "balance" of the transmitter and receiver windings in the searchcoil, resulting in power being induced into the receiver winding. When this induced power is sensed by the detector circuits, the detector alerts its operator to the presence of the iron mineral.

Iron mineral detection is a major problem for both manufacturers and users of metal detectors. Of course, the detection of iron mineral is welcomed by a gold hunter who is looking for black magnetic sand which can often signal the presence of placer metal. On the other hand, the

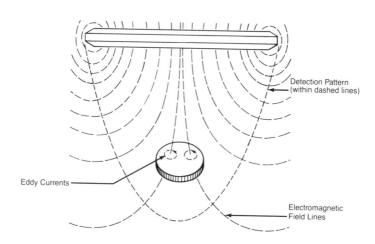

Detection Pattern
(within dashed lines)

Eddy Currents

Electromagnetic
Field Lines

When any metal comes within the detection pattern of a searchcoil, *eddy currents* flow over its surface, resulting in a loss of power in the electromagnetic field, which the detector's circuits can sense.

27

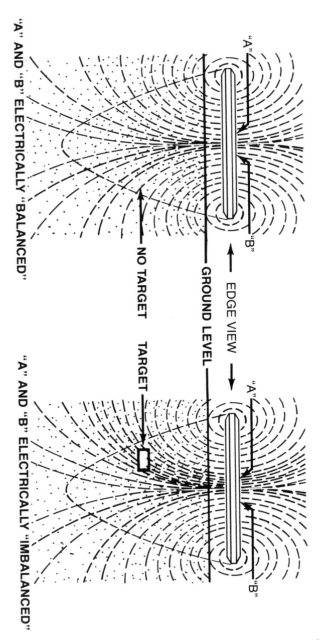

When a target comes within the detection pattern, searchcoils windings become imbalanced at Points A and B, and electromagnetic field lines are redistributed as shown in this drawing.

28

treasure hunter, who is looking for coins, jewelry, relics, gold nuggets, etc., usually finds iron mineral detection a nuisance.

Search Matrix

Any substance penetrated by the electromagnetic field is "illuminated." Many elements and different combinations of minerals are within the soil, including moisture, iron and other minerals, some detectable and some not. Of course, it is hoped that the targets being sought are also present.

A detector's response at any given moment is caused by conductive metals and minerals and ferrous non-conductive minerals illuminated by its electromagnetic field as shown in the drawing below. One detector design criterion requires the elimination of responses from undesirable elements, permitting signals only from desirable objects. How this discrimination is accomplished depends on the type of detector.

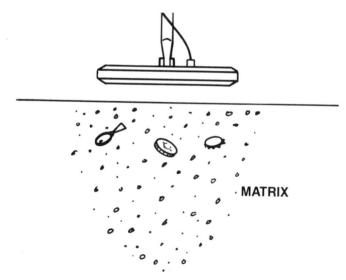

This typical matrix beneath a metal detector's searchcoil illustrates how the electromagnetic field generated by the antenna in that searchcoil *illuminates* every metal target in the area it reaches.

Electromagnetic Field Coupling

"Coupling" describes the penetration of the electromagnetic field into any object near the transmitter antenna. There is perfect coupling into some objects such as wood, fresh water, air, glass, and certain non-mineralized earth materials as shown in the drawing below. Coupling is inhibited, however, when the electromagnetic field attempts to penetrate iron mineralization, wetted salt, and other substances. This inhibiting of the electromagnetic field, as shown in the drawing on the facing page decreases the detection capability of the metal detector. Even though modern instruments, can eliminate the effects of iron minerals, the electromagnetic field is still inhibited (distorted), which results in reduced detection capability and performance.

Salt Water Detection

Salt water (wetted salt) has a disturbing effect upon the electromagnetic field because salt water is electrically

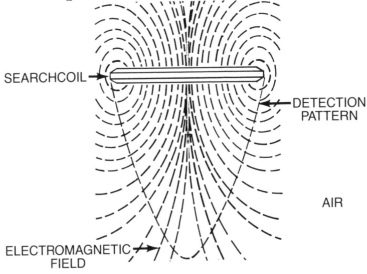

This diagram of "perfect coupling" illustrates the general shape of a detection pattern that occurs when the electromagnetic field from a searchcoil penetrates earth or any other nearby object.

conductive. In effect, salt ocean water "looks like" metal to some detectors! Fortunately manufacturers are able to design detectors capable of "ignoring" salt water.

Depth of Detection

Numerous factors determine how deeply an object can be detected. The electromagnetic field generated by the searchcoil transmitter antenna, flows out into the surrounding matrix, generating eddy currents on the surface of conductive substances. Any detectable target that sufficiently disturbs the field, is detected. Three factors determine whether the disturbance is sufficient for detection: electromagnetic field strength, target size and surface area.

Electromagnetic Field Strength

How far does the electromagnetic field that flows out into the surrounding matrix extend? Theoretically. to infinity...but you can be certain it is extremely weak when it gets there! In fact, only a few feet away from the searchcoil,

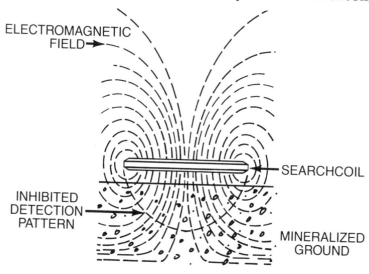

Detection depth capability is inhibited in some elements such as iron mineralization and wetted salt where coupling is inhibited when the electromagnetic field attempts penetration.

the field is greatly reduced in strength. Several factors, including attenuation (absorption by the earth, matrix materials, etc.) and distance, reduce the field strength. When all things are considered, a detector may have several thousand times less detection capability at six feet than it does at one foot, so you can understand why detectors are limited in their depth detection capability.

Target Size

Targets can be detected better and more deeply simply because of their size. Larger targets are easier to detect because they produce more eddy currents. One object with twice the surface area of another, will produce a detection signal twice that of the smaller object but it will not necessarily be detected twice as far. By the same reasoning, a larger target will produce the same amplitude detection signal at a distance farther away from the bottom of the searchcoil than the smaller target. Size is also an important factor in target discrimination, a metal detector characteristic discussed elsewhere in this book.

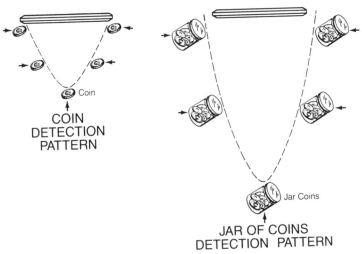

COIN
DETECTION
PATTERN

JAR OF COINS
DETECTION PATTERN

Any detected object has its own pattern, as shown above, with the detection pattern for the jar of coins being wider at the top and extending farther away from the searchcoil's bottom.

Surface Area Detection

Metal detectors are, for the most part, *surface area* detectors. They are not metallic volume (mass) detectors. The larger the surface area of a metal target that is "looking at" the bottom of the searchcoil, the better that target will be detected. The actual volume or mass of the target has very little to do with most forms of detection. Prove this for yourself.

Turn your detector on and tune it to threshold. With your hand, bring a large coin in toward the searchcoil with the face of the coin "looking at" the bottom of the searchcoil. Make a note of the distance at which the coin is first detected...say, eight inches.

Now, move the coin back and rotate it ninety degrees so that the edge of the coin "looks at" the bottom of the searchcoil. Bring the coin in toward the searchcoil. You will see that the coin cannot be detected at eight inches. In fact, it probably will be detected only at a distance of four inches or less.

Another proof of surface area detection is to measure at what distance a single coin can be detected. Then stack several coins on the back side of the test coin and check to see how far this stack of coins can be detected. You'll find that the stack can be detected at only a slightly greater distance, illustrating that the increasing the volume of metal had very little effect on detection distance.

Fringe Area Detection

Fringe area detection is a phenomenon of detection, the understanding of which will result in your being able to discover metal targets to the maximum depth capability of any instrument. The detection pattern for a coin may extend, say, one foot below the searchcoil. The detection pattern for a small jar of coins may extend, perhaps, two feet below the searchcoil as illustrated in the drawing on the facing page. Within the area of the detection pattern, an unmistakable detector signal is produced.

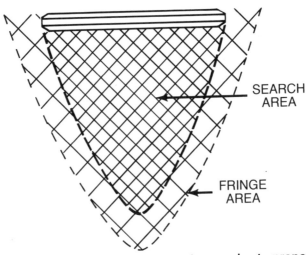

SEARCH
AREA

FRINGE
AREA

This illustration shows the location and approximate proportional size of the fringe detection area in which faint target signals from around the outer edges of a normal detection pattern can be heard.

What about outside the detection pattern? Does detection take place? Yes, but the signals are too weak to be discerned by the operator *except* in the fringe area around the outer edges of the detection pattern as shown in the drawing above.

A good set of headphones is a must, if you desire to hear fringe area signals. The next most important thing, is training in the art of discerning the faint whispers of sound that occur in the fringe area. Skill in fringe area detection can be developed with practice, training, concentration and faith in your ability. Develop fringe area detection ability to a fine art and you are on your way to some great discoveries that many detector operators will miss. The ability to hear fringe area signals results in greatly improved metal detection efficiency and success.

Detector Applications

The uses to which metal detectors are put are limited only by mankind's imagination. During the past 50 or so years, they have been used to detect and locate practically every kind of metal and detectable mineral.

Approximately 95% of those who use metal detectors for treasure hunting do so to search for coins, jewelry and other small objects which might be found on beaches and playgrounds and in parks and various other places where people congregate. Practically anyone can learn to use a metal detector and find places to search. Coins have been lost everywhere people have been, and people have been practically everywhere. This aspect of treasure hunting is relatively easy; it is not necessary to travel long distances to find good coin hunting locations.

Other treasure hunting activities such as gold hunting, relic hunting and cache hunting often require some travel to get to good locations. Too, more metal detector expertise is usually required for greatest success in these specialized fields.

Industrial users such as utility, construction and electrical companies save time and money by employing detectors to locate pipes, electrical conduits and land markers. Imagine, for instance, the inconvenience and repair expense involved if a bulldozer's blade rips into a buried cable containing thousands of telephone lines. To avoid needless destruction, field crews scan the ground with metal detecting devices before digging, trenching or disturbing the ground.

Law enforcement personnel use detectors to locate

guns, knives, weapons, stolen goods, physical evidence and other metal objects concealed and hidden in the ground, buildings, water, and other locations. Often, detectors are used to locate metal objects possibly hidden in clothing or body cavities of a suspect. Archaeologists use detectors not only for locating and retrieving metal objects but for many other applications as well. See Chapter 31 for a discussion of archaeological uses of metal detectors.

Various manufacturers require different types of detectors for unusual metal detecting jobs. Lumber mills use instruments to search for nails, spikes and wire in trees and logs. A single nail or spike can damage expensive sawblades in the twinkling of an eye. Correctly designed metal detectors can prevent this kind of destruction.

One lumber mill foreman needed a detector to take into a jungle, deep in the heart of Africa, to scan saw logs to locate embedded metal objects before they damaged sawblades. He could hardly believe the quantity of metal objects that were embedded in the trees in this isolated forest. Apparently, the spikes, nails, and other metallic trash had become part of these trees during World War II.

Metal detectors are widely used in food processing plants to locate "tramp" (unwanted) pieces of metal that may have broken loose and fallen into food processing containers.

One food processing plant manager had another problem...someone dropped a meat hook into two thousand pounds of sausage, and it was ground up along with the sausage. The pieces of metal had to be located, but the sausage had already been processed and packaged into links. Use of a metal detector enabled the plant manager to locate all of the meat hook metal pieces easily.

Another manufacturer had a problem with a foam rubber reclaimer. As foam was processed in his plant, it came out of the machine in sheets six feet wide by six inches thick. His manufacturing process required a heated wire to be stretched across the opening of a machine to cut the foam into layers of various thicknesses from one-half to two inches. Oftentimes metal objects, such as pins, were present in the foam. When the foam was pushed into the heated wire, the metal pins touched the wire, causing it to break. The manufacturer used a detector to locate these tiny pieces of "tramp" metal before they could reach the wire.

Modern Applications

Some metal detector applications are listed below. This list is by no means complete, but it will suggest the extent to which metal detectors are used.

Electronic Prospecting

Hunting gold nuggets.

Hunting silver nuggets.

Locating veins (gold, silver, copper, lead, zinc and other conductive metals).

Searching for isolated natural gold and silver pockets.

Lumber mill inspector in Pacific Northwest uses metal detector to search for nails, spikes, wires or other objects made of metal that could damage blades of the cutting saws.

Locating mineral zones by prospectors.

Identifying metal/mineral ore samples (bench testing.)

High grading mine and rock piles to detect conductive metal ore specimens.

Identifying various rock and mineral specimens by rockhounds.

Detecting high grade ore, as well as certain gems that contain iron and/or conductive metal.

Detecting minerals and metals bearing uranium.

Grading conductive metal ore by electronic prospectors.

Locating black sand concentrations by gold pan and dredge operators.

Industrial

Tracing electrical wiring and conduit.

Tracing and locating pipe.

Detecting nails, spikes, barbed wire, staples, bullets and other metal pieces in trees and logs that are to be milled.

Detecting foreign or "tramp" bodies in food processing.

Detecting nails and other metallic devices for ease in building construction. (Nails indicate location of studs, etc.)

Detecting spikes, nails and other metal objects that have become embedded in non-metal tires prior to recapping.

Locating underground pipe, lawn sprinklers, sprinkler heads.

Locating staples, nails, and other metallic objects in paper before further processing.

Locating staples during automatic processing of paper money.

Detecting pins, staples and other metallic objects in foam processing plants.

Locating manhole covers and other underground metal objects in the ground, under highways, and in building construction.

Detecting the presence of electrical pipes, conduits, etc., ahead of bulldozers and other earth digging and excavating equipment.

Counting quantities of items going through food processing plants, such as cans, etc.

Detecting the illegal removal of books from libraries.

Locating steel reinforcement rods in concrete slabs, highways, etc.

Detecting metal in plant vats by glassware manufacturers.

Checking bales of hops for "tramp" metal. (Hops are used to flavor beers.)

Locating pipe, cable and reinforcing rods in floors by pest control personnel to determine correct sites for pest control chemicals.

Locating all metal objects concealed (in fields) in the path of reapers and other farm machinery.

Detecting metal objects mixed with ore or coal, etc., in processing plants.

Locating concrete re-bar to determine if construction meets specifications, standards, etc.

Locating steel reinforcement in atomic reactor plants prior to drilling and installation of additional reactor strengthening devices.

Locating nails, spikes, etc., used to attach sheet rock and other wall coverings.

Law Enforcement

Locating weapons concealed on individuals and/or hidden in various parts of their anatomy.

Locating guns, knives and other metallic evidence hidden in buildings.

Detecting bullets and metal arrow points in animal carcasses by wildlife officers when investigating poaching cases.

Locating all metal objects at aircraft and other crash and wreck sites.

Searching crime scenes to locate physical evidence.

Locating evidence at arson and bombing sites, such as gas cans, bomb parts, etc.

Detecting illegal fishing nets by fish and wildlife officers.

Detecting I.D. tags implanted in fish by fish and wildlife officers.

Locating buried bodies through detection of rings, jewelry, fillings in teeth, etc., by crime scene investigators.

Medical

Locating and tracing metal particles swallowed by humans.

Detecting foreign metal particles accidentally lodged in various parts of the human body, such as the feet and eyes. (People step on needles and pins, and metallic slivers from grinding wheels are occasionally propelled into eyeballs.)

Detecting bullets in the human body. (Bullet locating might seem easy until you consider that a bullet may enter into a person, strike a muscle or a bone, and be deflected, traveling a long distance through the body before it finally comes to rest. Detectors can locate bullets much more easily and quickly than can x-ray processes.)

Tracing the flow of metallic objects through various body cavities in experimental medicine.

Military

Locating bullets, or other metal objects in cadavers by medical examiners.

Locating land mines, booby traps and other dangerous devices.

Locating unexploded bombs at practice sites.

Locating underground ammunition storage vaults.

Locating weapons, ammunition, etc. buried in foxholes.

Locating underwater obstacles, equipment and other submerged objects.

Professional

Detecting metallic objects at archaeological sites.

Locating lost rings and jewelry by insurance agents.

Locating stakes, corner posts and other markers by surveyors.

Locating only bronze, brass and other highly conductive metals at archaeological sites. (These items are more likely to bear legible inscriptions of names, dates, etc., than corrosive metals.)

Defining site perimeters on archaeological sites.

Verifying the presence of metal objects at archaeological sites to assist in determining whether ground level of dig has been reached.

Locating metal building hinges, locks, reinforcement rods which will help define building outlines, etc. at archaeological sites.

Locating pipes and fire hydrants covered with snow, sand or mud.

Use by Civil Defense personnel to locate automobiles, fire hydrants, emergency equipment and countless other things covered during snow and mud slides, flooding, earthquakes, etc.

Security

Detecting weapons on people at airports, in business establishments, courtrooms, etc.

Detecting the presence of weapons on prison visitors and inmates.

Detecting dangerous devices concealed in letters and packages.

Detecting weapons on people at sports and cultural events.

Traffic Control

Counting vehicles on roadways.

Controlling signal lights and other traffic flow devices.

Treasure Hunting

Finding coins.

Finding rings.

Finding jewelry.

Finding caches (buried money usually in some type of container.)

Detecting relics, buried in the ground and concealed in buildings.

Locating bottle and trash dumps (usually by persons who want to dig for bottles and relics.)

Locating money, caches and relics in buildings.

Finding coins under clotheslines and fence rows where clothing has been hung.

Locating discarded mile marker nails along railroad tracks.

Locating buried barbed wire.

Locating fence post holes from prior years by detecting differences in soil mineral content.

Identifying targets to determine value. (Most commonly illustrated by discriminating metal detectors where coin and treasure hunters determine whether objects are worth digging; accomplished by "measuring" the conductivity of the metal. Fortunately, gold, silver and copper are good conductors; iron, foil, bottlecaps and other junk are not.)

Underwater

Locating underwater sunken shipwreck treasure.

Locating sunken boats, motors, toolboxes, etc. (One woman used a detector to locate a toolbox that was dumped from a boat in which her husband was riding. The husband had drowned and she was attempting to locate the exact spot where the boat overturned.)

Locating sunken helicopters. (A helicopter was located in a North Central Texas lake.)

Locating weapons, money, and other metal objects thrown into wells and cisterns.

Locating metal objects to define a wreck site, archaeological perimeters, etc.

Detecting whether sonar-detected sunken objects are metal (underwater searchcoils). When only metal objects are searched for, this technique saves valuable diver time.

Miscellaneous

Detecting metallic particles in stomachs of domestic animals.

Locating buried caskets. Oftentimes, underground caskets shift beneath the ground because of water flow or earth movement. One company produces a casket with metal rings embedded in each of the four corners. Specialized metal detectors can then be used to locate the rings and prevent grave digging machines from penetrating these "misplaced" or "lost" caskets.

Analyzing and determining purity of metals and coins. (For example, determining the relative purity of silver and silver coinage).

Detecting the amount of iron mineral placed in paper currency. (This mineral is placed in U.S. paper money to give it certain long-wearing qualities. It can be detected with some metal detectors).

Locating valuable valves and other brass fixtures in junk yards and metallic junky areas.

Detecting underground earth anomalies. (Certain types of detectors can be used for detecting underground anomalies, such as voids, crevices in ice, caves, etc.)

Detecting razor blades, metallic slivers, or other metallic trash in Halloween candy.

Determining if lead sinkers have been used to increase fish weight at fishing competitions.

I close these listings with an account of how one lady envisioned a detector should NOT be used. A dealer, demonstrating a detector to a lady, told her that very large metal objects could be found to depths of more than 15 feet:

"Oh," the lady exclaimed. "I don't want that detector. I wouldn't have it!"

"Why not?" the dealer questioned.

"Well," replied the prospective customer, "Since I'm buying this detector for my husband, I'll be the one who digs all the holes. I sure don't want to dig holes 15 feet deep...

"I'm not even that tall!"

Around the World

Thus, metal detectors of all types are in use throughout the world. As in the United States, the majority of metal detector operators search for lost coins, jewelry, and money caches. In some countries, however, specialized forms of hunting take predominance.

In Western Australia, where it seems the ground is literally paved with gold, seekers of this precious metal make up the majority of metal detector owners and operators. It is not known how much gold has been taken out of Australian gold fields, but the amount is in the multiple tens of millions of dollars. Peter Bridge of Perth, Australia, who is President of Hesperian Detectors and is the "Father" of Australia's modern-day electronic "Gold Rush," reports that one gold nugget found with a Garrett metal detector brought one million dollars to its finder.

There are numerous reports of finders receiving fifty thousand, one hundred thousand, and even a quarter-million dollars for single gold nuggets. There seems to be no end to the Australian gold supply. While Australians make up the majority, a surprising number of gold-seekers, scanning the Outback, are from other countries. Australian gold tours often originate in the United States. Even Royalty gets into the act! When crown Prince Charles, heir to the British throne, made a state visit to Western Australia in 1979, a highlight of his visit was a metal-detecting, gold-hunting safari to the rich Murchison gold fields located approximately four hundred miles north of Perth.

Beach hunting around the world is on the rise. For well over a hundred years sunbathers enjoyed the beautiful Australian beaches, and it was not until the early 1980s that metal detectors were used to search these lucrative areas. On a trip to Australia in 1979, several American and English treasure hunters spent some time scanning a popular Sydney beach. We were amazed at the large quantity of coins and jewelry we uncovered in a very short time.

There is a considerable number of shipwrecks that lie in shallow waters all around Australia. Since all treasure belongs to the Crown, apparently very little activity with underwater metal detectors is taking place.

The Australian government has been using modern deepseeking detectors for years, to clean practice bombing ranges of unexploded bombs.

In Central and South America, metal detectors are used primarily in the gold and silver fields and in areas where known caches are buried in the ground or concealed in building structures. It seems everyone in Mexico knows a story about a rich treasure cache that was secreted away and never recovered by its owners. Countless ruins dot practically every area of Mexico. A 115-pound coin cache was discovered by the author during one treasure hunt in Mexico. Gold and silver coinage and caches are often reported. Sales of deepseeking equipment take the lead in Mexico, with cache hunting detectors being sold at a much swifter pace than coin hunting models.

Author uses a detector to seek metal relics, coins, jewelry or other valuables in the area of these Mexican ruins near the location where a 115-pound cache of silver was found.

There is often brisk electronic prospecting activity in the gold and silver regions of Central and South America. The quantity of silver being recovered far outweighs that of gold, but that is primarily because of the abundance of silver that can be found with metal detectors.

Since the government controls mineral resources in Central and South America, and metal detecting is restricted, it is questionable whether successes to equal Australian gold finds will take place. Of course, coin hunting on thousands of beaches can be very good as most have never been scanned with a detector.

In Canada, coin hunting is quite popular; electronic prospecting comes in a close second. Coin hunting is most popular near the populated areas, and beachcombing is on a sharp increase. Ghost town hunting is popular because of the numerous ghost towns dotted all across Canada.

Electronic prospecting is an extremely active metal detecting hobby. For instance, in the Cobalt, Ontario, region, a steady stream of electronic prospectors scan their searchcoils back and forth searching for, and finding, native silver. During the early part of the 20th century, countless miles of underground ore tunnels were dug in this region. The majority of this rock that was removed can still be found lying about in road beds and monstrous rock piles throughout the region. Electronic prospectors are having success in locating silver in these rocks that early-day miners missed. Large quantities of silver float are found all around the mining areas. Silver chunks weighing hundreds of pounds are often found. One such piece was sold to a smelter for ten thousand dollars. I have found silver in Canada, the largest piece weighed fifty pounds worth five thousand dollars.

Hunting with a Garrett Freedom detector, a hobbyist in England discovered this religious pendant believed to have been worn by King Richard III in the 15th century.

The majority of hunting in the United Kingdom, takes place on private land areas. Very little underwater work is being done. A good situation exists in England between individuals and the government. The Crown requests that all finds be turned into the British museum. All artifacts are evaluated, and if the Crown so decides, the relics will be purchased from the finder at fair market value. Those finds the Crown does not wish to purchase, are returned to the finder. Occasionally, large hoards of Roman coins are found. A fifty-thousand-coin hoard was found in the early 1980s.

Even though the private possession of hand guns is prohibited in the United Kingdom, guns and other weapons are smuggled into the country. The famed Scotland Yard has purchased hundreds of miniature hand scanning detectors to use in their investigative work.

Even during the height of the Cold War, it was reported that metal detectors were being smuggled into Russia and other Iron Curtain countries. Russian tourists in England and various Western Europe countries continue to purchase metal detectors to smuggle back into their home country.

Our West Germany distributors W. A. Albrecht and H. G. Scholz, owners of A&S Handelsgesselschaft mbH & Co. KG in Dusseldorf, relate that laws relating to metal detecting are reasonably liberal. Searching by means of locators is permitted, but excavation is permitted on private ground only. Many areas have been declared "cultural-historic areas," and are off limits to metal detecting. It appears that regulations there are similar to those in the United States.

Metal detectors are used in law enforcement all over the world; an Italian diver here prepares to take a Garrett Sea Hunter down in the Mediterranean Sea.

The ground all over European countries is a true treasure chest. Sites of old battle areas are particularly productive. Countless individual, family and even government treasures were buried for safekeeping during the various wars. Tons of treasure are still waiting to be found in the ground.

Often, reports of extremely valuable treasure finds come to my attention. Several of these finds have been written about in our *Searcher* Magazine and in various other treasure publications. Coin and cache hunting is very popular in Western Europe but since the government controls the use of metal detectors possibly no more than one percent of the potential lost wealth will ever be discovered. Certainly, millions of war relics can be found. However, relic hunting on World War II battlefield sites is considered highly dangerous because of the vast quantity of unexploded munitions.

Plebe Ciro of Livorno, Italy, has worked out a unique arrangement with his government. The government sanctions his land and underwater metal detector searches, and all finds are turned over to them. Plebe is awarded a small, yet agreeable, percentage of his finds.

Throughout Western Europe, historians and research teams are using metal detectors to scan historical sites, battlefields, ancient cities, etc. It will require several lifetimes to examine all the battlefields mentioned in the Bible alone. Researchers are using detectors at these sites to locate relics that will establish dates, define perimeters and ascertain other details of these battles.

Because oceans and lakes have been used extensively for thousands of years, tens of thousands of shipwreck sites, many sunken harbors and cities and much lost treasure await the underwater explorer. It is estimated that ten times more treasure is "lost" in water than in the ground. Metal detectors are finding treasure under water as they are on land: locating sites, defining perimeters, establishing dating, determining ship and cargo types, etc.

Sales of equipment to South Africa have been steadily increasing for several years. E. G. Beaton, owner of DECO, in Durban, South Africa, reports that the hobbyist and electronic prospectors are about equal in number. Coin and cache hunting is very popular in the more urban areas.

Throughout the world, the use of metal detection equipment shows continual signs of increasing. Terrorist attacks, bombings, hijackings and other lawlessness necessitate the use of walk-through and portable hand-held body scanning detectors. Letter and mail bombs are increasing at an alarming rate, which causes an increase in the use of instruments to detect such devices.

Industrial applications of all types of metal locating and tracing equipment are increasing. Underwater equipment continues to grow in popularity in most countries.

Three factors prevent rapid growth in world-wide detector usage:

Author and fellow treasure hunters from Holland use metal detectors to scan the site of Napoleon's 1815 Waterloo battle, where they found coins, buttons, numerous projectiles and other relics.

— Stiff governmental restrictions and high import duties and taxes,
— Complexities of reaching those who have need for metal detection devices,
— Failure of the majority of the world's population to understand the value of the metal detector. A vast number of people have never heard of metal detectors, and a good percentage of those who have don't believe that they work and do not understand the simple procedures required to locate concealed metal objects.

Nevertheless, the demand for metal detection equipment throughout the world is growing, and will continue to increase. Designers and producers of quality high tech, computerized metal detectors who are now developing world markets will be the manufacturers who will prosper as they continue to supply these markets.

Physical handicaps did not deter Otis Rood from electronic prospecting in the Paradise Valley of Alaska's Brooks Mountains, north of Fairbanks, where he found this 5 1/2-ounce nugget.

Of The Handicapped

Of the many ways metal detector owners can be of service to their communities, working with the handicapped often proves to be the most rewarding. Since President John F. Kennedy's Mentally Retarded Awareness Program of the early 1960s, the public has more clearly recognized and sought to improve the world of the handicapped. Metal detector users in every community can participate.

One of the desires of blind citizens is to participate in outdoor activities and sports. Metal detecting is an excellent outdoor hobby. The late Roy Sexton of Grand Island, NY, was a leader in the movement to introduce the blind to the world of coin and treasure hunting. For many years Roy and his family were active treasure hunters, traveled widely and enjoyed their hobby. They rarely missed a treasure hunt and have ventured as far south as Texas to attend competition treasure hunts and other metal detecting activities.

As the years went by, Roy lost most of his sight. Yet in his strange new world, Roy diligently fought to maintain a normal life. Of the many activities he pursued, metal detecting occupied much of his time. He found great enjoyment and satisfaction in being able to continue to find coins and treasure with his metal detector. During his training at a special school, Roy made friends with many people. Because of the happiness he experienced when detecting, he suggested to his school instructors that his fellow classmates might also enjoy detecting.

His instructors agreed, and Ms. Judith Engberg of the

Blind Association of Western New York set up a program. Several students enrolled in a vocational exploration program employing metal detectors. Roy volunteered to take the students out to local school yards where they explored with detectors for two hours each day, once a week for four consecutive weeks. He instructed the students in the proper use of the metal detectors. This school is believed to be the first formal metal detector school for the blind.

In a letter Roy wrote to me, he said he realized great satisfaction in helping these students do something new. The course proved that metal detecting could be a hobby for anyone with perseverance. Roy related that the students enjoyed their new hobby very much and were thrilled at being able to find a penny or even a bottlecap! He believed that metal detecting classes would continue to be taught at the school.

Mental Retardation

Mental retardation can be severe or minor. Metal detecting programs can be developed that will provide much enjoyment for almost all of the mentally handicapped and help them instill greater confidence in themselves and their abilities.

In a Utah school for the retarded, teachers developed a special metal detector Easter program. The teachers acquired a quantity of chocolate Easter eggs that were wrapped in conductive foil. Several Pocket Scanners were obtained for the students to use in this historical Easter egg hunt. A group of students, who were selected to be the first to use the detectors, were taught how to use the instruments, and the other students hid Easter eggs in their hats and pockets of their clothing.

The searchers then began scanning and were permitted to keep all the eggs they found. Later, the searchers exchanged places with the "hiders." Teachers could hardly believe the excitement that this most unusual hunt generated among the children. It was certainly one of the most enjoyable activities in which the children had ever participated.

Various other metal detecting programs have made history at schools for the mentally retarded. Treasure "maps" were placed in metal containers. The containers were buried or hidden at various locations. Working in pairs, or small groups, the youths began their search with metal detectors. Teachers put them on the right trail and helped find the first treasure map. When the young people dug up the container and found a map inside, they were very excited. This first map gave instructions on finding a second map. It was then up to the children to search, on their own, for the second container. Slowly, but surely, they found all the maps and eventually found the treasure which was theirs to keep. Who can doubt that these boys and girls enjoyed this treasure hunt as much as chocolate pie, a ride on a school bus or a trip to a movie!

At all schools for the mentally retarded, as many activities and facilities as possible are provided. With soft drinks and candy vending machines available in canteens and cafeterias, the young people think it grand to have their own money and be able to buy candy and drinks from the vending machines. Providing metal detecting coin hunts has proved a perfect way to provide a real fun day by letting these youngsters "earn" their own canteen money. Within a designated area, coins are buried at shallow depths (about one inch). The youths are given preliminary instructions on the use of metal detectors and retrieving coins with spoons or other non-dangerous digging tools. Then, in pairs, the kids can begin hunting in the area where coins have been "planted."

If you think these boys and girls are not capable of enjoying or understanding what they are doing, you must reshape your thinking. The mentally retarded of all degrees are just like you and me. When it comes to finding buried treasure, we are all the same...just like kids. Summer heat or winter cold doesn't slow these young people down. And, the finding and recovery of treasure is only half the fun! The trip to the canteen rounds out a perfect day for them.

The Disabled and the Handicapped

The disabled, including those on crutches and confined to wheelchairs, can also enjoy using metal detectors. They gain further confidence when they are successful in finding treasure with their detectors. The elderly, whose handicaps prevent them from pursuing more active hobbies, are finding that metal detectors can provide just the right amount of exercise, and they can work at their own speed. There is no time limit imposed on this hobby. A person can hunt for as long or as short a time as he or she chooses. And, there's no expensive travel involved. Sure, THing in exotic, faraway locales is fun, but the truth is that treasure also is waiting to be found literally in your own back yard.

Many older persons report that coin hunting is a sport that they wish they had begun at an earlier age. They find metal detecting to be a healthy and body improving activity! My father, who lived until his 80s, enjoyed finding treasure almost to the day he died!

Over the years, as I have watched disabled people using metal detectors, I could only stand in amazement. These people go about their metal detecting activities in spite of their handicaps. One young lady especially stands out in my memory. She enjoyed her hobby of coin hunting even though she had to use crutches to get around. She and her husband came by our factory and explained their dilemma. If we could attach a searchcoil to one of her crutches, she could both scan and walk at the same time.

We installed a searchcoil mounting bracket on the lower end of one crutch. We positioned the searchcoil so that as she swung the crutch, the searchcoil moved over the ground. We installed a detector hipmount kit so that she could carry the control housing on her belt. All of this can be seen in the photograph on the facing page.

56

Although this young lady must use crutches, she is well equipped to continue her coin hunting activity with a "rig" that connects a searchcoil mounted on her crutch with a hip-mounted detector.

She and her husband came back to visit with us later and related how the searchcoil and housing arrangement had permitted her to spend lots of enjoyable time pursuing one of her favorite hobbies. Needless to say, everyone at the factory experienced great satisfaction knowing that we had been able, in this small way, to help her.

Handicapped Awareness Programs

The Boy Scouts have always been active in handicapped awareness programs, holding them at meetings, outings and even International Jamborees. They blindfold themselves and, for a certain period of time, carry out all activities just like a blind person. The Scouts sit in wheelchairs and play basketball and other games in order to get the true "feel" of the handicapped.

One group of Utah scout leaders suggested that Scouts go on a metal detector treasure hunt. The boys thought that would be easy until their leaders placed blindfolds over their eyes. Then, the situation changed! But, that is what handicapped awareness programs are all about...to give a first-hand idea of what it is like to be handicapped.

In writing this chapter, my goal is to bring to *your awareness* what *you* can accomplish by developing and sponsoring in your community metal detecting and other programs for the handicapped and disabled individuals. These children and adults have feelings and desires just like you and I. Their problem is that they must depend upon others to help them do the things they want to do...the things that you and I take for granted. Why don't you devote some of your free time to help the less fortunate people enjoy life a little more?

Is there any greater found treasure?

Detector Development

Over the years detectors for individual, professional, and hobby use have reflected, generally, an evolution in circuitry. This evolution ran from BFO (Beat Frequency Oscillator) to TR (Transmitter-Receiver) to VLF (Very Low Frequency)—with manual and/or automatic ground balance—to the computerized instruments of today featuring microprocessor controls.

Of course, there were improvements within each of these evolutionary steps, and the progress was by no means regular. Certain hobbyists and treasure hunters continued to prefer certain circuitry over all others.

Still, it can be generally stated that TR detectors represented an improvement over BFOs, and that VLF instruments offered advantages over TRs. And, the happy result of this evolution today is the computerized VLF detector with microprocessor controls...vastly superior to everything that has preceded it.

Since all of today's modern metal detectors feature circuitry that operates in the very low frequency spectrum (even the new microprocessor-controlled instruments), there no longer exists any need for the use of this terminology. Almost *all* modern metal detectors are VLF instruments!

There is another type of circuitry that must be discussed, however...pulse induction, entirely different from all of the other types, yet still representing the modern metal detector that is now used for underwater searching.

Detectors for commercial use (industrial, military, medical, surveying, etc.) also use these same circuit types (with a few exceptions), and they may be manufactured in different configurations designed for specific applications such as public utility metal locators, airport security metal detection systems, ore sampling detectors and so on.

Basic Types

In the interests of history alone, the BFO and TR detectors will be briefly discussed in this chapter, along with pulse induction types. Later chapters will concern only the modern detectors which constitute all of those now being sold commercially, with a special all-new section of this book devoted to the computerized versions, which more and more treasure hunters are coming to welcome as their...*detector of tomorrow.*

Some of you oldtimers may immediately cry out that I'm neglecting your favorite detector, that wonderful old BFO or TR instrument that's found so many coins, rings and gold nuggets for you over the years. Well, I'll just say three things about those old detectors and promise not to mention them again after this historical chapter:

First...congratulations on your success.

Second...your detector is *obsolete.* Newcomers to the hobby have no business trying to use a BFO or TR (or an early VLF model, for that matter). And neither do old-timers, either! I wonder just how many valuable metal objects those "wonderful" old detectors have actually scanned over?

Finally...if you insist on using one of the older detectors, you must already know more about them than I do since I wouldn't try to use one to hunt...*anywhere!*

The pulse induction detectors are discussed separately because this is a different type of instrument than the VLF. Let me state, here and now, that pulse detectors are highly capable detectors. I rate them very highly for most types of treasure hunting, especially on the beach, in the surf or in the ocean's depths. The fact is, however, that the only pulse detectors now being commercially manufactured are submersible models intended for hunting under water. Our Sea Hunter, for example, is protected to depths of 200 feet. Since this is a feature not especially desired by most treasure hunters, the pulse induction type of instrument will be discussed separately.

The BFO

This venerable instrument, the BFO detector, saw its introduction at the very beginning of today's modern detectors. First models were produced after World War II. Transistorized BFOs in the '50s were lighter, more compact and used fewer batteries than earlier vacuum tube-types. BFOs performed every detecting job but were used primarily for general THing and prospecting.

The first metal detector manufactured by Charles Garrett in 1963 contained a crystal controlled Beat Frequency Oscillator circuit with vernier tuning, speaker headphones and a meter indicator.

While it is generally true that BFO circuitry and searchcoil construction were technically simple when compared with other types of detectors, it is not true that top quality, all-purpose BFO detectors were any cheaper to construct. Quality equipment of any kind costs more to build than does cheaply built equipment, even of a more complex type. Much care and skill went into the production of stable, sensitive BFO equipment.

The block diagram below shows the various BFO circuits and how these circuits are interconnected with the power supply, searchcoils and other components.

A BFO consisted of two electronic radio frequency oscillators that are designed to oscillate at the same frequency. The *reference* oscillator was generally controlled by an electronic crystal and other stable components and, consequently, could not change (or, should not have changed) its frequency. The *search* oscillator was constructed using two variable type components and, consequently, its frequency could change if one or both components changed their "value." Thus, the search oscillator's frequency was controlled by two variable components: tuning control and searchcoil. The tuning control was generally a variable capacitor. And, believe me, there was a real art to tuning this type of detector.

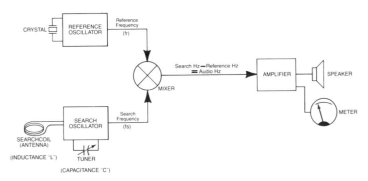

This block diagram of a crystal-controlled BFO metal detector illustrates circuit connections and electronic oscillators mixing to produce an audio Beat Frequency tone.

There was something about a BFO that made you fall in love with the instrument. The audio was especially pleasing. This detector was respected for its all-purpose capability, extreme reliability and field ruggedness. That's not to say that other types of detectors are not rugged or field worthy. It's just that back during the days when so many new and different types of detectors were coming on the market there were abnormally high failure rates. When the new whatchamacallit detector failed, the BFO was used while whatchamacallit was being repaired.

A BFO could perform most treasure hunting tasks relatively well. In fact, there was very little a BFO couldn't do, especially once the operator had mastered its capabilities. With it a THer could search for coins, money caches and relics...ghost towns and structures of all types. The BFO was right at home while performing every prospecting task.

The limits of the BFO were that it did not have the depth capability nor the ground canceling ability of later VLF types. It did not have the ability to neutralize salt water effects. Yet, even while these detectors couldn't probe as deeply as other types, nor cancel iron minerals, there were BFO experts who mastered their instruments and could literally make them "talk" in such a way that they seemed to outperform average detector operators using even the very latest of the new types of detectors.

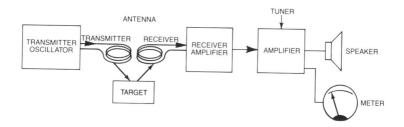

Simplified block diagram of a Transmitter-Receiver (TR) metal detector shows how an oscillator feeds signal current into the transmitter antenna which generates an electromagnetic field.

This would not be true today! Even a novice with a computerized instrument could find treasures that would elude even the most experienced and qualified veteran hunting with a BFO.

Alas, the days of the BFO have been over for years now. It has gone the way of the manual typewriter, the pinball machine and the push-type lawn mower. If you own a BFO and plan to keep it, occasionally turn it on, check it out and replace weak batteries. Spend a little time working with it and learning a little bit more about its capabilities. Take it along on a treasure hunting or prospecting excursion. Let it search the walls and ceilings of deserted houses. Someday that old detector may pay for itself many times over...if it hasn't already!

The TR

Transmitter Receiver (TR) metal detectors became popular in the '60s. Transistorized versions were lighter, more compact and used smaller batteries than did the earlier vacuum tube types. TRs were primarily very good coin hunting instruments, with excellent detection depth possible. Countless millions of coins and other treasures were found with TRs.

Their history follows a path parallel with that of BFO detectors. Both types were developed during the same time period; together, they rose to the pinnacle of popularity and then fell from prominence as newer and then-modern VLF's became popular.

The electronic circuit design and construction of TRs is based upon electronic parameters different from BFOs. The earlier summary of BFO circuitry indicated that the

The Garrett Master Hunter CX II, a wrist action configuration whose perfect balance lets the detector "float" in the user's hands, is computerized with microprocessor controls.

presence of conductive metal and non-conductive iron mineral within the detection pattern caused the antenna inductance to change. A search oscillator frequency change resulted.

TR detector reaction to the presence of metal or mineral within the detection pattern is caused by two phenomena: eddy current generation on the surface of conductive targets, and inductive imbalance between the transmitter and receiver antennas.

The name transmitter-receiver is not fully descriptive because a phonomenon called Induction (searchcoil) Balance (IB) "magnifies" the effects of target detection by the Transmission/Reception (TR) method, thus improving sensitivity and detection depth. The simplified block diagram at the bottom of Page 63 shows a transmitter oscillator connected to a transmitter antenna. The oscillator feeds a radio frequency signal current into the antenna. The current, circulating in the winding, generates an electromagnetic field that flows out away from the antenna in all directions. It resembles the electromagnetic field described in Chapter 3. An amplifier boosts any detection signal that is sensed by the receiver antenna. The amplified signal is fed into a speaker, or earphones, and these suitable indicators alert the operator to the presence of targets.

TR detectors were not as versatile as BFO types, however. While a few cache (money) hunters used TRs, they were never popular with electronic prospectors because they were ineffective over mineralized ground and had non-uniform searchcoil detection characteristics. TR popularity waned with that of BFOs in the mid-'70s.

With a pistol-grip detector like the Garrett Ultra GTA 1000, the instrument becomes an extension of the user's arm and scanning is as easy as pointing a finger.

The VLF

The first Very Low Frequency (3-30 kHz range...lower than those of BFOs or TRs) ground balancing detectors were developed in the '70s. These lower frequencies allowed responses from iron minerals to be balanced, or isolated, from other types of metal targets. Because VLF detectors responded only to metal and "ignored" effects of iron mineralization, they were not subject to troublesome responses (like TRs) when operated over ground high in iron mineralization. Detection depth was also increased.

Because iron mineral composition varies so greatly throughout the world, developing VLF ground balanced detectors with a wide tuning range was necessary...if detectors were to operate satisfactorily in all locations.

The first VLF detectors were produced with only one mode of operation; that being, ground balanced all-metal detection. Operators, who soon grew tired of digging to great depths only to find junk targets, demanded detectors with discriminating capabilities that would facilitate the elimination of trash.

When manufacturers added TR discriminating circuits to VLFs, the VLF/TR ground balanced detector was born. A VLF/TR detector features two modes: a VLF ground balanced (iron-mineralization canceling) all-metal mode and a TR discriminating mode. Since early TR discrimination modes responded to iron ground minerals, they had limitations, but eliminated some junk targets.

Most VLFs operated at approximately 5 kilohertz. Excellent depth was achieved at this frequency. Frequencies near 15 kilohertz produced an improvement in operation in the TR discrimination mode. Thus, two classes of VLF/TRs emerged. While detectors in both frequency ranges were superb instruments, the VLF 5 kHz range produced greater depth and the higher frequency 15 kHz detectors had an edge in coin hunting because of the better TR mode characteristics while operating over iron earth minerals.

68

Next came VLF detectors which incorporated ground balance and discrimination simultaneously. At first, these "motion detectors," as they were called, required extremely fast whipping of the searchcoil. Circuit complexity and an almost "insane" use of far too many integrated circuit components left much to be desired as far as field reliability was concerned. Improvements and refinements continued, however, and today we have VLF circuitry of all types that is far superior to that of early models.

Further improvements in VLF circuitry resulted in greater versatility, detection depth and target identification. These instruments are being used to re-scan "worked out" THing sites, and operators are finding treasure at depths greater than was possible with BFOs and TRs. VLFs are used in practically every metal detecting situation, from coin, cache and relic hunting to gold hunting in mountains and streams. A wide variety of searchcoils and probes greatly expands VLF capabilities. Land and shallow submersible detectors are available, as well as versatile instruments for law enforcement and industry.

Pulse Induction

Pulse Induction detector popularity began to increase in the early '80s when moderately priced, high quality and versatile detectors were introduced. Pulse instruments were available in the '70s, but they were designed primarily for underwater work and their cost was considerably higher than present models.

Pulse instruments work especially well in hostile salt water environments. Consequently, convertible types for use both on land and under water increased the popularity of pulse instruments . Salt water beach hunting had been somewhat non-productive in salt water environments that also contained iron earth minerals (magnetic black sand). Pulse detectors changed all that and opened up a new sport. Consequently, Pulse Induction metal detectors have become the most popular of all underwater types.

Industrial

Metal detection equipment is used widely for industrial, commercial and law enforcement purposes.

Industrial detectors have essentially two applications: metal locating and pipe tracing. Metal locators are used by construction crews, utilities, plumbers and others to locate buried and concealed metal objects, such as manhole covers, meter and valve boxes and sprinkler system components. In prior years field crews used whatever metal detectors were available including BFO, TR, VLF and a deepseeking RF (radio frequency) or two-box type.

Beginning in the early '80s, however, sophisticated VLF circuit types with a multitude of searchcoils became popular. Attachments that convert standard VLF configurations to the two-box type are preferred because of their deepseeking capability and their ability to ignore subterranean water and mineral pockets, a problem that plagued users of the older types.

Tracing equipment is used world-wide to locate and trace the countless millions of miles of metal pipe, cable, and conduit that is buried or otherwise concealed. Modern-day instruments not only can locate these metal objects, but they can trace, measure depth, and locate breaks. A great amount of time and money is saved by users of this equipment.

Modern-day industrial equipment manufacturers have combined metal locating and pipe tracing circuitry into one versatile instrument, which can be used as a deepseeking locator to find manhole covers, valve boxes, etc., and as a tracer to locate and trace pipes, cable, and conduit. These multiple-use instruments do all the jobs and functions that formerly required two or more instruments. In addition, the new instruments are more capable and deeper seeking.

Metal detection systems in such industries as lumbering and food processing locate nails, wire, spikes and other metal objects in tree logs prior to sawing. Detectors also

This "modern" metal detector, appearing in the September 1930 issue of *Popular Science* magazine, was described as an "amateur treasure finder...a homemade radio prospector."

locate metal objects that may be present in food products in plants where they are being processed.

Traffic control systems abound with metal locators that sense the presence and flow of vehicular traffic. Airport, industrial and others in security management use both hand-held and walk-through metal detectors to locate weapons, tools and other metal objects hidden on people as they pass through gates, out of buildings or anywhere in and out of controlled areas.

Law enforcement personnel, particularly crime scene investigators, utilize almost all types of detectors in their search for metal evidence and in searching individuals for hidden and concealed weapons. Both land and underwater types have proven themselves many times in these exciting fields.

Military Equipment

Military mine detection equipment is continually being improved. Private industry, through military grants, develops much of this equipment. Military equipment is extremely rugged and environmentally protected. Some instruments are sensitive enough to locate tiny metal pins in otherwise all plastic mines. Mine detectors are produced not only for the use of the individual soldier, but highly sensitive vehicle-mounted detectors are also in widespread use.

"Detectors" have been perfected that locate all-plastic mines and voids. Instruments have been developed to find underground caves, tunnels and storage areas, such facilities that might be constructed prior to an enemy's withdrawal from captured battle areas. I helped develop one such type in the early '60s during the Vietnam War. Of course, military operations often include commercial, deep seeking detectors for such applications as locating unexploded bombs that must be removed from practice bombing ranges and war-torn battlefield sites.

Equipment Styles

This chapter contains discussions about metal detector configurations available for any and every kind of treasure hunting. Detectors are manufactured or can be adapted to fit any style of hunting or any physical limitation. These configurations include standard models, pistol-grip types, hip mounts, chest mounts, as well as models designed to be convertible or used only under water. This material is designed not only to inform you about the various detector styles but to help you select a configuration to fit your specific personal requirements.

Detector Configurations

The traditional metal detector represents the *standard* configuration with control housing attached to the handle and stem. Several sizes of searchcoil are available. This style is restricted to land or very shallow water hunting. Our Garrett Master Hunter configuration, illustrated on Page 65, is often called the *wrist action* model, which is one of the most popular styles. Lightweight models such as the Grand Master Hunter whose balance lets the detector "float" in your hand can be used for long periods without causing much fatigue.

This style of detector is popular with THers of both sexes and all ages. Most important of all, it is easy to handle and responds instantly to even the slightest wrist movement. Plus, well-balanced detectors such as the Grand Master Hunter expose hand or arm muscles to little, if any, strain...even after a long day of hunting. All controls are readily accessible, and the meter is easy to see at all times.

Our Ultra computerized detectors feature the *pistol-grip* configuration with built-in arm rest. A pistol-grip detector such as the Ultra, illustrated in photographs accompanying this chapter, is suitable for hunting anywhere. Lightweight, properly balanced models can be used for long periods without causing undue fatigue. Some hip mount models, such as the Garrett AT4 (All Terrain), have a pistol-grip stem, and still other models are convertible to hip mount with this type stem. An example of such a convertible detector is the Ultra design, which features a slip-off battery back that clips to the hip. The detector's weight is cut by more than 35%, yet all controls and the Graphic Display are still easily accessible. Best of all, the Ultra requires no "conversion kit;" hip mount adaptability is "built into" the detector.

The pistol-grip style is popular with many treasure hunters because of the immediate response of the detector to any movement of the arm and hand. As some like to point out, scanning with this style of detector is as easy as pointing a finger.

For various reasons, some detector operators desire that the housing of their instrument be body-mounted. This can be done to relieve weight on the hand and arm or to raise the detector for use in shallow water.

The *hip-mount* configuration model is especially popular for hunting in rugged terrain as well as on the beach and in splashing surf waters. The control housing, mounted on a belt, can be worn around the waist (hip-mounted) or slung over the shoulder. This not only relieves the arm and hand of weight but permits the operator to retain a better sense of balance when difficult terrain or conditions are encountered.

Some hip-mounted models are non-convertible because they cannot be assembled into a standard wrist-action or pistol-grip detector configuration. An adjustable-length stem and an armrest are supplied. Belt clips are attached to the control housing. Some hip-mount styles permit use of more than one searchcoil. Ideally, the meter is easily visible and all controls are quite accessible.

A special accessory kit is available with many detector models that permit you to convert your *standard* configuration into *hip-mount*. Generally, the control housing is mounted on a belt and slung around your waist or across one shoulder. Equipping your detector with hip-mount components may require minor fabrication such as drilling a hole and/or mounting one or more strap clips. If you are hesitant to put a tool to your detector, ask your dealer for instructions. Some dealers are factory-trained in this procedure.

Use of the *hip-mount* configuration generally requires searchcoil cable that is longer than the normal length of 90 inches. Using a standard-length cable on a hip-mount unit necessitates the use of an extension cable two or three feet long with mating conductors. If the unit is to be used under water, the connectors must be waterproof.

When used as a hip-mounted unit, a Garrett GTA detector does not require extra cable because the coiled cord emerges from the handle of the detector as needed to connect with the battery box.

Our new Ultra detectors are a happy exception to the rule of "hip-mount accessories." This detector converts to a hip-mount configuration merely by slipping the battery pack from its normal position and clipping it on one's belt. The coiled cable cord is designed for hip-mount use at any time.

The *chest-mount* configuration with control housing mounted high up on the chest just under the chin proves quite functional, but has never enjoyed much popularity. Usually, the control housing is suspended with a cross-shoulder x-type strap that holds the housing flat against the upper part of the chest. The control housing should be as slim as possible to permit an unrestricted view of the ground. If a meter is provided it must be mounted either on top of the control housing or on the lower part protruding away from the body so that it can be readily viewed. The knobs should be readily accessible, but should not interfere with clothing.

Convertible configuration detectors are designed to permit the control housing to be attached to the stem (standard operation) or worn on the body. The *body-mount* configuration requires a cable length of about 90 inches. The extra weight of this cable is noticeable when the detector is used in the *standard* configuration.

Flotation mounting locates the control housing on some sort of a device that will float when the detector is to be used for searching in the surf or in shallow lake and stream waters. Almost any type of detector is suitable for flotation mounting if extra searchcoil cable is available. Flotation mounting is satisfactory for lakes and ponds with calm water but is generally risky when operating in ocean surf or fast-moving streams. Some floats are made from such inflatable articles as large plastic bottles; others are made of styrofoam. Most surf hunters build their own flotation devices.

They can be built with a wire mesh sifter, preferably one that is hinged to facilitate quick dumping of accumulated rock and debris. Of course, metal trash should not be dumped but brought in for proper disposal. Compartments on the float are designed to hold treasure finds and trash. Hook arrangements can support digging equipment, and some THers carry food and drink to permit a snack without leaving the water. The float can also be used as a "life raft" when flotation support is needed.

That Second Detector

Probably two-thirds of all active treasure hunters own more than one metal detector. Usually, they have a main instrument — the one they search with most often. They keep on "standby" one or two additional detectors...usually older models. Should their primary instrument fail, or get stolen, the hunter always has a backup unit.

Many hobbyists have more than one detector because they enjoy *more than one type of hunting.* They may like to find treasure on both land and in the water. In that case,

Because so many THers "cut their teeth" with the Freedom Ace Plus, it is a popular second detector that is still used even after hobbyists have "moved up" to a more sophisticated instrument.

77

they probably need a dry land model and one they can get wet. Many THers have several models, perhaps a specialized coin hunting type, a deepseeking cache hunting type and a model for gold hunting.

Some hobbyists purchase a new detector almost every year as newer, deeper seeking and more capable detectors are introduced. They know how just a slight bit of extra detection depth can pay dividends.

Some detectors are all purpose; they can perform many treasure hunting and prospecting tasks. All purpose detectors eliminate need for more than a single detector unless the hunter is concerned with primary detector failure. Also, there is no all purpose detector built that can be submerged for surf hunting.

Should you obtain a *second* detector? In the event of primary detector failure — which, by the way, is not likely to occur — a backup detector is necessary. If you don't travel far from home and rental instruments are available, your need for a second instrument is reduced. Your first purchase will probably be for a coin hunting model. After all, that's what most people go after. But, later, you may become interested in surf hunting or you may be going into gold country. You may then wish to equip yourself with a different model for more effective performance in those other fields.

A second detector is especially beneficial when there is someone to use it. Perhaps your spouse or other family member could hunt with the second detector, yet be willing to temporarily give it up (or maybe do the digging...?) if the primary detector fails or is stolen. Let me urge, however, that you purchase wisely any and all instruments you buy. Choose reliability no matter how many instruments you need and you may never have to purchase again.

Characteristics

An understanding of the operating characteristics is important, whether you are buying, using or just trying to understand metal detectors. First must come familiarity with the general characteristics of any metal detector, followed by specific understanding of a given instrument. Such knowledge will help you analyze manufacturers' product reports, advertisements and dealers' explanations of their products.

Fifteen specific characteristics are discussed in this chapter. They are listed in alphabetical order, with no particular "weight" given to their importance. In fact, rating these characteristics by their *importance* can be the subject of some lengthy conversations (arguments?) among THers!

Balance

Metal detector balance is a physical characteristic. It refers to the ease with which a detector rests in the hand when held in the normal operating position. A detector with good balance is one that requires little effort to hold the searchcoil in the air at operating height. The better the balance...the less fatigue you will notice during and after your search.

Manufacturers strive to produce well-balanced detectors, and there is really no excuse today for a detector that is not well-balanced. At one time, it was somewhat difficult to produce perfectly balanced detectors because of searchcoil weight. The old, heavy coils just destroyed balance. Searchcoil windings by some manufacturers required large amounts of a foam substance (which had weight) for mechanical strength and to improve durability.

Newer and lighter searchcoils feature better and sturdier mountings for windings that require little, if any, foam. Still, it is important that they be hardy and durable, because flimsy searchcoils can lead to problems and expense for the user. After a certain amount of field use, poorly constructed searchcoils may begin to deteriorate, resulting in erratic operation, drift, and other undesirable characteristics. Only the purchase of a new searchcoil can remedy the situation.

Searchcoils larger than seven-to-eight-inch diameter (general purpose size) may imbalance some detectors. In these situations, an armrest or hipmount can prove the answer. An armrest can dramatically improve detector balance. Hipmount configurations can solve an imbalance problem by removing the control housing from the handle and placing it on the operator's belt.

Capability

A capable detector is one that satisfactorily performs all of the functions for which it was designed. Do not confuse "versatility," discussed later, with "capability." A versatile detector is one that can perform many different metal detecting tasks. A capable one can perform specified tasks in a satisfactory manner. For example, a 100%-capable coin hunting detector will locate all coins in a given area when controls are properly adjusted for that area and the detector is being properly used. If that detector cannot locate all the coins, then it is only partially capable.

Remember that a detector can be capable, but not be capably used. Of the many limitations that prevent total metal detecting success, more often than not, the greatest is the lack of operator ability. The degree of success achieved with any instrument depends primarily upon how well an operator has mastered the equipment.

Construction

Outside of design, the construction of a metal detector is the most critical factor affecting capability, performance, dependability, versatility, overall quality and, certainly, all the other operational characteristics by which that detector can be judged.

A detector that is well-made will show it. There will be no sharp corners to rip clothing or cut hands and arms. It will have a solid feel; the handle and stems will be securely attached to the control housing. The finish (or, paint job on older detectors) will be uniform...without chips and scratches. The instrument will *appear* well-designed, with the best principles of human engineering applied to every component. It will have good, comfortable balance...not requiring a great amount of effort to hold at operating height when fitted with a general purpose searchcoil. Labels and decals will be attractively designed and will be applied with no peeling corners to deteriorate further in the field.

The detector that was used properly by this treasure hunter demonstrated its capability to locate the small Civil War relics in the palm of his hand as well as the large pistol.

Look closely at the detector. Does it give the impression of quality? Does it have rough edges and unfinished parts? Do the controls turn smoothly? Do the meter and/or other detection indicators function properly?

Turn it on, adjust the controls, and put it through its paces. Bump the control housing with your hand. Does the instrument seem solidly built and does the audio remain at its threshold setting without having to be continually readjusted?

Quality of construction of a detector is best determined, not by looking at photographs, but by *testing the detector for yourself.* As with any product, there are differences in construction quality among manufacturers. If you want to spend your money for a detector that will stand up in the field, you should *do your own testing.*

Dependability

Dependability is the measure of how well a given metal detector performs in the field. How long that detector can be used without a disabling malfunction is also a measure of dependability. If mechanical or electrical malfunctions don't limit or prevent operation, that detector is dependable. No detector, of course, should be expected to give a lifetime of trouble-free performance. Even the most dependable, highest quality detectors occasionally malfunction in the field. When you consider that there are perhaps two thousand components and assembly steps in the manufacture of a metal detector, and that each of those components and assembly steps are made by a human, you can understand that sooner or later something may fail. Of course, the chances of malfunction can be almost entirely eliminated in manufacture by the use of

Noted prospector Frank Chapman understands that proper design and high quality construction are essential if a detector is to operate properly in rugged gold country.

quality components and construction techniques. Manufacturers who regularly update their products, improve quality and field test their instruments on a continuing basis will produce the most dependable products.

It is a fact that some detectors are more dependable than others. Unfortunately, there is no cut and dried method of locating the most dependable products. Your own experience is the best measure. Join a metal detector users' club; talk to other detector owners and dealers; read books and magazines. Gradually you'll learn of the brands and types of metal detectors that are dependable and that represent consistent high quality.

Detection Depth

Usually the first question people ask when they begin thinking about metal detectors is, "How deep will that detector go?" This question simply cannot be answered with complete accuracy because many factors influence detection depth.

The major factor is how well the detector was designed and manufactured. Other factors are truly too numerous to list, but among them are the size of the target object, its shape and composition, how it lies in the ground, how long it has been in the ground, whether detectable metals and minerals are in the search area, moisture content of the ground, influence of nearby metallic objects, what type of instrument and searchcoil the operator is using, the condition of the detector and its batteries, the extent of operator expertise, how well the operator can hear the detector responses, how alert the operator is...and, the list could be continued. These, however, are the primary factors that determine depth.

Quality metal detectors are meant to be used...not babied; and, if properly maintained, should be expected to perform satisfactorily for many years in all types of environments.

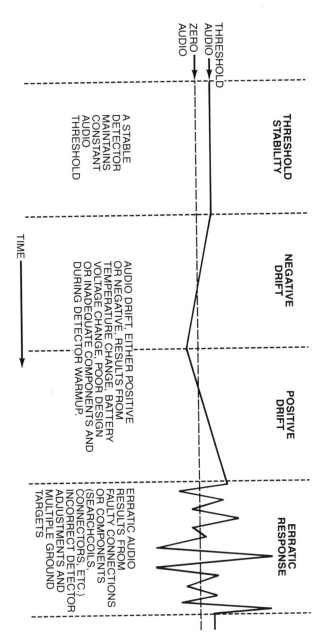

This diagram illustrates metal detector drift by depicting the audio level of a metal detector during times of threshold stability, negative and positive drift and erratic response.

86

Drift

Drift is a troublesome and undesirable change in the threshold of a metal detector.

To understand drift, consider this example. Turn on your radio and tune it to a station. If the station continues to come in loud and clear, then the tuning does not drift. If the station fades out, the radio has drift. The same thing can sometimes happen in metal detectors. If the detector is tuned to the desired audio threshold operating point but gets louder or fades out, the detector has drift.

Drift results from many conditions, including temperature changes, component aging, battery malfunction, searchcoil expansion, contraction and others.

Many people do not understand drift and confuse it with ground mineral pickup. When a detector, operated over mineralized ground, is not balanced properly to eliminate ground minerals from detection, audio can fluctuate. This fluctuation, as the searchcoil is scanned over the ground, is often erroneously termed drift. Frequently, customers write to a manufacturer, claiming their detectors *drift,* when, in reality, the instruments are improperly ground balanced and are picking up (reacting to) iron minerals.

The new computerized detectors with microprocessor controls are truly drift-free, but most other detectors still have some amount of drift. Drift can also result from temperature changes, such as those that occur when a detector is taken from a warm car into cold air, or when a warm searchcoil is thrust into a cold mountain stream.

False Detection

In the strictest sense, quality metal detectors do not give signals unless *something* has been detected. A quality detector will never lie to you! When an instrument that is working correctly gives a signal, some thing or some condition caused that signal to be produced. Many times detector operators get a signal, dig a hole and find nothing.

Actually, of course, there was a reason for the signal, though the operator may not understand what it was.

On getting a signal when coin hunting, the operator may cut a plug, check it with the detector, and get no reading, then scan over the hole and get no reading. What is wrong? The coin may have become dislodged from its flat position, fallen further down into the hole, and came to rest in a vertical position. A deeply buried coin standing on edge is more difficult to detect because of the relatively small surface on which eddy currents can be generated. So, even though the operator sees nothing, and thinks there is nothing in the hole, he would be wise to explore a little deeper.

Again, a detector signal from no apparent target can be caused by tin cans or bottlecaps which have completely rusted. Carry a small, powerful magnet and rub it into the dirt. If iron rust is present, it will become attached to the magnet and the mystery of another false hole will be solved!

A detector may give its metallic signal as a response to bit of foil or a gum wrapper. The operator begins to dig. The piece of foil crumples or disintegrates and cannot be as readily detected.

To avoid being fooled by apparently false signals pinpoint carefully and learn to distinguish among responses. You will soon learn, for example, that small bits of foil generally produce a *high squeal* from a detector.

Another small object that can produce a big response is a .22 caliber shell. After these shells have been buried for a year or longer, they produce a very large signal. Because of their size and color, they are often overlooked after they are uncovered and the hobbyist may continue digging a deeper and deeper false hole.

In another instance, the operator gets a positive indication as he scans across a hole he has dug. So, he digs a little deeper, scans again and receives another metallic response. This sequence can be repeated until signals are being received from a monstrous, gaping hole. You may ask, "Why does a detector give a metal indication over such a hole? Especially, when there is no metal in it!" The explanation for this is somewhat complex, but can be quite easily understood.

Most ground contains some mineralized negative-reaction iron. If the detector searchcoil is lowered to the ground, it drives the oscillator in the "negative" or "mineral" direction. In order for the operator to search correctly over such ground, the detector must be adjusted. This manual, positive adjustment of the detector circuitry, cancels the negative reaction caused by the ground and, as the operator scans across the ground, the detector, thus, "ignores" the "minerals" that were producing a response.

If, however, the searchcoil is scanned over a place in the ground where the negative-reacting iron has been removed, the detector may produce a positive indication because the negative, disturbing force was removed, allowing the positive adjustment to sound through the speaker.

Spots of ground which have an absence or a low concentration of mineral, can be caused in several ways. A hole might have been dug for a post which was later removed with the hole refilled with non-mineralized ground. A wash can also cause this problem, and a fire can create the same effect.

In ground containing conductive salts, metal detectors can react positively to the salt. Wetter ground causes an even greater positive indication. Ground that is predominantly positive, yet containing very little moisture, will appear as neutral. However, in a shallow place or sink hole with moisture, the salts will become conductive. As the detector is passed over this area, a positive indication is produced. Salt occurs naturally in certain areas. Also, the farmer or rancher who sets out a block of salt for animals unknowingly creates a "metal" target as rain slowly dissolves the salt, and it seeps into the ground.

Fringe Area

Fringe area describes the extreme outer limit of the search matrix (pattern) where detection of targets can occur. Within the detection pattern, audio and meter target indications are pronounced and easily recognized. Near the outer edges of the matrix, targets produce weak signals. Unless the operator is using headphones and paying careful attention, fringe area signals will go unrecognized.

Life Expectancy

Any well-made detector given reasonable care can be expected to provide many years of service. Skid plates (coil covers) will protect searchcoils from wear caused by constant abrasion against ground and rocks. Carrying bags are available for storage and transportation. Speaker covers allow some instruments to be operated in light rain. Newer models are specifically designed to protect the speaker from the elements

Keep your detector clean by wiping it occasionally with a damp cloth. Dismantle and clean the stems to remove any buildup of dirt that might lock or freeze the stems. Install fresh batteries as often as needed. Never leave batteries in a detector longer than one month without checking them. Even that much time is risky if the batteries are already in a run-down condition.

Screws that hold the various parts of the detector together should be occasionally checked and tightened when necessary. Follow all maintenance instructions in your owner's manual.

Do not be afraid to use your detector when and where you need it, even under apparently poor environmental conditions. Detectors are electronic instruments, but they are designed to be used. They are built to be rugged and to give dependable, trouble-free operation for a long time. Land detectors are made to be scrubbed over the ground, occasionally bumped into trees and rocks, back-packed and hauled around as the need arises. Most can be sub-merged in water to the control housing.

Any detector that cannot take normal usage is poorly designed and manufactured. So, again, don't be afraid to use your detector. Put it to work! Make it do what you want it to do and what it should do. If it's a good one, it will hold up and give many years of dependable service.

Limitations

Although metal detectors are built that will do just about everything except dig the target, they all have limitations. Detectors are getting "smarter," however, as proved by the new microprocessor-controlled instruments. Instruments of tomorrow will seem be even more improved. Let's look, however, at some of the ways in which detectors may be limited.

Metal detectors cannot penetrate all earth materials. In areas where ferrous and conductive minerals are present, penetration will be restricted to an extent. The greater the mount of minerals, the greater will be the

Because newly designed elliptical searchcoils can scan their full length from toe to heel, they can be considered to have an effective wide scanning capability as well as knife-edge penetration.

reduction in penetration. In locations where the matrix (area to be searched) is non-uniform, such as mine dumps, penetration may be seriously reduced.

Under no circumstances can metal detectors ever "reach out" to locate targets. In order for a metal target to be detected at any time, some portion of it must be lying within the area of the detection pattern directly below the searchcoil.

Metal detectors can classify or identify metal targets with only limited accuracy. Audio and meter indicators can classify metals into groups, called "probability" indication. Because different targets can fall into the same groupings, what a detector indicates to be a coin sometimes turns out to be a bottlecap. Probability indicator meters are getting better, however, and are definitely valuable in increasing the efficiency of the operator by helping make the decision whether to dig and to locate coins among metal trash.

Some other limitations are also being overcome. Depth of detection is a good example. A few years ago, single coins could be detected to about six inches deep; today, coins are often found at depths of twelve inches and deeper! A few years ago, a gallon bucket of coins could be detected at two feet; today, that same bucket can be detected to six feet-plus!

Penetration

This refers to the capability of a detector actually to *penetrate* earth minerals, air, wood, rock, water, and other material to locate metal targets. Although the terms "penetration" and "detection depth" are sometimes used interchangeably, penetration is actually one of the limiting factors in depth detection. While a detector may penetrate sand to detect an object at six feet, that same detector may only penetrate an iron mineralized matrix to detect that same object at only two feet. Of course, air is easier to penetrate than any solid or liquid substance.

Scanning Width

Scanning width is a function of detector type and searchcoil design. All detectors can be built so that detection of shallow metal objects occurs across the full width of its searchcoil. As detection grows deeper, the search pattern decreases in width as the distance from the searchcoil bottom increases.

In the early days of metal detection, some searchcoils had an effective scanning width of less than one-half their diameter. An eight-inch searchcoil had an effective scanning detection width of less than four inches on shallow targets, with width diminishing on deeper objects. Most of today's detectors feature full searchcoil-width scanning.

Sensitivity

Sensitivity, a measure of the ability of a metal detector to sense conductivity changes within the detection pattern, must be regarded as one of the most important operational characteristics of any electronic metal detector. Sensitivity is measured by the degree of change in conductivity of a suspected target that is required to produce a detector signal. The smaller the change in conductivity it takes to produce a detector signal, the more sensitive the instrument.

Detector sensitivity and depth detection are phrases often used interchangeably. Since sensitivity is a measure of the ability of an instrument to detect very tiny objects, it follows that a detector with poor sensitivity will have poor depth detection. Sensitivity is mostly dependent on, or related to circuitry and design features of a detector: operational frequency, searchcoil design, quality or low-noise characteristics of its amplifiers, and sensitive high-gain receiver circuits.

Sensitivity is illustrated by the fact that gold nuggets weighing less than 0.05 grams are often found with certain detectors to depths of about three inches (7.5 cm.). Such gold nuggets are only about the size of a pin head!

Stability

This characteristic measures the ability of any detector to hold or maintain its threshold level during a wide range of varying conditions. If the detector drifts, it is unstable. A perfectly stable detector is one that, once adjusted, never requires any type of threshold adjustment. Any number of factors may affect stability...temperature changes, battery conditions, moisture, mechanical shock (bumping a tree, for example), mechanical and electronic change due to poor detector design, change in the preset tuning due to faulty controls, loose wiring, poor connections and others.

Versatility

How many different jobs a detector will perform is the measure of its versatility. Some models are so versatile they will excel at every treasure hunting task. Others may perform only one or two tasks efficiently. Extremely versatile detectors always have more than one available searchcoil. Searchcoils vary in size, with the application depending upon what they are designed to do.

Capability is a factor that affects versatility. Two instruments may be equally versatile, but one of them may be far more capable, in that it can detect a given object much more deeply than the other. Some instruments are designed specifically for certain applications, such as coin hunting, weapons detection and underwater searching.

Components/Controls

This chapter will be concerned with a number of the various components and controls on a modern metal detector. In the following chapter, I will discuss the important detector functions of Ground Balance, Discrimination, Pinpointing and Audio. Searchcoils, headphones and other accessories are discussed in Section IV.

Battery Systems

Various types of batteries are used in detectors. Our Garrett models, for example, use AA and C cells, as well as 9-volt. All of our battery systems are interchangeable between regular and NiCad rechargeable batteries. As long as detector circuits are designed properly, battery type is of little importance in determining the quality of the detector or how well it performs.

One of the most reliable battery types is the carbon-zinc. Carbon-zinc batteries are, however, more likely to leak acid when the battery is in a discharged state, than are alkaline and NiCad units. Alkaline batteries give longer life, but they cost more. If you use your detector quite often, NiCad rechargeable batteries may save money.

Arguments continue as to which is best...non-rechargeable or rechargeable batteries. Manufacturers promote their rechargeable batteries, claiming up to $1,000 in savings during the life of the rechargeables. Let's study the situation.

Rechargeable batteries cost more than other battery types, and battery rechargers are expensive. It doesn't matter whether the NiCads come standard with the detector or whether they are purchased separately. The purchaser pays the cost. The detector operator who uses a detector one hour every day will spend from $40 to $80 per year on disposable batteries. Rechargeable batteries can pay for themselves (if they suffer no catastrophic failure), but, obviously, the length of this "payout" depends upon the battery drain of the detector, how often the detector is used and other operating factors.

To help prevent premature failure, keep NiCads fully charged. Recharge them as soon as possible after you use the detector.

If you use standard, off-the-shelf NiCad rechargeables, what do you do about spare batteries? It may be wise to purchase a set of carbon-zinc batteries and keep them in the refrigerator, except during the time when you take them on your detecting trips. If your detector is equipped with specially designed rechargeable battery packs, with no provision for standard off-the-shelf batteries, then you should purchase an extra rechargeable battery pack from the manufacturer.

Battery containers for Garrett's GTA Ultra series (above) and the Grand Master Hunter series (facing) illustrate the innovative battery systems available on modern detectors.

Keep spare carbon-zinc batteries on standby for about six months, then use until they are discharged. Purchase a fresh set for spares, and repeat the process each six months. A spare set of carbon-zinc batteries may cost a few dollars, but the lost time and frustration they can avoid make the cost seem small indeed.

Generally, detector manufacturers provide a meter or audio indication of battery condition. Determine how accurate the meter is by continuing to use a set of batteries in your detector until it is obvious that the detector is no longer performing correctly. "Motorboating," or some other erratic signal, will tell you your detector is not operating as it should. While you are letting these batteries run down, note the position of the meter pointer that checks batteries and listen to the audible tones. If the "low battery" signal is given a considerable time before the batteries actually ran down, you can obtain extra battery mileage by not replacing the batteries as quickly as your detector indicates.

Always carry a spare set, however!

There is an amusing story told about one treasure hunter who was paying no attention to the condition of his detector's batteries. He began to hear a da-da-di-da sound. The speaker was producing what he thought to be Morse code signals! The treasure hunter jumped up and down, yelling to his buddy, "Hey, I've detected a cave or something! I've located an underground radio transmitter!" Actually, the electronic circuits were "motorboating," a condition that occurs when the battery voltage level drops too low to supply adequate power to the circuits. Internal battery resistance creates a feedback situation that causes the electronic circuits to oscillate in a da-da-di-da fashion.

Chapter 34 of this book, "Maintenance and Field Repair," gives additional information and tips on how to get more from detector batteries and how to prolong their life.

Control Housing

Control housings in which electronic printed circuit board(s), batteries, switches, etc. are generally placed come in all sizes, shapes, configurations and materials. Some control boxes are quite large, while others are matchbox size. The size of the box has nothing to do with the performance of the detector, provided it's large enough for adequate housing of all components, and that components are arranged in such a way that creates no electronic interference or other detector operating problems.

Detectors manufactured today use aluminum and plastic control boxes. Metal boxes are in themselves a Faraday-shield, whereas plastic boxes require certain special shielding or circuitry construction if the manufacturer wishes to prevent outside electrical interference.

Metal and plastic both can be used to advantage in the construction of metal detectors. The right type of plastic, such as ABS, is very strong and lightweight, and when properly used, can perform as well as aluminum. Plastic can be manufactured in colors that produce a very attractive finish. Aluminum parts may be anodized and/or spray painted, and plastic parts may also be painted. Extremely durable epoxy paints are available which can even be applied with various attractive "finish" patterns.

Many detector components are now made of lightweight plastic, such as searchcoil housings, meter covers, knobs and controls.

Some old-timers may try to claim that housings with control panels mounted on the left are intended for use by right-handed people only. They say, these detectors cannot be held with the left hand because the controls cannot be reached with the right hand.

Rubbish!

When you think about it, most all detectors are "right-hand" designed because detectors that have top-mounted controls, have main knobs that are located on the left side

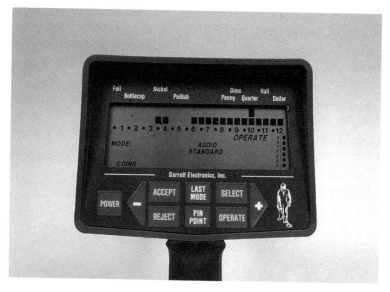

This close-up of the control panel on the Garrett Ultra GTA 1000 detector illustrates its touchpad controls and the LCD display that presents a continuous "on-line" report of all detector functions.

of the handle. Consequently, when the detector is held in the left hand while scanning, it would be difficult to reach over the handle, past the arm, to adjust these controls.

With the "set-and-forget" detectors, very few adjustments are *ever* necessary after initial settings are made at the beginning of a search day.

Controls that are recessed give protection if the detector is ever dropped. Also, controls are less likely to be accidentally "adjusted" by shrubs or tree branches when the detector is being used in brushy country.

Handle

The handle on a wrist-action detector such as those in our Master Hunter series is used to carry the detector and to maneuver the searchcoil over the ground, up a wall or along and over any surface to be scanned. The handle should have a comfortable plastic or rubberized grip. Even more important is its location for the detector to have optimum mechanical balance.

Some manufacturers have sought to avoid the problem of balance by converting all their models to the pistol-grip configuration. At Garrett we believe that a well-balanced wrist-action detector can be a good one for both beginner and professional alike, and we will continue to manufacture them.

Facing

Electronic prospectors Virgil Hutton, left, and Roy Lagal examine impressive gold nuggets that were found with modern metal detectors.

Over

Although only one of the many treasures that can be discovered with metal detectors, coins are the most common target of THers and are surprisingly easy to find.

Some say the handle should not obstruct the view of meters or other indicators. In actual practice such obstruction has never been the problem competitive advertising made it out to be.

Connecting Stem

The stem connects the control housing to the searchcoil. Most are adjustable, while some have a fixed length and cannot be adjusted. There are times, however, when a metal detector operator will *need* a longer or shorter length stem. It will sometimes be necessary, when scanning a building, to lengthen the stem for ceiling scanning. When reduced to the shorter length, the detector can be stored in a suitcase, a bag, or carried in a backpack.

Locking mechanisms for telescoping stems are generally of two kinds: a friction device or a spring clip producing "buttons" that lock into place in holes in the outer stem. Friction devices are good, but they do not provide automatic searchcoil alignment. Spring clip holes keep the searchcoil aligned automatically.

Target Indicator Meters

Meters are visual indicators and serve several functions. A meter permits the operator to observe detection functions. The indicator pointer and/or lights generally operate in synchronism with speaker sounds. When the audio increases in volume, the meter pointer deflects upward or the LCD indicator illuminates. When the speaker sound decreases, the meter pointer drops downward and the LCD indicator disappears.

The Graphic Target Analyzer™ on Garrett's new GTA Ultra detectors is a totally new kind of "meter." It reports

Treasures discovered by Charles Garrett include this 16th-century Spanish religious icon found under a coral outcropping on the Caribbean island of Guadeloupe.

continuously and visually on an LCD display such information as depth and type of target, audio and tone levels, sensitivity, battery condition, etc.

A meter and/or graphic target analyzer can also be used to pinpoint buried objects exactly. As you scan the searchcoil across a buried object, note where the maximum deflection of the meter pointer occurs. Maximum deflection indicates target center. If the target is large, or shallowly buried, it may be necessary to elevate the searchcoil several inches and scan over the target so that the meter pointer stays on scale. Otherwise, you will not be able to determine the point of maximum signal.

Another important meter function is the parallel indication function. Let's say that while scanning, you hear a very weak sound...so weak, in fact, that you are not sure you detected a target. Scan back over the spot, and pay careful attention to the meter pointer and the LCD lights.If you see the pointer deflect upward or a light appear, however slightly, while you are scanning over the spot where you heard the weak audio sound, you may be assured that some target has been detected.

Certainly, this is not always true for all detectors under all conditions because some detector meters are less sensitive than the speaker. Too, some people have developed what is called a "musical ear" and have the ability to hear sounds that either are extremely weak, or are composed of harmonic frequencies that occur when the detector detects metal. People with this exceptional ability can hear detection signals that would not show up on any kind of meter.

For additional information on the GTA and its functions read Section III and, especially, Chapter 19.

Contouring

The meter can be used to indicate a fairly accurate outline of the target. When the operator has detected a target, he can approach it from various angles with the side edge or "toe" of the searchcoil. The meter pointer or LCD can be watched, and when it deflects upward or lights, say, one division, a mental note can be made where on the ground this occurs, and the outline or contour of the target can be plotted.

Classifier meters and bar graphs such as those on Garrett detectors with a GTA (Graphic Target Analyzer) can be of great value in giving a general or probable indication of the identity of detected targets. Manufacturers print various target data to help a hobbyist determine what has been discovered. Always remember that numerous targets can produce similar readings. Experiment with your detector and its meter. Conduct bench tests with various targets and observe the meter indications. This will help you use a meter more effectively in the field.

Controls

There can be from one to a dozen touchpads, control knobs or switches found on a metal detector. These various types of controls may be hidden within the housing or they may be in plain sight. They are all designed by manufacturers to permit an operator to manipulate electronic circuitry that enables the detector to perform as desired (and advertised).

Knobs and switches often make detectors more complicated to operate. Numerous knobs, all of them the same

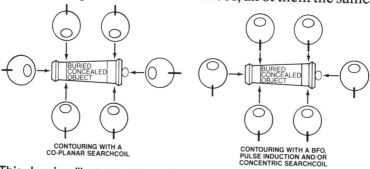

CONTOURING WITH A
CO-PLANAR SEARCHCOIL

CONTOURING WITH A BFO,
PULSE INDUCTION AND/OR
CONCENTRIC SEARCHCOIL

This drawing illustrates the various methods by which a detected target can be contoured, either by moving into it with the toe of the searchcoil or from the side of the coil.

type and size, lined up in neat rows, can add to this complexity. The design trend, and the desire of most manufacturers, is to produce instruments with as few knobs and switches as possible. Some people just won't take the time to learn to use detectors that are controlled by an excessive number of knobs. Even if they did, the manipulation procedures are forgotten when the equipment is not used on a regular basis.

Similar advice can be given for the "programming" features of a computerized detector. It should be as simple as possible, with preset detection modes instantly available for the detector operator who simply wants to hunt for coins or on the beach and has no special discrimination requirements. See Section III of this book for more information on computerized detectors.

Most people prefer a highly capable and versatile detector that they have only to turn on.

This statement is just as true today as I rewrite this edition as it was six or seven years ago when I first wrote this book. In that First Edition, however, the statement was followed by this sentence: Some day there may be instruments like that, but for now, and in the foreseeable future, universal, advanced circuitry detectors that can perform many functions, need certain controls for the operator to achieve desired operating characteristics.

Well, the future is now!

By the 1990s detectors were already on the market that were ready to hunt *under any conditions* simply at the touch of a single control. I can specifically cite our Garrett Master Hunter CX, Grand Master Hunter CX II and Ultra GTA models. Each of these three performs flawlessly at the simple touch of the **ON** touchpad with *absolutely no other adjustment necessary.*

Controls on any detector should be correctly located to facilitate ease of operation. Those controls designed to set single functions often have no knobs; that is, the control shaft is brought out beyond the panel just far enough so that the operator can turn it and make the single adjustment. Since there is no knob to get in the way, the operation of other controls is not hindered. Some manufacturers purposely leave knobs off "set- and-forget" controls, to encourage operators to leave these controls alone. Many people cannot resist the temptation to turn every knob. Let me urge you, however, not to manipulate knobs *just to be turning them*. If they have to be adjusted...fine. Do so. Otherwise, *leave them alone!*

Touchpads or the older toggle and rocker switches generally are used for dual-function purposes, such as power, mode selection and checking batteries.

Cut-Out Switches

Some detectors feature a mercury tilt switch that cuts out (removes) power from the speaker when the detector is laid horizontally on the ground. The sound is eliminated when targets are being dug, and battery power is conserved. Dirt clumps cannot be checked, however, if the mercury tilt switch cuts power to the speaker.

Some detectors feature a mercury tilt switch that activates a semi-automatic tuning mode. When the detector is laid horizontal, an automatic mode takes over the tuning and maintains sound threshold.

Mercury tilt switches should be housed in an unbreakable capsule, because mercury coming in contact with a PC board can damage components and dissolve solder connections.

Connectors

Several types of connectors are used both inside and outside the detector. Outside connectors link the searchcoil cable to a bulkhead connector, mounted usually on the lower end of the detector control housing. This cable provides the pathway for electronic signals to travel back and forth between the printed circuit board and the searchcoil windings.

Inside the detector, you may find one or more connectors, either of the PCB or pin type. These are used for quick connect/disconnect of the speaker, meter and the primary PCB.

Indicator Lights

Indicator lights are sometimes installed on metal detectors to give the operator a visual, flashing-light indication when a target is detected. Lights are not as good as speaker and meter indicators, however. Targets that produce only faint audio and meter signals may not cause illumination of indicator lights, especially during bright daylight. Lights should be used only in conjunction with speaker and meter, unless absolutely silent operation is required. Since some detectors may not have a cut-off switch for the detector speaker, a headphone plug can be inserted into the headphone jack to disconnect the speaker.

Indicator lights can be of several types: neon, light-emitting diodes (LEDs) and incandescent. Neon or high voltage lights take the least power, but they require voltage amplification circuitry, an added expense that offsets their other advantages.

LEDs create appreciable current drains, but they can be made to blink to diminish power usage. Because sunlight significantly reduces their visibility, LEDs are especially effective for night work.

Incandescent lighting is good — and sensitive — but requires more current than the other types and is therefore seldom used.

Remember that indicator lights are just that. They indicate the presence of a target, but with considerably less sensitivity than either a speaker or meter. Under no circumstances should they ever be counted upon to alert an operator to any fringe area signals.

Miscellaneous Hardware

Detectors use dozens of kinds of miscellaneous hardware. Any particular detector may need a bolt, a lock washer, a flat washer and a wing nut to hold the searchcoil to the end of the lower connecting stem. There may be one or more screws to hold the battery door in position. Occasionally, screws and nuts hold the handle to the detector. When you lose or break a piece of hardware, always replace it with exactly the same type, whether purchased from the factory, a dealer or a hardware store. Always use a replacement part made from the same type of metal. In other words, if the bolt and wing nut that attach the lower stem to the searchcoil are nylon (non-metallic), be certain to replace them with similar nylon hardware.

Instruction Manuals

Most detector manufacturers place a great deal of forethought into each of their Owner's Manuals. Our Garrett manuals include considerable general information about searching with a metal detector as well as specific instructions about operating that particular instrument. In addition, our Garrett Owner's Manuals are even pocket-sized and designed to be taken into the field.

Study of the proper books such as those from Ram Publishing Company can be a valuable aid in learning more about the hobby of treasure hunting with a metal detector.

In many cases the manual is the chief reference from which a detector operator learns to use his equipment. As important as it is, however, often the manual is the very last thing the new detector owner reads. As the saying goes, "When all else fails, read the instruction manual!"

The seller of the instrument should instruct the buyer in correct operating procedures. It then becomes the responsibility of the owner to learn how to use the detector, by paying careful attention to the manufacturer's instructions and what he has been taught. Chapter 23 of this book will be invaluable here.

An owner's manual should clearly identify and explain the function of each touchpad, switch, knob and major component. Full instructions should teach the owner how to test and replace batteries. It should give complete operating instructions, as well as a listing of precautions and basic instructions on field usage. Each capability of the instrument should be explained. The instruction manual should also include field repair data, so that in the event of a minor problem, the operator could run through a check list for a clue to the cause of the difficulty.

Before buying any detector, it might be well to check its instruction manual!

Kits

Metal detectors that need to be assembled from kits probably will not use the latest detector technology. For a number of reasons, Garrett offers no such models. A well-constructed kit detector, however, will probably perform as it was intended, according to published specifications. Extra care should be taken in reconstruction of the kit instruments. The builder should follow instructions exactly as specified. If the completed kit does not perform satisfactorily, the builder should take the detector to a qualified technician for troubleshooting.

Key Features

Four important features are common to the use of all metal detectors. A thorough understanding of each of these four is essential to your success in finding treasure with any kind of detector:

— *Discrimination*
— *Pinpointing*
— *Audio*
— *Ground Balance*

Of course, each of the four subjects is vital in almost any aspect of metal detecting. Because these topics are so important to the hobby, any time two or more treasure hunters get together, you're liable to hear several different opinions about each of them. So, here are my thoughts on these important matters:

Discrimination

You can minimize digging and still not miss valuable targets by using discrimination properly. This is especially true in most parks, beaches or other public places, where you're likely to find literally *pounds* of trash metal.

It's sometimes difficult for those of us who have hunted with metal detectors for a quarter-century or more to accept the ease and precise nature of modern discrimination circuits. We remember when any discrimination was considered "too much," and many veterans still urge you to *dig all targets*. Yet, I must admit that many of these same oldtimers can be found dialing in "just a little" discrimination to permit them to miss some of the trash that now seems to be present in the soil everywhere.

Some models classified as *universal* detectors, such as Garrett's Grand Master Hunter CX II feature two basic modes of operation – Discriminate (motion) and All Metal (non-motion). In the Discriminate mode the operator can utilize discrimination controls to designate the type metal targets that are desired. In the All Metal mode, of course, all targets are audio-detected. But, remember this one very important point...in *both* modes the target ID indicator continues to identify all detected targets. So, here's a tip...operate in the All Metal mode to achieve the greatest possible depth. Then simply read the meter to identify detected targets and decide whether to dig or not!

Detectors feature three basic types of discrimination. Most have a single dial, while some of the newer instruments feature notch or dual discrimination controls. These more modern methods of discrimination offer multiple selectivity and the ability to reject and accept specific targets. Those instruments with dual controls usually split the full range of discrimination between ferrous and non-ferrous. Detection of iron objects such as nails, some foil, iron bottlecaps and small pieces of junk is controlled by one knob. The other control governs discrimination of such non-ferrous items as aluminum pulltabs and aluminum screwtops.

The single-dial type of discrimination is quite simple to understand. When it is at its Zero (0) setting (extreme left on Garrett instruments), it provides no discrimination and all metallic targets are signaled. As the dial is turned to the right (counter-clockwise) more and more discrimination is dialed into the instrument, and various types of targets are detected. Use the bench-testing method described in this chapter to test your detector out with various targets and learn the setting at which they will not be detected.

It is important to remember that the discrimination control operates *cumulatively;* that is, all targets previously rejected at a setting will also be rejected at a higher setting, along with the new targets to which that higher setting pertains. This dial is illustrated below.

When setting detectors with dual discrimination controls (see next page) or notch, it should be remembered that each of the controls operates independently. The setting of one has no effect whatsoever on the other dial or any other notches.

On an instrument with two dials rotate the ferrous control of your detector to zero (fully counterclockwise on Garrett controls) if you wish to detect all ferrous materials. As you advance it back to the right to higher numbers, you will reject more and more ferrous materials. Like all discrimination control dials, this one operates cumulatively; that is, if you have it set at bottlecap rejection, most nails and some foil will be rejected along with the bottlecaps. We urge that you advance this control no farther clockwise than necessary to eliminate the troublesome ferrous junk metal where you are searching.

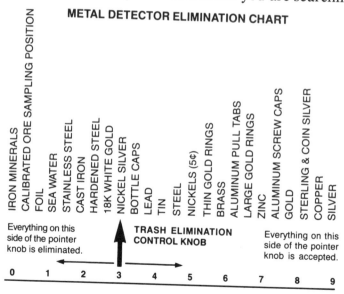

Various targets placed in order of conductivity illustrate a single-dial discrimination control that enables a detector to "compare" a target's conductivity with the setting its operator has dialed in.

Operate your non-ferrous control in the same manner. When it is turned fully to the left, few of the non-ferrous materials will be rejected. To eliminate, say, pulltabs, rotate the control clockwise to the manufacturer's suggested setting for them. Keep in mind, however, that there appear to be as many different kind of pulltabs as there are canning companies. Some few pulltabs, especially those that are bent or broken, seem to be acceptable to any detector at any setting. Set your controls for those you are finding just in the area where you are hunting.

Here's how to set any controls precisely by bench testing. Collect examples of all the types of junk you want to reject—a nail, bottlecap, pulltab and, perhaps, small pieces of iron trash. Place your detector on a non-metallic, preferably wooden, surface with the searchcoil at least three feet away from all metal. Make certain you are wearing no rings or jewelry on your hands or arms that

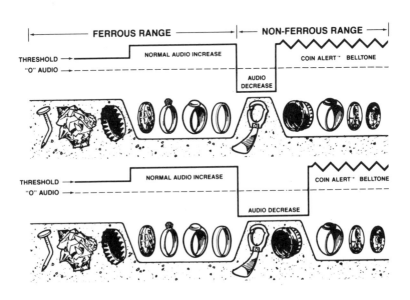

Garrett's multi-range controls offer four discrimination levels. Junk targets have been eliminated at top with rings and coins accepted. Non-ferrous control adjustment, below, eliminates screwtops.

116

could be detected. Rotate both control knobs (or only one, if your instrument is so designed) fully counterclockwise to the lowest settings. If you have a notch instrument, set it so that all metallic targets will be accepted.

Turn the detector on and listen for the tone telling you it is ready to operate. Adjust the audio control for threshold sound.

Pass the iron bottlecap across the bottom of your searchcoil about two inches away from it. Your detector will probably make a signal. Rotate the control (ferrous, of course, on dual-discrimination instruments) to the approximate bottlecap reject position or the setting suggested by your manufacturer, and pass the cap across the searchcoil's bottom again. You should hear nothing more than, perhaps, a slight blip. You may be able to rotate the control counterclockwise back to a lower number and still not detect the bottlecap. Practice so that you can set your control as far to the left as possible because you always want to use the lowest setting that is required.

Using the same technique, adjust the non-ferrous control just far enough clockwise that you do not detect the aluminum pulltab. This should be approximately the manufacturer's suggested setting point, which should probably prove to be your optimum pulltab setting, with the settings necessary for other style pulltabs being both above and below this one determined point. Again, let us stress that you should rotate these controls no higher than necessary to reject the junk items in the ground where you are searching.

Dual controls offer a greater adjustment range than single controls. You have more resolution which allows you to set the controls precisely to reject specific junk targets. A most important feature is that you can reject most aluminum pulltabs while accepting the majority of gold and silver rings. When searching for rings in a pulltab-infested area such as a public park or beach, set your non-ferrous control no farther clockwise than necessary to eliminate most of the pulltabs. Rings with a higher conductivity — and, especially, mass — than pulltabs will be accepted. Remember, however, that some rings will fall into the lower, or ferrous, range. Thus, dual discrimination lets you select rings that register both "above" and "below" pulltab rejection. So, don't advance either control any farther clockwise than absolutely necessary.

Here's where the new notch instruments (below) really offer you selectivity. You can accept or reject individual targets. So, when you are hunting in All Metal mode and are continually bothered by a specific type of pulltab or piece of metal junk. You can pass that target across your searchcoil, press the **REJECT** touchpad and not be bothered by that type of trash again.

There is another important reason for setting your discrimination controls conservatively. When a modern detector locates a junk target that you have asked it to discriminate against, it cancels out this junk target with a negative audio response that you normally cannot even hear. You know, however, good targets generate a positive

Notch discrimination on Ultra GTA detectors enable the treasure hunter to be highly selective in choosing those specific types of targets that the detector will either Accept or Reject.

response which you love to hear. If both positive and negative targets are beneath your searchcoil simultaneously, the two responses tend to cancel one another, and you may miss a good find. Of course, the situation is rarely that simple. Depth of targets, their metallic content, size and many other factors must be considered. So, simply remember this: never use more discrimination than you absolutely need.

Pinpointing

Electronic pinpointing can hasten your recovery of targets and make it far more pleasurable as well. Most veteran treasure hunters pride themselves in their ability to pinpoint targets using only the detector's normal search modes. Modern instruments make pinpointing so much easier that we oldtimers should swallow our pride and take advantage of the electronic assistance available to us. I know that I do! Who knows? The time we save might let us recover that "big one" that's always just a searchcoil sweep away.

Of course, you should check the Owner's Manual of your detector for proper understanding and use of its pinpointing function. But, a button or trigger somewhere on the detector will usually activate All Metal (non-motion) pinpointing circuitry. After you have detected a target, move the searchcoil off to the side, press and hold the Pinpoint touchpad (or switch) and scan your target area again. You will notice that signals have probably grown sharper to aid you in locating your target more precisely.

Here's a tip for the ultimate in target pinpointing. Once you have determined the surface location where you believe the target to be buried, place your searchcoil lightly on the ground above it and activate the pinpoint control. Continue holding this control and slide the searchcoil back and forth over the target at the same operating height. You will notice very slight blips when the target is directly beneath the center of your searchcoil. If you can't notice these blips at first, perhaps you have elevated the searchcoil from its level when you first selected the Pinpoint mode. Try the procedure again a few times. Maintain constant searchcoil height, and you'll be amazed at your precise electronic pinpointing ability. Warning: this technique requires practice...but, *practice pays off!*

Here are two methods that might prove helpful if your instrument does not offer electronic pinpointing. After you locate your target, continue moving its coil over the spot while reducing your audio level down almost into the quiet zone. You'll soon find your target signal weakening to a soft audio "blip." Your find will be directly beneath the center of your coil where the loudest signal over your detected metal object now occurs.

The second method is to begin raising your searchcoil higher in the air each time you pass over the detected target. Once again, signals will get weaker and weaker until you can hear only a "blip." Again, the target will be underneath the maximum signal area. This second method is obviously more difficult because the height of your coil will make it harder for you to locate the exact spot on the ground.

Rely on electronic pinpointing! That's my advice.

Audio

Because the audio setting is one of the most important adjustments you make in learning to hunt coins with a metal detector, your close attention to this subject is strongly urged.

Use of the "Bloodhound" two-box deepseeking searchcoil permits a treasure hunter to look for deeply buried caches and not be troubled by small metal targets.

There has been considerable talk recently in metal detector advertisements concerning audio. Searching *silently* is being touted as if it is the *latest thing* in metal detection.

Rubbish. Searching "silently" (and missing out on some good targets!) has always been possible with ANY detector. And, some people have always seemed to prefer this technique, but I could never figure out why.

I believe today, just as I always have, that maximum capability can be achieved with any detector only by adjusting the audio volume until you hear just the faintest sound coming from your speaker or headphones. *This is very important!* This faintest sound that you can hear is the detector's most sensitive operating point. It is called your threshold, a common term in all metal detector literature. You will notice that when you set the threshold to a very faint sound and then plug in your headphones, the threshold may be too loud. Simply turn the audio control knobs lightly to reduce the sound level back to your faint threshold level.

It is my contention, based on decades of operating experience and success, that a minimum threshold level is the best method...whether you're hunting with a new Garrett Ultra GTA 1000...a Grand Master Hunter CX II...or if you've borrowed one of the antique BFO models from our museum!

As I have observed, there have always been those who preferred to operate a detector with what is called a silent threshold; that is, with absolutely no sound coming from the speaker or head phones. If you are determined to use this silent threshold, I urge that you achieve it by setting

Concerned with detecting faint whispers of sound, competent THers will always wear headphones, especially where ambient noise interferes with hearing.

your audio to a slight level of sound, then backing off just enough to achieve silence. This adjustment insures that you miss the fewest possible targets. Be sure to check occasionally to make certain that you remain at this audio level just below sound. Otherwise, the farther below this level your audio drifts, the more targets you will miss!

For maximum success a treasure hunter should use headphones whenever searching with a metal detector. They are essential in noisy areas, such as the beach and near traffic. They enhance audio perception by bringing the sound directly into one's ears while masking outside noise interference.

Most persons can hear weaker sounds and detect deeper finds when quality headphones are used. They come in several sizes and configurations, the most popular being stereo types that cover the ears. For those detectors without volume controls headphones can offer the control that allow a wide degree of loudness adjustment without degrading the sound quality.

As discussed, you know that reducing sound volume to silent on a detector is accompanied by loss of detection depth and sensitivity. I strongly recommend that detectors always be operated with the audio control adjusted so that just a faint sound (threshold) can be heard. Headphones allow this threshold to be set much lower than with a speaker, giving improved performance. As an added benefit, headphones use considerably less power than a detector's speaker which results in the economy of longer battery life. And, you don't have to take the trouble to change them as often, either!

Ground Balance

This section that is always included in each of my books has been totally rewritten several times just during the past year or so. Changes are coming so rapidly in the field of metal detection!

Ground balance is a metal detector feature that will

always remain one of the most important for treasure hunters—whether it be performed manually or automatically. Yet, it is not so important as it once was for numerous reasons. Many of the modern type detectors are of the *motion* type (description follows) that features automatic ground balancing.

And, I must add here that new detectors such as Garrett's Grand Master Hunter CX II and Master Hunter CX (Computer Express) are causing the very subject of ground balancing—once so important—to become obsolete. Microprocessor circuitry is handling this former "problem" quite effectively. In fact, there is no longer any problem because microprocessor circuitry eliminates ground minerals even while the detector is being used...automatically and continually.

Still, ground balance is an area of considerable concern—and some difficulty—to all users of metal detectors...if we can measure it by the volume of calls received at the factory. And, our dealers tell us that their customers also appear to have problems. Therefore, I feel that it is a subject that must be covered in any book dealing with treasure hunting. After all, this text is designed to be of service to *any* treasure hunter...no matter *what* type of instrument is being used...or, to anyone generally interested in metal detection.

As discussed in Chapter 3, the majority of the earth's surface contains various densities of iron mineralization. Iron distorts the electromagnetic field to create an imbalance between transmitter and receiver windings that causes an instrument to detect the presence of iron. This characteristic caused great difficulty for early manufacturers (and hobbyists) until they finally utilized available circuitry knowledge and techniques to overcome this problem.

Electrical engineers have long known of three main circuit components (characteristics): resistive, conductive and capacitive. When alternating electrical voltage was connected across a circuit containing these three elements, a phenomenon called *phase shift* occurred that caused the current to lag or lead the impressed voltage by 90 degrees.

Metal detector design engineers employed this knowledge to discover that phase shifting could be measured and used to eliminate the troublesome aspects of ground minerals. This made possible the development of ground balanced metal detectors.

The diagram on the facing page illustrates the basic circuitry and components of a ground balanced detector, which allows most of the iron mineralization in the earth's surface to be "dialed out," permitting mineral-free operation. Only signals from detected metallic targets are amplified and conditioned to power the audio and visual indicators. More information on this circuitry can be found in Chapter 11, which deals with non-motion detectors.

There is still no doubt that ground balance, whether performed automatically or manually, will always be one of the most important features of a metal detector. Many veteran treasure hunters would argue the importance of the depth feature, and some might opt for discrimination. The simple fact remains, however, that without precise ground balance—performed either automatically or manually—hunting with a metal detector as we know it today would not be possible in most soil. Why? Because most soils contain just too darned much mineralization.

Beginning treasure hunters with a new detector quickly grow accustomed to the excellent ground balance now available on today's modern automatic detector. Many even take this feature for granted. *Please don't!* Some of the oldtimers are still in awe at the ease with which today's automatic detectors ground balance themselves. These veterans will assure you that ground balance is very important, and as you progress in the hobby, you will soon agree. In fact, there will be many times when precise ground balance will be demanded if you are to achieve optimum results. Learn how to ground balance your particular detector if it doesn't have automatic ground balance. It will probably be as important as anything you ever do after you turn on the instrument and set the audio.

Motion vs. Non-Motion

You should know that there are two detector modes of operation that permit ground balance: motion and non-motion. Before we discuss these modes, let's first understand just exactly what is meant by the term "ground balance." As discussed earlier, there are two predominant ground minerals that concern us. They are wetted salt and iron, and they can be found literally all over the world. Wetted salt can be found predominantly at ocean beaches but also at numerous upland locales. Iron minerals, generally classified further as non-conductive (not metal) minerals, can be found practically everywhere.

Both wetted salt and iron are readily detectable and cause untold grief to conventional detectors unless some means is available to cancel or "ground balance" them out. The term *ground balance*, then, is our description of the method of circuitry that enables a modern metal detector

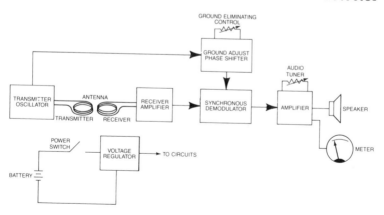

Block diagram of a VLF ground balancing detector shows basic circuits and components and electrical phase relationship between metal and iron mineral targets that permits ground balancing.

to ignore these minerals completely...to go about its business of detecting other metals, as if iron and wetted salt were not even present.

The motion mode of ground balancing has been around several years and is available on detectors from a number of manufacturers, including Garrett's Ultra, Beach Hunter and Freedom Plus models. It is also available on Master Hunter CX instruments (more about this...soon). As its name implies, the motion mode requires that the detector be continually moving (in motion) to detect objects. This mode is very efficient and quite good for hunting most types of treasure. Both iron and salt minerals are essentially ignored, permitting the hobbyist to concentrate on finding jewelry and coins without being bothered by detection of minerals. This mode, however, does not provide optimum performance and the deepest detection when the detector is used for prospecting or hunting for relics and money caches.

The non-motion mode (permitting a detector's searchcoil to hover perfectly still) which had previously given the best performance for these other types of hunting was achieved only through manual adjustment of ground balance controls. While such adjustments could be made with relative ease, it has been the desire of Garrett and other manufacturers to produce detectors that are fully automatic.

The Master Hunter CX, Grand Master Hunter CX II and our brand-new Grand Master Hunter CX III, each of which features computerized circuitry based on microprocessor controls, offer both motion and non-motion ground balance. The motion mode features not only automatic ground balance but also full discrimination control. Treasure hunters have come to love their performance.

Until now non-motion ground balancing of the Grand Master Hunter was possible only through adjustment of manual controls. Now, Grand Master Hunter CX II and the new CX III are equipped with automatic ground balance modes called Fast Track® and Ground Track® that balance out iron ground minerals automatically, even as the searchcoil is scanned. Such ground balancing continues whether the searchcoil is moving or not. Even when the earth minerals themselves change density beneath the searchcoil, the Ground Track circuits sense these changes and properly adjust the detector's ground balancing characteristics while the detector is scanning for targets.

The new computerized Master Hunter models, indeed, are *thinking* detectors, the instrument of tomorrow. But, today there remain in the hands of treasure hunters thousands of detectors that respond to manual ground balancing controls in the non-motion mode. This "how to" discussion is concerned with such detectors and will be important to their operators.

To Ground Balance

The following instructions will apply to Garrett detectors with non-motion (All Metal mode) manual ground balancing capabilities and to most other instruments as well, but you are urged to study the Owner's Manual for your particular detector. Read especially carefully the section concerning ground balance.

Now, to ground balance a detector manually in the field! Begin by holding the detector with the searchcoil away from any metal and about two or three feet above the ground. Listen to the audio as you lower the searchcoil to operating height. If the audio signal grows or fades to any degree, you will require manual ground balancing.

This procedure, of course, may differ from one brand to another. Basically, however, if the audio signal grows louder, turn down the ground balance control dial or press the touchpad on your manual ground balance controls marked minus (−) several times. Lift your searchcoil again, press the audio (threshold) control and lower it again to operating height. If the sound level now decreases, you have made too great a negative adjustment. It will be necessary for you to press the touchpad marked plus (+) a few times or turn up your control dial. Remember that with the dial on a Garrett or other quality detector you are dealing with a 10-turn control for precise adjustment. Don't be afraid to turn it several times! Repeat these procedures until the audio does not change or changes only slightly when the searchcoil is lowered to operating height. When performing this ground balancing procedure, make certain there are no metal targets in the ground beneath your searchcoil.

When searching extremely mineralized ground, we recommend that you operate the searchcoil two inches or more above the ground. You will not lose depth, but will actually detect deeper because ground mineral influence is greatly reduced.

Non-Motion Detectors

This chapter is devoted to the history, theory, characteristics and field applications of the Non-Motion Ground Balanced (iron mineral canceling) type metal detector. This type of detector can be manually adjusted to ignore the effects of iron mineralization and detect only metal targets. Because of its circuitry, it can detect such targets while motionless; hence, the name, non-motion.

Until the development of the automated (motion) ground balanced detector, the manual adjust models dominated the treasure hunting field. They represented such an improvement over the old BFO and TR detectors which had but limited (perhaps, *non-existent* would be a better description) ability to eliminate iron earth minerals and wetted salt. Quality manual adjust motion instruments are still highly popular instruments capable of performing all coin hunting, treasure hunting and prospecting tasks. They detect very deeply and are offered with an array of desirable features.

Some modern computerized detectors, such as the Grand Master Hunter CX II and Master Hunter CX, already include the automatic ground balancing feature. As I have pointed out earlier in this book, I believe that in just a few years all quality detectors will provide automatic ground balance. In fact, it will be an aspect of metal detecting that hobbyists will finally be able to take for granted! What an improvement this truly is...especially after all the problems that veteran THers have experienced over the years with ground balance.

Today, however, a large number of quality detectors

already in the hands of treasure hunters permit the treasure hunter to adjust ground balance manually. All of these instruments will fulfill every expectation of most coin and beach hunters. In addition, the detectors can meet the requirements of cache hunters, relic hunters and gold hunters with ease and efficiency. Since quality non-motion detectors are so highly capable, they can be selected and used with the utmost confidence.

I especially commend this type of detector to the individual who is interested in hunting for all types of metal detecting. As noted above, many hobbyists use motion-type automated VLF detectors for tasks other than hunting for coins and jewelry. The simple truth of the matter is, however, that manual adjust non-motion models will generally detect deeper than motion models.

Because of those very same "manual" controls from which it gets its name, this type of detector is capable of more precise ground balance. Such precision will rarely be required by the average coin and beach hunter. Not so with relic and cache hunters who seek deep targets and gold hunters working over highly mineralized ground. They demand absolute ground balance that will enable them to hear faint signals from faraway or tiny targets.

Any kind of pinpointing technique is possible with the manual adjust non-motion detectors since they can be hovered over a target at will. Still, the matter or pinpointing is not especially important since modern, quality instruments all offer precise electronic pinpointing circuitry.

The fact is that manual adjust non-motion detectors are just a little more difficult to use than the automated motion models because they have to be ground balanced. At the same time, however, they offer more versatility and will usually provide greater satisfaction in areas of metal detecting. A manual adjust detector, therefore, can prove to be a valuable addition to your metal detecting equipment.This type has been in use since the mid- 70s and is referred to as the *manual ground balance VLF.* In order for the metal detector to "ignore," or eliminate from detection, iron earth minerals, the operator manually adjusts a control knob to achieve iron earth mineral elimination for each location where the metal detector is used.

This type of detector was originally known as a Very Low Frequency (VLF) ground balancing (canceling) type detector, and derived its name from its radio frequency operating range which is within the Very Low Frequency radio spectrum of 3 to 30 kilohertz. Since virtually all modern metal detectors operate in that range, that nomenclature is no longer appropriate. The old VLF was actually a transmitter-receiver (TR) type detector with two main differences: they operated at a much lower frequency than TRs (see *Frequency Designations* on Page 413), and they balanced, or eliminated from detection, iron soil minerals.

Because the non-motion detector is not bothered by the disturbing effects of iron minerals, circuit gain can be made higher, improving sensitivity (smaller targets can be

One of the finest non-motion detectors available today is the Garrett Grand Master Hunter CX II, a truly universal instrument, that features microprocessor-controlled circuitry.

detected) and greatly increasing detection depth. Operating at a lower radio frequency, eddy current generation will be greater. Since the depth to which eddy currents can be generated (skin depth) increases as the frequency of the electromagnetic field source decreases, larger amounts of eddy currents are generated in a metal's surface. Thus, all targets with surfaces that generate good eddy currents can be detected deeper.

The early VLF detectors were part of an era in the history of metal detector manufacture that I like to distinguish as *alphabet soup*. We already had our BFOs and TRs, and now we had the VLFs, which were given various additional alphabetical designations (GEB for Ground Exclusion Balance, MF for Mineral Free, etc.) by manufacturers in their marketing efforts. The VLF/TR designation was made when an additional circuit was added because discrimination could not be accomplished simultaneously with iron mineral elimination. Thus, a detector was created that had a VLF iron mineral elimination circuit mode and a TR discriminating circuit mode. Both circuits operated at the same VLF frequency, thus, was born the VLF/TR dual mode detector.

As the mid-80s approached, acceptable ground balanced discrimination circuits were developed and the modern distinction became merely between the non-motion detectors discussed in this chapter and the motion instruments studied in the next.

Theory of Operation

Non-motion detectors are very similar in design to TR detectors, described in Chapter 6. The block diagram on facing page shows the main VLF circuits and components and how they are interconnected. An electronic oscillator feeds a signal into the transmitter antenna, extending the resulting electromagnetic field into the space that surrounds the searchcoil. The portion that extends below the searchcoil creates the detection pattern. Detectable metals and minerals have a disturbing effect upon the electromagnetic field.

At this point, similarity with TR detection ends, as ground balancing circuits are brought into play. An electromagnetic signal transmission phenomenon called phase shift occurs. Phase shift refers to a time delay between electrical voltage and current signals, one occurring before the other. Phase shift has been known and used for many years, especially in military radar systems, (See the discussion on *Iron mineral ground balancing* in Chapter 10.)

Eddy current "loss" signals are *electrically phase shifted* or *time delayed* with respect to the transmitted electromagnetic field. The Synchronous Demodulator "measures" this time difference and separates the phase-separated signals.

When purely non-conductive ferrous targets (iron minerals) cause field distortion, transmitter/receiver antenna imbalance occurs but there is no phase shift.

When a composite signal containing both in-phase and phase-shifted components is fed into the Synchronous Demodulator, the two phase-related signals are separated. The earth iron mineral signal is discarded by the circuitry, but the metal target signal is amplified to enable it to power the speaker or headphones and/or in-

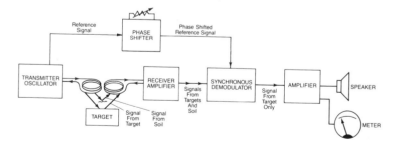

Block diagram of a VLF (non-motion) detector with main circuits, components and interconnections shows transmitter and receiver windings electronically balanced until upset by detectable targets.

135

dicators. Thus, the effects of the earth's iron minerals have been effectively "eliminated" or "ignored."

A Ground Balance Control is provided by the manufacturer so that the operator can adjust his detector to "match up" with almost any mineral matrix. When "match up" occurs, minerals are eliminated from detection and target signals alert the operator to the presence of metal.

Wetted Salt Cancellation

Wetted salt is electrically conductive (looks like metal to a metal detector) and cannot be eliminated from detection in the same manner that iron minerals are. It can be eliminated, however, because its conductivity can be determined the same as conductivity of any conductive (metal) element. Using the Discriminate mode, the operator can "dial out" ocean beach and other wetted salt.

Hot Rocks

Non-motion detectors will respond "positive" to "hot rocks" (mineralized rocks that contain a highly concentrated magnetic iron/conductive element content differing from the matrix to which the VLF detector has been adjusted). Hot rock response is troublesome in some areas, but the non-motion detector will not indicate its presence unless the hot rock is close to the searchcoil, a maximum distance roughly equal to the diameter of the searchcoil. If a detected target is "suspect," switch into the Discriminate mode (set to "zero" elimination) and pass back over the target. If the sound decreases from the audio threshold level, the target is a rock or mineralized hot spot. If the audio remains the same or increases, investigate the target. It has some metallic content.

If you are prospecting, be certain the Discrimination control is set to "zero." Nuggets and ore samples may be rejected if greater discrimination is used. Even the "zero" setting on non-calibrated detectors may result in rejected nuggets and ore. Consequently, always use the All Metal mode.

Sensitivity Problem

Because non-motion detectors are very sensitive to even small pieces of iron, you may find yourself digging extremely deep holes for bits and pieces of iron when operating in the All Metal mode. Be prepared!

When coin hunting, you can use discrimination to remove most of the problem, but when you are cache hunting and don't want to use any amount of discrimination, you will detect small, deeply buried targets. To be more efficient when hunting large caches you should consider using the Depth Multiplier "two-box" attachment which ignores small metal pieces. These handy accessories are discussed more fully in Chapter 21.

Deepseeking Detectors

Non-motion detectors are well known for their deep-seeking capabilities...detecting all metal objects to great depths. Availability of large searchcoils greatly extends depth capabilities of these instruments. They can ignore the iron minerals and wetted salt that are found on some

The Garrett CX (Computer Express) is an easy-to-operate non-motion detector with touchpads and a sensitive meter that indicates type of target as well as depth for pinpointing.

137

salt water beaches, although not simultaneously. In these situations, Pulse Induction detectors with discrimination are generally recommended along with motion detectors with circuitry designed to ignore salt.

Meters

Many non-motion detectors such as our Master Hunter models are equipped with coin depth-measuring circuits and indicators that, to an excellent degree of accuracy, classify or identify detected targets, increasing the operator's efficiency. (See Chapter 10.)

Audio Threshold

Non-motion ground balanced detectors give the greatest detection depth when set to minimum audio level threshold. When operated in the "silent" zone, some ability to detect in the fringe area is lost. Also, when the detector is operating "silent," it is difficult to know *where* in the null zone the operating point is set. Certain signal strength meters do give a fair indication as to where this audio threshold is located.

Since a certain amount of detection signal is "used up" in bringing the audio out of the "silent" zone to a level where it can be heard, some sensitivity (and detection depth) is lost. The farther the detector is operated down into the null zone, the worse the problem. Thus, most manufacturers stress that detector audio be set to the lowest possible threshold level that can be continuously heard.

Using non-motion Pinpoint circuitry, this THer was able to locate her target precisely, then determine its depth by observing the meter on this Grand Master Hunter CX II.

Versatility

The versatility of the non-motion ground balanced detector is legendary. There just isn't much that it won't do! Formerly, the BFO was really the only all-purpose detector that we considered for every metal detecting job. Of course, the non-motion detector is far more versatile because of its ground balancing and extreme depth capabilities, and the availability of such a wide range of searchcoils and usable attachments.

The Little Iron Kettle

In Chapter 3 a hypothetical situation was described in which a little iron kettle filled with gold coins was buried beneath a large rock lying in a field. Unfortunately, there were nine hundred ninety-nine other flat rocks in the field, and many of them were highly mineralized. From the discussions already given in this book you should be able to locate that pot of gold without overturning every rock in the field. How?

Use a non-motion ground balancing detector equipped with one of the larger searchcoils. Use the All Metal mode, tuning out ground minerals. Use headphones and maximum detection depth and scan the rocks one at a time. With luck, you might get a positive signal over the very first rock. Raise the rock and dig down a few inches to find the gold! But, what if you dig and find nothing? What happened? The rock is a hot rock! Do you dig beneath every rock? No, set the Discrimination circuit control to "zero," and scan over the rocks one at a time, still using your All Metal mode. When you get a positive response, pinpoint at the spot where you hear the loudest signal. Place the

Garrett's Scorpion Gold Stinger is a highly versatile detector, incorporating three modes, All Metal (non-motion), TR discriminate for ore-testing and Discriminate (motion).

searchcoil directly upon the rock. Press your mode change switch to activate the Discriminate mode. Maintain searchcoil contact with the rock as you slide the searchcoil to one side. If the signal does not change or it decreases, dig the target. You have located metal and, hopefully, the little iron kettle! Another, easier way to locate the kettle if it is large enough (about quart-size) is to scan with the Depth Multiplier attachment. Minerals and hot rocks do not create false signals. The Depth Multiplier detects just metal with only minor influences from minerals.

Spend the contents of the kettle wisely!

Motion Detectors

The motion-type detector with automatic ground balance is probably the most popular model generally used today for coin hunting in parks, on the beach or anywhere else. First of all, it is easy to use. Added to this are its capabilities for finding coins and jewelry that are almost equal to those of the higher priced detectors. This capability becomes particularly apparent when both expensive and average-priced models are in the hands of a novice. Yet, while most models from reputable manufacturers are capable, some will definitely detect coins and treasure deeper than others.

Primary difference between the motion and non-motion detectors is expressed by the very names. But, there is another important difference. On the motion detector there is no manually adjustable VLF ground balance (iron mineral elimination) control. That function is performed automatically and electronically.

On some detectors there is a manually adjustable ground balance control, which is not needed when the motion mode is in operation, but provided so that the hobbyist can improve electronic pinpointing accuracy over highly mineralized ground. Also, some instruments feature both the motion and non-motion modes. Thus, when the non-motion (or, All Metal) mode is being used, these same manual ground balance controls can be adjusted to achieve precise iron mineral elimination.

Of course, various models of the automated detectors are manufactured today. Some offer more features than others, and some are simply better than others. Working with a dealer and trying out various detectors will enable you to determine which model is best suited for your needs.

These instruments with their "automatic" ground balance are often referred to as "motion" detectors since target signals will fade out if the searchcoil is not kept moving. They can be hovered over a target for only a few seconds because of their automatic circuitry. Consequently, slight searchcoil motion is always necessary. Certain models, however, can be scanned much more slowly than others. You must learn the capabilities of your instrument through practice.

Another technique you will have to practice is pinpointing, especially in manicured lawns or other areas where exact location is important. Since hovering over a target is not possible, manual pinpointing will be more difficult. Electronic pinpointing offered on all the better models overcomes this deficiency.

The motion instrument ranks high among all types of detectors in detection depth. Not only is it capable of reaching to great depths to detect coins, but its extremely sharp, fast-response signal is unmistakable when rings, coins and other such objects are detected.

It would be well to warn against confusing automatic ground balance with the "automatic tuning" feature on some models of older detectors. The tuning feature is concerned only with the *audio* threshold of the detector and has no relationship to ground balance.

All quality motion detectors will offer some form of trash elimination through discrimination control(s). I urge you to read the section on this feature in this book to insure that you realize the full benefits offered by your detector.

I should point out here that many hobbyists find the automated motion models fairly satisfactory for types of metal detecting other than beach and surf hunting. This is particularly true of those instruments produced by quality manufacturers. In fact, I've used our automated Ultra models for shallow relic hunting. Some hobbyists even report they have found gold nuggets with an automated instrument. If you're interested in a detector that will perform satisfactorily in situations other than primarily coin hunting, however, I suggest that you learn more about the non-motion and computerized models.

Motion ground balancing detectors utilize what is called in engineering jargon "non-linear" circuitry. Automatic ground balancing circuitry results in the audio being mostly either *off* or *fully on*. There are very few "in between" signals. Whenever target signals of sufficient strength occur, the audio is driven from "silent," or minimum audio threshold, to full audio volume. Notice the word "sufficient." Because some target signals are insufficient, they do not result in maximum audible alert.

Precise contouring and subtle target characteristic determining capabilities may also be lost. When the audio threshold is set to operate "silent," as recommended by some manufacturers and hobbyists, there is really no way

Garrett's Freedom Ace, the instrument that introduced countless men and women to the hobby of treasure hunting, has proven itself one of the world's most popular motion detectors.

145

of knowing *where* in the null the detector is operating. Although manufacturers go to great lengths to build stable detectors with steady audio threshold, improperly designed circuits may permit some drift from the preset point. Detectors with preset factory threshold settings may have no provision for adjusting the operating point. Since audio threshold location should be a concern of all who want to achieve maximum performance from their detector, perhaps operators should not consider purchasing preset instruments with no adjustment provision.

Motion detectors should be used primarily for coin and beach hunting and searching buildings. Prospecting, cache hunting and relic hunting should be performed with standard, non-motion ground balancing universal VLF instruments.

Wide Operating Latitude

Correctly designed motion detectors have an extremely wide adjustment latitude. Zero ground minerals, or any magnitude of iron minerals up to the greatest density that a metal detector operator is likely to encounter, will be eliminated from detection. There is nothing the operator can do to effect this operation as there is no control knob provided.

You must remember that these instruments operate continuously in an automatic "tuning" mode. You can prove this to yourself by stopping or hovering the searchcoil directly above a metal target. The signals will die out, indicating that the detector's functions are controlled automatically. While this may seem like a disadvantage for certain types of hunting, it is not. Since most people use these detectors for coin hunting only, there is generally no need to hover the searchcoils. Some users report occasional difficulty in pinpointing, but this disadvantage is overcome by models that feature an electronic pinpointing mode.

The first time you use a motion detector you will notice

that the audio signal, when a coin is detected is generally much more quick and sharply pronounced than the non-motion type. Most coin hunters have no difficulty in getting accustomed to this different audio sound, many preferring it.

Designed for Coin-Sized Targets

Motion detectors, especially when some amount of discrimination is used, are most efficient when detecting coin-sized targets. They are not recommended for cache hunting, relic hunting and gold hunting. As you gain experience with this type detector you will learn that the detector sometimes has difficulty analyzing large and irregularly shaped targets which can cause the signals to break up or be erratic.

Silent vs. Audible Threshold

All motion detector manufacturers state that their machines can be operated silently with no audible sound emanating from the speaker or headphones except when a target is detected. Some claim that no sensitivity and/or

Simplicity of operation, deepseeking capability and revolutionary notch discrimination of Garrett's Ultra GTAs took the THing world by storm when these motion detectors were introduced.

detection depth is lost in the silent mode. Let's analyze silent versus threshold operation.

In other chapters in this book, threshold operation is clearly defined and the metal detection process is described. Whenever a detector is adjusted to operate with slight audio threshold, the least disturbance of the electromagnetic field by a metal target can be heard in the headphones. This is fringe area detection. Whenever the operator is intently listening to audio threshold these very slight perturbations can be heard.

In silent operation, the detector is now operating in a null or quiet zone. In all but the most extremely precise audio adjustments, there is a finite difference, electronically speaking, between the silent audio level and threshold audio level. In other words, when the detector is operating silently, it takes some definite amount of signal power to move the audio from silent to the point where the audio can just be heard. As long as the detected target is large enough or buried shallow enough to drive the audio from the silent point into the discernible range, the target can be located. But if the target is extremely small or deeply buried, it is possible that it cannot produce sufficient drive to cause the audio to break into this range. Thus the presence of the target is not revealed to the operator.

The sensitivity or detection depth that is lost with the motion detector at silent, rather than at slight threshold, is often referred to as the lost fringe area detection. Admittedly, the amount of loss could be very small, especially if the silent operating point is set very close to the "break point" into threshold audio. Each individual must decide if the lost detection depth is of any consequence.

Electronic Pinpointing

As previously stated, a motion detector may occasionally be found lacking in its ability to pinpoint a target manually. This problem occurs because these instruments operate in an automatic mode. The operator must continually move the searchcoil and cannot hover above targets to pinpoint.

High quality motion detectors, however, feature three-step pinpointing capability. Scanning speed is extremely slow, almost to the hovering point, because the circuits permit almost as wide a range of scanning speeds as a non-motion detector. If the operator wishes more precise pinpointing, two additional pinpointing methods, electronic pinpointing and detuning, can be brought into play.

To activate electronic pinpointing, a switch or control must be operated as described in the Operator's Manual for the instrument. This mode sharpens detection signals and activates a non-motion All Metal mode. The detector can then be hovered, and detection signals are sharpened. Thus, the target can be more accurately pinpointed. If even more precise pinpointing is needed, detuning (tuning to the target) can be brought into play. The operator draws an imaginary "X" on the ground, and determines the area where maximum signal occurs. The searchcoil is placed directly upon the ground. The pinpoint switch is pressed and released, momentarily, and then depressed and held. This switching action tunes the detector to the target. As the searchcoil is scanned over the target, a sharp audio sound will be heard when the target is directly below the center point of the searchcoil.

Operation is Easy!

To operate one of the motion type detectors simply turn the instrument on and start scanning. No ground balancing adjustments are necessary. You can set the audio to either silent or threshold and make the desired adjustment in discrimination. If you need more precise pinpointing, you can use non-motion electronic pinpointing (or the old detuning method) if your detector is equipped with these circuits. Always wear headphones for

Charles Garrett congratulates Ted Seaton of Great Britain, who found the priceless historical religious pendant shown on Page 47 with a Garrett Freedom 2 motion detector.

improved efficiency. Scan the searchcoil in front of you in the side-to- side motion as explained in this book. Keep in mind that you cannot hover the searchcoil over a target, but don't consider this a problem. Just scan as you normally would at a rate of about one to two feet per second, and you will get good depth.

Although these detectors do not shape up for gold, cache and relic hunting, they do a superb job of finding coins anywhere, and you can count on them to produce quite well in most phases of ghost towning.

Pulse Induction Detectors

Pulse detectors came into their own during the '80s. Their tremendous value to the ocean beach hunter became apparent soon after the first discrimination models became available. Several characteristics not only set them apart from other detector types, but result in superior performance during extremely adverse conditions.

Pulse induction detectors are very easy to use. Just set the audio to your preferred threshold level and start scanning. No adjustments are required because these detectors ignore practically all types of minerals. If your detector is equipped with a discrimination (trash elimination) circuit, dial in the desired amount. Wetted ocean salt and black magnetic sand are both ignored simultaneously. Pulse induction models are capable of detecting targets to extreme depths.

Quality pulse detectors are very stable. Some models feature interchangeable searchcoils which expand their capabilities. Some have a very pleasant "bell ringing" audio sound. Meters are found on most models.

Pulse Induction Theory

Pulse induction detectors are intermittent transmission types (see the diagram on the next page). They use searchcoils similar in construction to those of BFOs. A large electrical current is pulsed, or caused to flow, in the winding. A very intense and powerful electromagnetic field is generated which illuminates, or flows out into, the surrounding matrix for a very short time during a given cyclical period.

The electromagnetic field contains a large amount of energy, some of which is "captured" by metal targets. The captured energy is in the form of eddy currents which flow on the surface of the metal. When the primary electromagnetic field dies out following transmitter shutoff, eddy currents are still flowing on the metal's surface. And, eddy currents will flow longer on those objects with a greater degree of conductivity. These currents generate a secondary electromagnetic field that flows outward from the target. A portion of this secondary field passes through the pulse antenna winding where some of its energy generates a signal in the winding. During the sample "window" period, this signal is amplified and conditioned to drive the "bell ringing" audio which alerts the operator to the presence of metal.

As stated earlier, wetted salt and most earth materials are somewhat conductive. The primary field power causes eddy currents to flow in wetted salt and soil mineralization, but the conductivity is so poor that they die out quickly. Thus wetted salt and soil mineralization are not

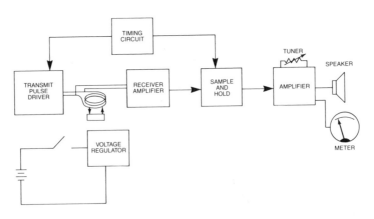

This electronic block diagram of a Pulse Induction metal detector shows the basic circuitry, components and wiring inter-connections that make this type of metal detector so successful.

detected. In other words, when the transmitter circuit shuts off power to the searchcoil, the receiver circuits "wait" past the time needed for wetted salt and ground mineral eddy currents to die out. Then, the receiver circuits "turn on" and receive the metal target signals. Therefore, conductive ground minerals are ignored and only metal targets are detected. Also, since iron mineralization is not conductive, nor does iron affect the antenna circuits, it is not detected.

Pulse Induction Characteristics

Pulse detector circuitry is different from all detector types discussed in this book. BFO, TR and VLF types use a continuous wave type circuit. That is, they transmit the electromagnetic field continuously. Any metal or mineral that sufficiently interrupts the transmitted field produces a signal alerting the operator to the presence of the target.

Pulse detectors are slow response with a target detection process somewhat slower than that of the other types.

This impressive collection represents but a few of the rings and jewelry items found by a New England couple on beaches and in the surf, where a pulse induction detector is so highly effective.

153

Consequently, target pinpointing is slightly more difficult. Pulse detectors require more battery power. They have an affinity for elongated iron objects; these are detected even in discrimination modes. Discrimination pulse induction detectors, however, do an excellent job of eliminating foil, iron bottlecaps, small rusty iron pieces and aluminum pulltabs. At pulltab setting, some rings and nickels may be eliminated.

Discrimination pulse detectors are popular beach and underwater instruments. It was once imperative that this type detector be used on ocean beaches that contain magnetic black sand. BFO and the early VLF detectors simply could not cope with magnetic black sand and salt water simultaneously. The new motion and computerized detectors handle such obstacles with ease, however, as do the non-motion instruments.

Because of the early difficulties with salt, countless beach swimming areas that have never been scanned adequately are now being worked very efficiently. Coins, rings and jewelry that could not be detected by other types, are now being found.

Underwater Hunting

Several underwater models and convertible types that can be used both on land and under water are available. Pulse detectors have long been popular with the diver, but pulse popularity was limited in early years because of high prices. Modern technology has resulted in reduced production costs, and pulse detectors — though still sold at prices higher than motion and non-motion models — are relatively reasonable. In addition, prices are competitive.

The availability of various size searchcoils has improved the underwater searcher's capabilities. The depth detection selector, installed on some models, improves diver efficiency and speeds up target recovery time.

Chapter 30 presents a considerably longer discussion of underwater metal detector operating characteristics and treasure hunting techniques and procedures. A study of this Chapter 13, however, will let you become better acquainted with the general features of Pulse Induction metal detectors.

Pulse Audio

Pulse detectors should be tuned for faint threshold sound. The "bell ringing" audio sound is different from other detectors. Not all pulse detectors feature this "bell ringing" sound, however. Whatever the characteristics, the audio should not be scratchy or irritating. The special "bell ringing" tends to prevent outside interference noise from masking detector target response, especially when underwater where its sound is especially pleasing.

Applications

Pulse detectors readily penetrate layers of black magnetic sand and wetted salt to extreme depth as they locate coins, rings and other metal objects. In fact, detection through layers of mineralized beach sand can be greater

Garrett's Sea Hunter XL500 has proven itself a dependable and effective pulse induction metal detector with a remarkable record of treasure recovery for divers and salvors all over the world.

155

than detection through air. Accounts of single rings and coins being detected 12 to 18 inches and deeper are often reported.

Cache and relic hunting with large searchcoils produces good results. Pulse detectors can be used to search buildings, but nails will probably present a problem. Pulse detectors can be used for any type coin hunting applications, but where small iron trash abounds, motion or non-motion types may have to be used.

Pulse detectors are not recommended for any form of gold hunting. The form factor of nuggets and veins prevents good detection. "Hot rocks" respond and appear as metal targets.

Pulse induction detectors fill a very important slot in the field of metal detection, for without the pulse much treasure and other sought-after metallic objects could not be found. You should not hesitate to acquire a quality pulse detector if your search for treasure takes you to the beach, especially salt water beaches. Deeply buried coins, gold and silver rings and other jewelry you should find will quickly pay off the investment.

Because pulse induction detectors have proven so effective in salt water environments, underwater detectors such as the Sea Hunter are popular on beaches.

156

Author's Comments

This section of the revised *Modern Metal Detectors* was written both for those who already owned one of Garrett's computerized and microprocessor-controlled metal detectors or had an interest in them. As I rewrite this introduction today, Garrett has just begun manufacturing its eighth such instrument, the GTI (Graphic Target Imaging) 1500 and has introduced the marvelous concept of imaging to the field of treasure hunting. The new GTI 1500 is the ultimate coin hunter, and this detector and its companion the GTI 2000 are simply *the finest metal detectors ever manufactured.*

They have proved themselves to me and to countless others who have utilized the concept of imaging to find treasure with them while avoiding numerous trash targets..

This is not to say that other Garrett detectors are not outstanding instruments that represent real value for the treasure hunter. And, there are numerous other manufacturers who produce fine detectors, although I would not feel particularly comfortable in commenting on them.

So, this section as written a few years ago, will concern itself entirely with Garrett's Grand Master Hunter CX II, the Master Hunter CX and the Ultra GTA models. These chapters are not intended to replace either the Owner's Manual or the

Development of Garrett's first Grand Master Hunter with computerized, microprocessor controls represented an historic breakthrough in metal detector technology.

video and audio instruction tapes prepared especially for these detectors. Indeed, this Section III is a *supplement* to those materials.

Plus, this section was designed to give just a peek into the future to those who had not yet sampled the sheer joy of working with a truly computerized instrument...a detector that incorporates the magic of incorporating microprocessor control throughout all its operating functions.

It is well to understand that only such detectors...those using a microprocessor as the integral control element...can be considered computerized detectors. Or, can be expected to give the performance that a treasure hunter should expect from a computerized detector.

Unfortunately, some who either make or sell detectors have confused the issue by abusing the term *computer* in advertising and promotional materials. Such terms as "computer-aided, computer-enhanced and computer-designed" have been used to describe detectors. To the best of my knowledge *none of these so-described detectors utilize microprocessor controls.* Perhaps some of their circuit designs were improved by use of a computer. (I know that those of Garrett detectors were.) Perhaps target responses were tested by a computer program. Perhaps a computer was used in some way to manufacture the detector.

Still, to qualify as a real computerized detector *in the field,* the only place that counts for a true treasure hunter, an instrument **must** incorporate microprocessors in its circuitry.

Of the Garrett detectors, therefore, the CX II and III, the CX and the Ultra GTA models were the only computerized instruments at the time this section was written. Now, of course, they have been joined by the two GTI imaging detectors. You can believe me when I tell you that the sensitivity and deepseeking capabilities of the earlier computerized detectors exceeded all our expectations. They have proven so simple to operate that even novices are pushing a single touchpad and beginning to find treasure immediately. And, now *Imaging by Garrett* is even more extraordinary!

Since the three detectors discussed in this section are such truly simple instruments to operate...why was this section included in addition to available instructional material?

Good question...particularly, since we who have designed and produced these fine instruments are confident they are the easiest metal detectors in use anywhere in the world today. Because they are also the most capable metal detectors available, we want all who hunt with them to be aware of their *full potential*...their characteristics and unique qualities.

Thus, this section of the revised *Modern Metal Detectors* was especially designed to enable anyone to understand how a computerized detector operates and exactly what it is doing that makes it find more treasure. Also, we wanted to insure to the best of our ability that hobbyists got the most from these then-new detectors in all their applications.

Simply stated, this was not intended as a "how-to-use" book. None is needed for any of the Garrett computerized detectors beyond the Owner's Manual that accompanies each of them. This book, while describing the full capabilities of a computerized instrument, seeks to guide every treasure hunter, novice and professional alike, toward achieving full potential in using one...no matter what phase of treasure hunting is selected.

The first drafts of this material on computerized detectors were written as initial models of the Garrett's Grand Master Hunter were being eagerly accepted by the treasure hunting public and we were introducing the Grand Master Hunter II. Such acceptance overjoyed all of us involved in producing this detector. Because we wanted you treasure hunters to appreciate its full capabilities, we began a book on the new detector. Yet, we knew that improvements would be made on the original Grand Master Hunter to make later models, such as the Grand Master Hunter CX II and III, even finer and more distinctive.

And, we foresaw development of the revolutionary new Ultra GTA, with its unique Graphic Target Analyzer (GTA) and "user-set" discrimination modes that can be precisely tailored to any and every kind of treasure hunting. Plus, plans for the GTI imaging detectors were already appearing on the screens of computers in our Engineering Laboratories.

As the time came to completely revise *Modern Metal Detectors,* we felt it appropriate that up-to-the-minute material on computerized detectors be included as a part of this new book.

To experience the greatest success with a computerized detector, we urge that you keep this book readily available and read Section III in conjunction with your Owner's Manual. The final chapter in this section reviews the Starter Phase operations of each of the three computerized detectors, and additional tips on their operation are given throughout Section V, "Using a Detector."

To use a computerized instrument properly we urge that you refer to all of this material often, as well as to your audio and video tapes...no matter what your level of experience with a metal detector, When you learn how to hunt with a computerized detector, we guarantee that it will provide you with multiple thousands of hours of enjoyment and success.

And, perhaps, we can enjoy this success together when...

I'll see you in the field.

Charles Garrett

Summer 1998

Electronic Design

The Grand Master Hunter CX II and III, the Master Hunter CX and the Ultra GTA are the finest all-purpose metal detectors ever manufactured. These computerized and microprocessor-controlled instrument are the products of more than 10 years of intensive research and study in the application of microprocessor technology to the field of metal detection. Along with this analytical investigation came the necessary laboratory and field tests to produce what are truly the world's first *thinking* metal detectors.

In one sense, they are not *new* metal detectors, since the capabilities of each are built upon 25-plus years spent by Garrett Electronics in developing technology and expertise...all this in addition to experience gained in the parks, woods and waters by tens of thousands of hobbyists the world over who have used Garrett instruments to find treasure.

In a real sense, however, the computerized instruments are *absolutely new* and revolutionary detectors. They utilize the very latest in microprocessor technology... expertise that has never been brought to any metal detection instrument.

Why Was It Developed?

The Grand Master Hunter was developed because we at Garrett have never been satisfied with any detector that we ever manufactured. *We always sought to do better!* It has been our continuing goal, year by year, to update and improve the quality, performance and capabilities of each piece of equipment that is sold bearing the Garrett trademark and, thus, representing the Garrett tradition of excellence..

We had long recognized the feasibility of using microprocessor chips in the circuitry of a metal detector to improve its capabilities with computerized technology. Garrett's first patent in this effort is now almost 15 years old. When ultra-low-power microprocessor technology made such chips available for metal detectors, we realized that the time had come to complete our design, then to manufacture and market this computerized detector.

Tracing the history and lineage of the Grand Master Hunter takes us back more than a decade to the manufacture by Garrett of the first Master Hunter ADS detectors featuring *Automatic Detection Systems*. Virtually overnight, these new ground balancing instruments were recognized as the most powerful, deepest-seeking detectors ever offered to the treasure hunting public.

They were capable of ignoring iron minerals and penetrating mineralized soil to unmatched depths to detect even the tiniest targets.

Garrett further enhanced performance of this Master Hunter ADS equipment by adding discrimination capabilities, target identification, pinpointing, coin depth measuring and a wide range of searchcoils. Throughout the world these detectors became recognized for their dependability, reliability and capability.

It is well known in metal detecting—indeed, in any design endeavor—that extensive laboratory and field testing are essential for success. In fact, for the development of field-worthy, high performance equipment, it is necessary that the amount of testing in the field—in hours, certainly—exceed that done in the laboratory. It is simply impossible to manufacture equipment that will perform at maximum levels under actual outdoor conditions unless countless days and weeks are spent in the field testing such equipment.

A continual process of building prototypes, testing them, building new models, testing them, continuing to improve designs, etc. must be carried out. In fact, it's a *never-ending* process! For a detector to respond fully to all demands such testing must be conducted in various locations over the world in addition to the United States.

This is the testing and development program of Garrett Electronics. The author, his field engineers, employee hobbyists and other veteran treasure hunters and electronic prospectors spend countless hours over many months and years testing all types of new equipment. Indeed, because of this testing, some new detectors are never offered to the public. All equipment is actually used under field conditions over ground mineral areas ranging from zero to absolute maximum mineralization. Every detector is subjected to rugged environmental tests.

Results from a quarter century of operations speak for themselves. Garrett Electronics would never consider

Garrett engineer Bob Podhrasky illustrates miniaturization with a small printed circuit board (PCB) designed to include all components and functions of the two boards being held by author

producing — much less, trying to market — any equipment today without complete initial field testing and thorough analysis of all prior test data, followed by extensive test programs in actual treasure hunting locations as the new equipment is developed. Such extensive testing at all levels is one of the reasons why the new computerized detectors exceed all other metal detectors available today in capabilities and in rugged, reliable performance.

Electronic Computer Design

Before the program of field testing, however, it was necessary for the first Grand Master Hunter to be designed in the electronics laboratory. This is the story of that procedure:

In developing a computerized design, using microprocessor controls, our first task was to simply mate existing Master Hunter ADS technology with the new computerized circuits we had developed. It became quickly and painfully apparent that we were placing severe limitations on ourselves and the capabilities of the new detector by developing it solely on existing circuitry. We recognized that an entirely new detector could be designed from searchcoil to audio...with significant improvements in every area.

Microprocessor technology gave us the capability to build equipment utilizing super low power circuitry with extremely low signal-to-noise ratios and fantastic gains. This technology, therefore, offered the capability of *pre-analyzing* the soil and all detected targets which would never have been possible with existing circuitry. It became readily apparent that the amount of data we were receiving from existing searchcoils through existing circuits — while the best in the detector industry — was woefully inferior to that which could be achieved through the technology of microprocessors and computers.

For example, data received from a searchcoil on a particular target is called a "target signature." It contains all the data about each target that can be acquired from the electromagnetic field. Iron minerals send similar signatures.

Microprocessor technology gives us the capability to analyze within a fraction of a second — and, on a continuing basis — every bit of this signature information.

It became necessary, therefore, for us to develop a new searchcoil that could gather as much signature information as possible...then, to design circuits with the capabilities of handling this vastly increased amount of electronic information.

Garrett Electronics was challenged as it had never been before. Talented new personnel and expensive equipment were required for Garrett to be able to respond appropriately. Essentially, we needed new laboratory electronic design equipment with computerized circuitry that permitted total analysis of all signature data as it was received from the ground. We could then take this data and compare it with what was being analyzed by Master Hunter equipment and technology.

Because our new computer equipment was also capable of systematically analyzing all existing circuitry and printed circuit boards (PCBs), an immediate benefit to Garrett and its customers was an upgrading of circuitry and PCBs in all models. We gained the ability to vastly improve current models even without the use of a microprocessor chip.

All of Garrett's detectors were upgraded through this program, and I must confess that our Freedom models even added the initials "CDC" — for Computer Designed Circuitry — to their name in one stage of development. At **no time,** however, did we ever refer to these instruments as *computerized detectors!*

We recognized that to utilize fully the capabilities of microprocessors in a detector itself, we needed to design and build an all-new instrument. Yet, we kept always in mind that such a new instrument must utilize the 25 years of field application and the experience in automatic ground balancing that were represented in Garrett's expertise. The result is two new series of detectors that can operate at 100% efficiency at the push of a single touchpad. No other control adjustment is necessary. In addition, the Grand Master Hunter CX II and III offer the exclusive *Fast Track*™ and *Ground Track*™ feature, and the CX also provides *Fast Track* ground balancing. The two Ultra GTA detectors make exclusive notch discrimination capabilities available that will satisfy the exacting requirements of the most demanding treasure hunter.

These revolutionary detectors give far better performance, detection depth, accuracy of detection and accuracy of target identification over all types of soil than any other instrument ever available. The CX detectors automatically analyze the soil and adjusts ground balance — continually and automatically — even as they analyze all detector targets. The GTA instruments offer discrimination capabilities that had previously existed only in the dreams of treasure hunters.

Automatically programmed into the circuitry of each detector is a wealth of information that treasure hunters previously had to retain in their heads — or notebooks. Veteran hobbyists remember how they had to be continually on the alert for changing ground mineral conditions...how they had to analyze various targets and, often, conflicting discrimination signals received from a detector. Now, much of this human analytical aspect that was formerly required has been assumed by the microprocessor-controlled circuitry in these detectors. This is why we believe them truly to be "thinking" detectors. Garrett Electronics is proud to offer each of them to treasure hunters of the world!

Mechanical Design

Before design can begin on any type of equipment, it is necessary for a set of *specifications* to be set forth that fully describe the equipment to be designed. Specifications for a metal detector must include both mechanical and electronic requirements. We at Garrett call upon countless years of experience in the field working with professional treasure hunters who use our equipment successfully...as well as the experience gained in designing new models.

Just as important is our work with novices to insure that beginners in the hobby of metal detecting are able to utilize all Garrett instruments to the maximum potential possible.

In designing a new detector, however, specifications must come first...and, then be followed up with specific performance goals set forth and sought throughout the development process. These design specifications become the objectives, the targets that must be met. It is impossible to achieve any goal without a target at which to aim.

As time progresses and prototypes are tested, however, specifications change as goals are modified and made more difficult. Garrett engineers and technicians continually seek new and improved methods of design and manufacture. We continually discard that which is inadequate and utilize improvements whenever they are discovered...all with the aim of providing the best equipment possible to the metal detecting public at the lowest cost possible.

Mechanical/Packaging

We began our concept of both the CX and Ultra GTA detectors with the idea of completely new design efforts — from searchcoils to battery packs. Completely new sets of mechanical and packaging specifications were presented. Such new and revolutionary pieces of electronic equipment demanded totally new housings.

Some initial resistance was expressed...justifiably so. The housings that had been developed over a decade for our ADS and Freedom equipment were highly reliable and extremely durable. But, in considering new and revolutionary pieces of metal detection equipment, existing housings proved to be totally inadequate...not only in esthetics, but in such practical areas as weight, balance, handling and environmental performance.

Many hours were spent in the field as well as around the design table in an effort to develop two packages that would be perfectly suited for instruments as new and revolutionary as the CX and Ultra. All types of designs were inspected and analyzed — arm action, chest mount, hip mount. For the greatest performance in all-purpose hunting it was decided to develop two totally different detector packages...one utilizing wrist action control and the other of pistol-grip design.

When a hobbyists is using any Grand Master Hunter for scanning, the instrument is held in the hand with the searchcoil gliding across the ground, side to side in a straight line. This is wrist action. With the instrument held comfortably, the detector is scanned or maneuvered by a combination of actions requiring minimum movement by only the wrist and lower arm.

On the other hand, the primary scanning methods used by coin hunters suggested that a pistol-grip configuration be utilized on the new Ultra GTA series of detectors. The revolutionary battery pack design that resulted in a "slip-off" hip mount that is an integral part of the overall package also lent itself to this design.

Developing searchcoils for a detector with these configurations became an important consideration. We knew that several different sizes would be necessary to produce an all-purpose instrument. We also knew that even the larger searchcoils must be ultralight to assure that long hours in the field would not result in more than minimal fatigue.

Positioning of the controls — along with the actual controls themselves — was also a vital consideration on both detectors. With our wrist action design, it was necessary that all primary controls be immediately available on the handle itself with secondary functions easily accessible on a side-mounted control panel.

Controls on the Ultra GTA had to be easily accessible and the meter had to be visible, no matter how the detector was being operated.

Weight

We set forth all specifications for both detectors, including weight, balance, comfort, function of components, meter controls, meter location, speaker location, battery

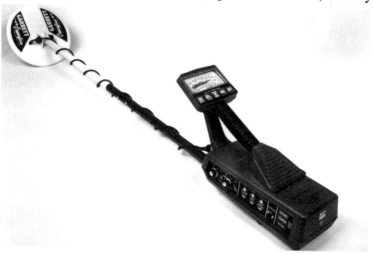

Clean, functional lines characterize the handsome design of the Master Hunter CX II, which was designed to be just as modern and efficient in appearance as it is in treasure hunting.

location and mounting, stems and other features. Weight and balance were two of the specifications that we spent untold hours developing. Those of you familiar with our Master Hunter 7 know that we shaved some one and one-half pounds of weight from it to achieve the lighter and more-easily-handled Grand Master Hunter.

The final weight result was even better than anticipated since our goal was for an instrument exactly one pound lighter than the Master Hunter 7. When we weighed our first production models at slightly less than four pounds, we were more than satisfied. Our new detector is a lightweight, well balanced instrument that can be used for countless hours with minimal discomfort or fatigue.

Of course, the Ultra is even lighter...in fact, that is one of the reasons for its name because we began referring to it as an *ultra lightweight* detector. Hence, the Ultra.

Balance

All of the CX detectors are particularly well balanced. Just a single finger placed beneath the forward end of the handle permits each detector to float perfectly in the air at the proper scan angle. The operator is not forced to raise the coil continually to keep it balanced. The detector's handle permits complete grip comfort. In fact, it is not even necessary to "grip" the handle, but simply to let the detector float comfortable as it is cradled in an individual's curled fingers. The meter is placed in a protected position on the end of the handle for both visibility and rugged performance.

Balance is equally as good in the pistol-grip Ultra model. Moving this lightweight detector around is as easy as pointing your finger.

Touchpads, the major controls of the instrument, are placed right at the hand of the operator on both detectors where they can be reached easily and operated instantly by the touch of a thumbtip. Speaker are placed for maximum sound direction to the ears of the operator, while being protected from an environmental standpoint. Below the rubber handle grip on the CX models and in the battery pack of the Ultra, the speaker is truly hidden on both models. The cross-louvered area on the CX is actually an opening for a multiple slit beneath which is mounted a waterproof speaker.

Batteries for the CX are mounted directly behind the speaker with a convenient door that slides open to permit immediate access to the drop-in battery tray. The Ultra's AA batteries are contained in two specially designed containers that fit snugly into the removable hip-mount unit.

Stem configurations for both detectors represented a completely new stem arrangement for Garrett detectors. The upper stem is aluminum, making it both considerably lighter yet stronger than stems of most other detectors. The lower stem is significantly changed.

New lower stems are a one-piece injection mold of full density polyethylene for extremely light weight yet the ultimate in strength and durability. We do not believe that any other metal detector uses a stem any lighter in weight.

Searchcoils

An intensive design concern throughout development of the Grand Master Hunter concerned searchcoils that would serve it and the Ultra. We were determined that they be electronically perfect and electronically stable. In addition they had to be environmentally protected, yet small and thin to keep weight to a minimum. We are extremely proud of the new Crossfire searchcoils that emerged from these design considerations.

The new searchcoils are much thinner than those previously used by Garrett, and they feature a modernistic design. In addition a new procedure for mounting them to the stem permits them to be locked easily and sturdily at any search angle.

Changing this angle requires only that the operator touch a toe lightly to the searchcoil while pressing on the

173

detector itself. The position of the searchcoil is adjusted and locked without the operator having to grapple with any knobs or bolts.

Of special interest to all hobbyists should be the fact that the electronic transmitter/receiver winding configuration is housed within our new searchcoils in a floating tri-point suspension system. Of course, prior models with the winding completely encased in a lightweight foam configuration represented excellent design for a rugged and long-lasting searchcoil. The new tri-point floating system, however, affords even better performance, greater stability and more rugged, durable operation.

In the new searchcoil the electronic winding is positioned to be protected against shocks that might occur when the searchcoil is bumped against a tree or boulder. The floating design transmits this shock directly to the upper cover of the searchcoil and into the stem. Temperature stability is also improved in the new models since there is no coefficient of expansion or contraction in the two plastic covers that can affect searchcoil windings which are connected only at the three pinpoint positions. Housing contraction or expansion because of temperature can have no effect on searchcoil windings.

All of Garrett's new Crossfire searchcoils are submersible. They can be fully submerged to the cable connector and continue to operate at 100% efficiency. Neither blowing sand, dust nor any other terrain feature will affect this searchcoil. Although they are rugged and extremely easy to maintain, we recommend the use of inexpensive skidplates (coil covers) for all searchcoils. Soap and water

Computerized analysis with colors showing various stress levels enables Garrett engineers to maintain light weight while designing stronger and more efficient equipment.

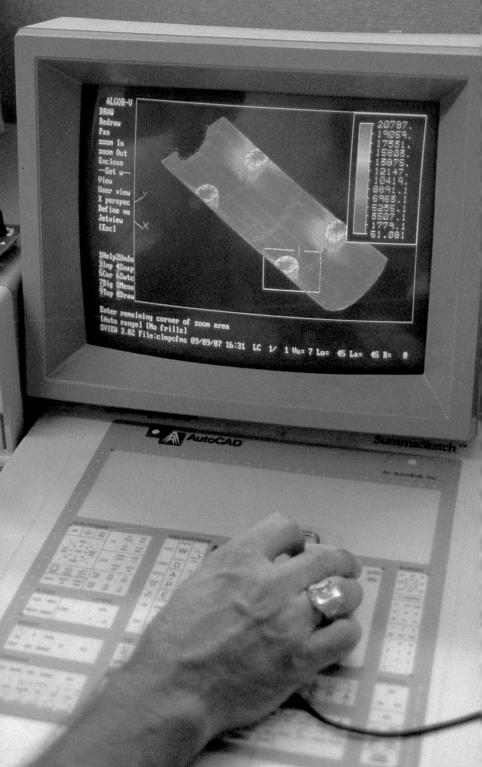

can be used to remove any excess soil or grime accumulated on the searchcoil.

Garrett has designed searchcoils in five distinct sizes to give the CX and Ultra detectors all-purpose capabilities. A searchcoil is available to perform every treasure hunting task professionally and efficiently.

The 8 1/2-inch searchcoil is designed for all-purpose use. It is very satisfactory for any type of treasure hunting...even to include the largest targets you will ever encounter. Its depth performance and pinpointing are excellent on all size targets. We particularly recommend this searchcoil for coin hunting and general treasure hunting. It is also suitable for nugget hunting, many other phases of prospecting and most general treasure hunting applications.

Our 4 1/2-inch searchcoil, called the Super Sniper™, has been designed especially for coin hunting as well as for some phases of electronic prospecting. The Super Sniper is small, lightweight and ultra sensitive. Highly maneuverable, it is especially good in areas of restricted surface movement or where there is metal junk in the ground. This small size lets the detector identify individual targets more accurately, which greatly improves their identification and resolution.

Metal junk in the ground increases the likelihood that an occasional good target might be blanked out. Since the Super Sniper covers such a small area, this possibility is virtually eliminated when it is used. This smaller searchcoil is the fastest selling accessory searchcoil ever manufactured by Garrett. It is impossible for us to recom-

The old meets the new as an "ancient" Garrett detector is scanned alongside a modern Grand Master Hunter CX II with computerized microprocessor controls.

mend it strongly enough. We urge you to you to try it for yourself in the various phases of treasure hunting and electronic prospecting.

The third circular Crossfire searchcoil is a large one that is 12 1/2 inches in diameter. It offers the greatest depth on all targets except the very tiniest, such as extremely small gold nuggets. When seeking deeper targets, especially those coin-sized or larger, this coil should be your choice. Its depth performance will fascinate you, and we guarantee you will reach depths you had not thought possible.

Despite its capabilities and actual size, this searchcoil is lightweight and easily maneuverable and offers excellent pinpointing characteristics.

Two elliptical searchcoils have also proven quite versatile. One is 5x10 inches in size, with the other 3x7 inches. Not only are they adaptable to searching in any environment that is not suitable to circular coils, but they have demonstrated great depth and sensitivity. With Garrett's exclusive 2D windings, these elliptical coils are especially sensitive in a relatively small strip down the center of the coil. Thus, they offer added depth and sensitivity with the effective scanning width of 10-inch and 7-inch coils.

For best results in seeking out really deep targets we recommend that the Grand Master Hunter CX II and III or Master Hunter CX be supplemented with Garrett's Depth Multiplier attachment, which most treasure hunters call the Bloodhound. In addition to its unbeatable depth performance on large objects, the Depth Multiplier offers another plus by not detecting targets smaller than a fruit jar.

To put this in terms any treasure hunter can understand, let's consider using the Depth Multiplier to search for a cache at an old farmhouse. As you know, around such places will be found literally hundreds of small iron targets such as nails and other pieces of junk metal. Also, as a cache hunter, you are probably hunting in the All Metal mode since you do not want to miss something like an iron pot full of money which discrimination could possibly cause you to lose. If you're using standard-type searchcoils with no discrimination, you'll certainly detect all the many small pieces of iron junk around any old farmhouse. Our Depth Multiplier, on the other hand, does not detect small objects but seeks only larger objects typical of a money cache. Therefore, you will not be bothered by small or individual targets, and you can become highly efficient as a cache hunter with the Depth Multiplier on your Grand Master Hunter.

Rugged Performance

Specifications for our new computerized microprocessor-controlled detectors demanded that the new instruments be rugged. We required that they be able to withstand shock, vibration and, even, dropping without damage to the instrument or any of its operating parts. Of course, Garrett has always built detectors designed for rough field handling. We have never required that any Garrett equipment be "babied." At the same time, however, we have always urged that hobbyists take good care of *all* their equipment...urged them to keep it dry and clean...to give it continual moderate care. But, rugged use? For a Garrett, the answer is, *Yes!* Never be afraid to use your Garrett equipment in any reasonable situation, no matter how rugged.

Easy to Use

This was still another specification that guided development of the Grand Master Hunter and the Ultra GTA. Our success here has spoken for itself through thousands of hours of field use of the initial Grand Master Hunter and CX models. As we have already explained, this detector can be easily transported by cradling it in the fingers. Its searchcoil can be swung over the ground in an easy, relaxed motion. The searchcoil can be swung up to search a wall in a house or a mine and swung back down easily to the floor. Hobbyists have reported amazement at the ease of handling shown by their CX detectors, even with large searchcoils such as the Depth Multiplier.

Those employee hobbyists and professional treasure hunters who have helped us field test the Ultra GTA 1000 report it equally as easy to use.

Appearance

The appearance of our detectors has been important to us throughout the history of the Garrett companies. We have always wanted them to be pleasant to look at...to be handsome and to have real eye appeal. This was particularly important for these new computerized detectors. We demanded a design as applicable to the 21st century as we knew that its circuitry and operating capabilities would be.

Immediately, we discarded all of the old folded metal box configurations, those *antiquey-looking* housings with sharp edges. We believe that these are truly for the horse and buggy days. A *little tin box* may be suitable for holding valuables, but it's not what we were willing to accept to enclose our detector's circuitry.

It's obvious now to see that the Grand Master Hunter and Ultra were designed for good looks throughout — front, back and both sides. We are confident that their designs will withstand the test of time truly into the next century. Owners of these detectors can be proud of them...their appearance, as well as their operation. The success of these two new designs advances the stature of all equipment now being made available to the treasure hunter.

Capabilities

Detectors in the CX series were designed to have capabilities superior to that of any detector available to the treasure hunting public...even greater than those of their legendary predecessors, the Master Hunter ADS detectors.

Our goals were achieved.

The Grand Master Hunter CX II, the just-introduced Grand Master Hunter CX III and the Master Hunter CX are capable of performing every metal detecting task, including coin hunting, cache hunting, relic hunting, ghost town searching, general treasure hunting, rock hounding and all phases of electronic prospecting.

Furthermore, each of them performs any one or all of the various treasure hunting tasks with real excellence.

The Ultra GTA detectors, with their graphic display and unique discrimination capabilities are the world's foremost coin hunting instruments. Yet, their capabilities far exceed the realm of mere coin hunting and make them almost universal detectors.

All of the varied performance capabilities of the Grand Master Hunter CX, the CX II and the Ultra will be discussed in detail in succeeding sections of this section. Always keep in mind when treasure hunting with a Grand Master Hunter or Ultra metal detector that you are limited only by your imagination. These instruments offer technologically advanced circuitry that will fully support treasure hunting capabilities at any level you desire.

No physical limits will be placed in your way. Even if your only concern today is hunting for coins, we assure you that on that day when you find yourself visiting a ghost town or hear about a money cache you can't ignore – even visit an old mining property or hunt anywhere for nuggets – your Grand Master Hunter or Ultra GTA will respond to the demands of these types of hunting and perform to your most extravagant expectations. Your computerized metal detector will provide you the greatest possible measure of potential success and rewards.

Trust and Reliance

At Garrett we have always urged that our customers *trust* the equipment we offer. Only with complete trust can maximum success be achieved.

This is particularly true with the Master Hunter CX, the Grand Master Hunter CX II and III and the Ultra GTA 1000 and 500...no detector before has ever deserved trust as much as these fine instruments. No matter how easy they may seem to operate, the capabilities of these detectors should never be doubted. None of them will never lie to you. You can trust them to perform to their maximum potential under all environmental and ground mineralization conditions.

Signals will be unerring. Of course, it is your responsibility to train yourself to listen for these signals and to learn what they mean...what your detector is telling you. But, this is simple. We have designed a unique system of target identification signals—both audible and visible—that instantly let you determine the type of target that you have detected.

Junk targets either are ignored or produce weak signals...just to let you know you have detected a target, but one that you should not be concerned with. Of course, any old-time treasure hunter will urge you to "dig all targets."

We agree, especially during your learning phases with any of these magnificent new detectors. You will soon learn to trust your instrument implicitly.

The Starter Phase

The Starter Phase was designed initially for those with little or no experience in metal detection. These individuals who were beginning their experiences in metal detecting and treasure hunting had complimented Garrett by their choice of a Grand Master Hunter CX-type detector or an Ultra GTA instrument. It was a wise selection, for they had decided to begin a treasure hunting career with the finest equipment available.

Yet, we understood that they would also want to begin finding treasure immediately with their new instrument with *no* prolonged training period. Because they are the finest universal detectors now available, this is possible with the Grand Master Hunter CX III with TreasureTalk™, the CX II, the Master Hunter CX...or either of the three all purpose Ultra GTA detectors. Even though all of these instruments include controls and present capabilities that satisfy even the most experienced and sophisticated treasure hunter, the detectors literally can be taken into the field *right out of the shipping container* and operated with only the push of a single touch-pad!

We developed a program that avoids all confusion, yet demonstrates how the detector can be operated to find treasure in a simple manner. This Starter Phase program proved an immediate success with those we assigned to test it. Because the Starter Phase was so important, it was explained initially in a folder separate from the Owner's Manual. As described on the cover, we wanted to make certain that all purchasers of the Grand Master Hunter would *Read This First!*

As we studied our success with this Starter Phase, however, it soon became apparent to us that *everyone* who uses our new detector would benefit from a few such hours of initial operation. Therefore, each Owner's Manual of all three of our computerized detectors now suggests to the new owner, *Let's Go Hunting,* and strongly recommends that every user of any CX or GTA detector—no matter what level of experience he or she has attained—operate in the Starter Phase for a minimum of **TEN HOURS** before advancing to the Professional Phase of each detector (which are also discussed in the various chapters of different kinds of hunting that are included as Section V of this book).

If you are just getting started with a metal detector, one of the most important steps you could take would be to go to a qualified and experienced dealer. One with field experience and knowledge of metal detectors can guide you in the use of either of these two types of detectors, their searchcoils and accessories.

Knowledgeable dealers welcome the opportunity to work with customers, to teach them the proper use of equipment. They know that a satisfied customer is their best advertisement.

Dealers can answer your questions about use of a new detector as well as problems that might arise in treasure hunting or your early efforts at research. Of course, no dealer can do more than help you with the basics and get you started. You will have to devote the necessary time and energy to learn your equipment and work with it under field conditions to become truly proficient. Still, a qualified dealer is absolutely worth his weight in gold!

No such dealer nearby? Then, join a treasure hunting club. If there's no club in your area, perhaps you can start one. Write to our company for advice.

Searchcoils and Accessories

The old days when detectors were purchased with only one general purpose-type searchcoil have indeed changed considerably. Various special "packages" are available today that present the new owner with numerous coil opportunities and other accessories at considerable savings. Before we studying each of the computerized detectors, let's look at the searchcoils and other major accessories available for them. It is well to remember, however, that the 8 1/2-inch circular and 5x10-inch elliptical Crossfire searchcoils will probably always be the most important.

The 12 1/2-inch searchcoil will be needed for extensive cache hunting, looking for relics at great depths and searching mines and gold fields for veins, float and other deposits. You'll also want this larger searchcoil if you simply desire the absolute maximum depth capabilities of your new Garrett detector.

The 4 1/2-inch Super Sniper searchcoil (shown below)could become an important tool for you to search junk areas for coins that other treasure hunters left behind, especially those who searched without this valuable smaller coil. You'll also find that the Super Sniper has important applications in gold hunting.

Two elliptical Crossfire coils are also very important. Developed initially for use primarily in areas where rocks and other physical conditions discouraged the use of con-

Small Super Sniper™ searchcoils enable opportunistic treasure hunters to search areas that others avoid because of the presence of trash metal targets, which the 4 1/2-inch coil can avoid.

ventional circular coils, these new models have proven themselves to be star treasure-finders under any conditions.

The coils are 5x10 inches and 3x7 inches in size and feature 2D windings specially designed and engineered by Garrett. Because these windings concentrate searchcoil power in a narrow strip down its middle, these new coils are proving to be deeper seeking and more sensitive to many types of targets.

Many treasure hunters are purchasing them as an alternate to circular Crossfire coils.

A carrying case, either a soft bag or a suitcase, should also be on your list of accessories. It provides you with protection during transportation and storage. Believe me when I say that a good carrying case is a wise investment.

Headphones are an absolute must! They are unquestionably the most important accessory you will ever purchase. Often, headphones can spell the difference between success and failure...especially when searching for ultra deep targets, seeking tiny targets or working around noisy areas. These noises can be man-made, produced by automobiles and traffic, or natural, such as those of surf or winds. Headphones will block out most ambient sounds while directing audio detection signals directly into your ears. Garrett offers a selection of headphones. We recommend sets with large ear pads and individual volume controls. In warm and humid climates you may want to consider a set with smaller earphones. The smaller pads do not block outside sounds quite as well, but do a reasonably good job of getting faint detection signals to your ears more directly.

To prove to yourself the value of headphones, perform this simple experiment: Bury a coin deeply in the ground. Pass your searchcoil over it and listen to the sound from the detector's speaker. Now use earphones and pass the searchcoil over it again. You'll notice the difference!

Computerized Hunting

Let's begin by assembling your new CX detector correctly! First of all, refer to your Owner's Manual. This is excellent advice, not only for a computerized detector, but for any instrument—at least, any of those accompanied by a Garrett owner's manual. We prepare these books to be invaluable to you as long as you use your detector. You'll notice that they are pocket-sized so that you can take them into the field easily.

First step in assembling any of the three CX detectors is to place the two black washers in the recesses of the white lower stem, then press and guide this assembly into the upright post of the searchcoil. Incidentally, if you purchased your detector with more then one searchcoil, we recommend that you first use the 8 1/2-inch size. Secure that searchcoil to the stem by inserting the white plastic screw through the holes and tightening the black knobs on each end of the screw. Hand tighten only. Tools aren't necessary, and you can damage the knobs or threads on the screw by using them.

Now, before you do anything else with the stems, make certain that spring clips are inserted in each of them with the buttons sticking out of the holes. These buttons permit you to adjust the length of the stem. If the spring clips haven't been inserted in the stems, compress the buttons of each and insert it, button-ends first, into the stem until the buttons pop out of the proper holes.

Next, insert the lower stem into the green upper metal stem. Press the two spring clip buttons and let them pop out into the second set of holes from the bottom of the metal stem. Press the buttons at the other end of the green stem and insert it into the receptacle under the detector housing. Let these buttons snap back out into the holes. You may find this a snug fit. In fact, you may have to work a bit to insert the stem into the detector housing. Whatever you do, resist the urge to use any kind of lubricant here or at any other time on your detector. Petroleum products and other lubricants will only attract dirt and various pieces of grit. Never use them on a detector.

Wind your searchcoil cable around the stem, letting the first turn come over the top. Wind it snugly, but not tightly. You want to be able to adjust the angle of your searchcoil without disturbing the cable.

Properly mate the cable connector into the control housing connector and press inward. Now tighten the nut a turn or two until snug. Sometimes this nut can be a little tricky, so make certain that it's tightly closed. Once again, however, use your hands only...no tools.

Your detector is now ready for operation. You're anxious to try it out, but we urge you to wait until you're outdoors.

Metal in a house or building can cause erratic operation. Of course, this won't harm your instrument, but you should let your new CX detector make its best *first impression* outdoors where it's meant to be used.

Using Your CX Detector

Of all universal metal detectors in general use today the Grand Master Hunter CX III is by far the easiest to operate from the first moment that you turn it on. The same statement is true about the CX II and CX, even though they lack some of the universal capabilities of their more sophisticated "big brother."

Yet, as you use any one of these fine detectors and learn their operating characteristics, you will quickly become more proficient in their operation and want to learn still more about them. Because the CX III includes some capabilites of the GTA detectors, owners of that instrument will want to read the following chapter as well. Simply stated, you can find treasure with these detectors from the beginning, but both the quality and volume of your discoveries will increase as you become more expert in their use. As you turn on your computerized Master Hunter instrument for the first time, a wonderful experience awaits you. It has unlimited capabilities that will continue to amaze you as long as you use it.

So... let's start being amazed!

In the Starter Phase you will use only *one* touchpad of the five located below the meter on the console. That's right, only one. (Well, two, counting the **OFF** touchpad!) As far as the controls on the side of the CX II are concerned, don't even think about them in the Starter Phase except to make certain the two knobs on the left are dialed to the Initial Setting (>) arrows.

Grasp the handle of your detector and place the searchcoil lightly on the ground. Make certain you are three to four feet away from any metal objects. Press the **ON** touchpad firmly and release. You have ordered your detector to check its internal circuitry. Millions of computations are made almost instantaneously to assure you that all circuitry is operating properly. You will also notice that battery condition is reported on your meter. After just a second or so, your detector will sound a beep tone indicating that it is ready to go to work.

If this is your first experience with a detector, now is the time to learn about an important subject called the *Audio Threshold.* This is simply the sound level projected from the detector's speaker or through your headphones while you are searching for targets. When a target is found, the sound level will increase perceptibly. I strongly recommend that you ALWAYS set your audio threshold at a level where you hear just a faint sound.

You'll probably find the audio on your detector already set at this level, but adjustments can be made to your individual preference on either of the instruments. On the CX II just push either the plus (+) or minus(−) touchpads adjacent to the word **AUDIO** on the side panel of your detector. Audio level on the CX is adjusted by holding down the **ALL METAL** touchpad and pressing the plus (+) or minus(−) at the right side of the touchpad console.

Now, you're ready to hunt! You are operating in the Discriminate mode. Circuitry of your instrument will detect items made of conductive metal, such as coins and rings, and other gold, silver, copper, brass, bronze and zinc items. With those two Discrimination knobs on the side panel at the Initial Setting arrows, your Grand Master Hunter has been programmed not to detect items made of junk metal such as nails, bottlecaps, pulltabs and other small iron and aluminum objects.

Scan or move the searchcoil in a straight line in front of you from side to side at a speed of from one to two feet per second. Skim the searchcoil lightly over the ground. Don't be in a hurry. Keep the searchcoil level as you walk and scan lightly over grass, weeds, rocks and other obstructions. If you prefer, hold it an inch or two off the ground, but try to maintain a constant searchcoil scan height. Be careful not to let the searchcoil swing upward at the end of each scan.

When your searchcoil passes over an acceptable target, you'll hear a pronounced audio signal over the detector's speaker or through your headphones. When you move the searchcoil back and forth over the object, the signal will be loudest when the target is directly beneath the center of the searchcoil. To pinpoint the location of your detected target scan the searchcoil across the object from different directions and draw an imaginary "X" on the ground where the signals are the loudest.

Listen to these sounds carefully and try to memorize them, along with indications being shown on your detector's meter, before you retrieve the object you have discovered. When you dig up the target, notice how deep it was and its position as it lay in the soil. Now, remember the signal your detector gave you and the meter reading it showed. By learning to correlate all this data, you will very soon become surprisingly accurate in identifying targets and in determining their precise location and depth, even before you dig.

Speaking of digging, always respect property rights of others. Never dig a hole any larger than necessary. Don't destroy grass or other vegetation, and don't damage manicured yards or buildings. A true professional treasure hunter will leave absolutely no sign that he or she has ever searched or dug in an area. Remember, always, to fill your holes; it's important! No matter whether you're hunting in a desert wilderness, on a lonely beach or in a crowded park, fill any hole you make. It's a great habit to get into!

Well, can you see by now just how easy it is to operate the Grand Master Hunter CX II or the Master Hunter CX? After using only *one* touchpad you can already tell that it's the world's most intelligent, capable metal detector! Remember that it is programmed automatically not to respond to most junk items. Occasionally, however, you will encounter junk targets that have detection characteristics that cause your detector to respond with a quick, sharp sound. It's what we call a "blip." It will not sound like the clear, strong signal made by a coin. Dig up and examine some of these objects that produce irregular blips. See how they register on your meter. You'll soon learn to tell the difference between junk and targets made of conductive metal.

The Discriminate mode in which you're now operating was designed primarily for coin hunting. Computerized circuitry of your detector properly identifies small junk targets with precise accuracy, but larger objects such as an aluminum or tin can may also produce a good audio signal. This is normal.

Always remember that your Grand Master Hunter CX II, CX or any other quality Garrett detector, is reporting accurately to you what it has detected beneath its searchcoil. The instrument will never lie, but will report what it finds. Because there are literally millions of buried metal objects of all types and sizes, it is quite common for more than one target to lie beneath your searchcoil at a detectable depth. When this happens, your detector must analyze all of the items simultaneously. Signals, therefore, may sometimes sound peculiar, and you may find it difficult to pinpoint a particular target. All of this is normal, and you will learn to understand it better after you gain experience with the detector.

This is one reason we recommend that you learn to appreciate the simplicity of the Grand Master Hunter CX II and the Master Hunter CX by operating in the Starter Phase for at least 10 hours...preferably more.

You can gain a good understanding of the characteristics of either of these fine detectors and the signals they give you. When you move into the Professional Phase and use the side controls, as you find them necessary, proficiency will come far more quickly. You will soon discover yourself accomplishing things you never thought possible with a metal detector. Devote just a few hours and learn to use it properly at first; then, enjoy the results the rest of your life. Start right and always be successful!

To turn off the instrument simply press firmly on the **OFF** console touchpad. All battery power is disconnected. The next time you wish to use your detector, simply press the **ON** touchpad. The detector will again automatically and simultaneously adjust its internal circuitry to proper operation of the Discriminate mode under existing atmospheric and ground mineralization conditions. Your audio threshold will also be restored at exactly the setting you selected earlier.

Who could have believed all this possible just a few years ago?

By closely following instructions for the Starter Phase in the Owner's Manual of the CX or CX II, it is possible to become proficient with the use of only a single touchpad.

192

Computerized Hunting

Instructions for assembling any of the three Ultra GTA detectors correctly are quite similar to those for a CX-type instrument. First of all, follow the advice about referring to your Owner's Manual.

Attach the searchcoil to the lower stem by placing two black washers in the recesses of the white lower stem, then pressing and guiding this assembly into the upright post of the searchcoil. We recommend that you first use the 5x10-inch elliptical or 8 1/2-inch circular size. Secure that searchcoil to the stem by inserting the white plastic screw through the holes and tightening the black knobs on each end of the screw. Hand tighten only. Tools aren't necessary, and you can damage the knobs or threads on the screw by using them.

Now, before you do anything else with that lower stem, make certain that spring clips are inserted in it with the buttons sticking out of the holes. These buttons permit you to adjust the length of the over all stem. If the spring clips haven't been inserted in the stems, compress the buttons of one of them and insert it, button-ends first, into the stem until the buttons pop out of the proper holes. The second clip will go into the control housing attachment that mates it to your upper stem.

With no dials to turn or controls to adjust the Ultra GTA detectors are so easy to operate that anyone can immediately begin using them to find treasure

195

Next, insert the lower stem into the green upper metal stem. Press the two spring clip buttons and let them pop out into the second set of holes from the bottom of the metal stem. Now use the buttons in the control housing attachment that will connect it with the green end of the overall stem. Let these buttons snap back out into the holes. You may find this a snug fit. In fact, you may have to work a bit to insert the stem onto the detector housing. Whatever you do, resist the urge to use any kind of lubricant on your detector. Petroleum products and other lubricants will only attract dirt and various pieces of grit. *Never* use them on a detector.

Wind your searchcoil cable around the stem, letting the first turn come over the top. Wind it snugly, but not tightly. You want to be able to adjust the angle of your searchcoil without disturbing the cable.

Properly mate the cable connector into the control housing connector and press inward. Now tighten the nut a turn or two until snug. Sometimes this nut can be a little tricky, so make certain that it's tightly closed. Once again, however, use your hands only...no tools.

Your detector is now ready for operation. You're anxious to try it out, but we urge you to wait until you're outdoors.

Metal in a house or building can cause erratic operation. Of course, this won't harm your instrument, but you should let the Ultra GTA 1000 or the GTA 500 make its best *first impression* outdoors where it's meant to be used.

Let's Go Hunting!

With a GTA detector there are no dials to turn...no controls to ad just. Just grasp the handle and hold the searchcoil at least three feet away from any metal. Lower the searchcoil to a level about one foot above the ground.

Press and release the **POWER** touchpad. After you hear two beeps, you are operating in the factory-set *Coins* detection mode.

The Ultra GTA begins operating with discrimination and other controls at factory-set levels. It is recommended that you use these settings the first few hours you hunt with your detector. Instructions for changing threshold, tone, audio, discrimination, etc. are given in your owner's manual.

Swing the searchcoil in front of you in a straight line and keep it moving at a rate of about one to two feet per second. Maintain a one to two-inch searchcoil height above the ground. Detection of a metal target will be indicated by an increase in sound.

Try to locate your target precisely by scanning back and forth over the target to determine where signals are loudest.

Notice all indications on the Graphic Display of the GTA's control panel. The Upper Scale of this display will indicate what type of target was detected. Use the Target ID Guide above the Graphic Display to identify the target before you retrieve it.

The Ultra GTA in its factory-set *Coin* detection mode will not respond audibly to most junk items. Occasionally, you'll encounter targets that cause the detector to respond with a quick, sharp sound...not like the clear, strong signal of a coin. Before you dig up some of the targets that make irregular audio "blips," see how they register on the Upper Scale of the Graphic Display. Learn to recognize them. Because your Ultra GTA is set primarily to hunt coins, it will also precisely identify small junk targets. Some larger objects such as aluminum cans may present a good audio signal. This is normal.

To turn off your detector simply press and release the **POWER** touchpad. All battery power is disconnected.

After 10 Hours

By now you are certainly impressed with the *super* sensitivity, depth capabilities and the target analysis of your Grand Master Hunter CX II, Master Hunter CX or

Ultra GTA. You may have encountered an occasional instance when the meter or graphic display seemed to be presenting conflicting information. This probably occurred when your detector was attempting to analyze two or more different targets beneath its searchcoil. Don't be alarmed. This condition happens with all detectors, but the array of visual data the detector presents just makes you more aware of it. Additional operating experience with these detectors will give you a better understanding of how their meters and graphic display combines with the audio to present target signals.

You will quickly master any of Garrett's computerized detectors, and you will love them! Most of all, you will probably love their simplicity. Yet, each of these instruments with patented microprocessor controls is as sensitive and effective as any detector ever manufactured...in fact, even more so!

Choosing a Detector

The selection of a metal detector is more involved than just finding one that costs the most or one that a magazine article said found 50,000 coins. *Quality can be found.* If you are diligent, you can become attuned to recognizing it when you find it. Metal detectors are actually easy to learn to evaluate and to use successfully. The purpose of this book to make both these tasks easier for you. Remember that your selection of any brand or type of metal detector should be based upon four proven features of that particular detector:

– Quality,
– Ability,
– Versatility,
– Capability.

Quality is not an accident. The more you study detectors, the better will be your ability to find quality. Study the advertising and sales literature of all manufacturer s. Make a chart, and list the various brands and types of detectors, their capabilities, the various available searchcoils and accessories. On the chart note what you like, and don't like, about them...also, their cost.

If a manufacturer says a detector will do a particular job, study his literature to determine if he gives you in-depth information regarding that detector and proving its capabilities. Or, has he simply made a flat competitive statement that his detector can be used for this or that with no proof whatsoever? Visit or contact several detector dealers. Talk to them about the various kinds of detectors.

199

Which instruments do full-time professionals use? Read the various magazines and books published. Notice which detectors people are using.

Testing the Instrument

Turn the detector on and set its audio level. If you are not able to do this, ask the dealer for assistance. See how easily he sets the detector. Does he seem to know what he is doing? If he cannot set the instrument and show you easy steps to operating it, perhaps you should doubt his ability to advise you properly. When the dealer hands you a detector, turn all the controls several times and then hand it back to him and ask him to reset it. If he can accomplish this quickly, perhaps it is safe to consider his recommendation.

Don't believe such statements as "Oh, that particular detector is junk," "No good," and "You don't want it." When you hear those kinds of statements, ask the person making them why he said that. Listen to his answer. Ask him for specifics and not generalities such as "All other brands of detectors are no good!" Try to judge for yourself the accuracy of such statements. Talk to detector owners and dealers about metal detectors and then try to average out what they say. Don't take the word of just one person on which detector is the best or which is the worst; talk to a lot of people. Perhaps a detector owner has experienced a problem with a detector. It may be serious, or only minor...or, in fact, the owner may have never learned how to use the detector correctly. Still, that person may forever be against that particular brand of detector...an opinion he or she expresses far and wide! Such information is scarcely the most desirable upon which to base your decision.

Select a detector built by a progressive company that has a continuing program of detector improvement. Does the manufacturer test his own instruments? Does he get out into the field and use them under all kinds of situations? Does he travel to various locations to test varying soil conditions to insure his detectors work regardless of conditions? Are company engineers active in the field?

Pay no attention to magical, fanciful and mysterious descriptions. A detector may be called a "super-duper triple snooper" or touted for its "unparalleled performance" or described as "rarin' to go" with amazing performance. You may be told that "this detector is not just a VLF detector but its trash rejection circuit is factory-computerized."

Pay no attention to that malarkey. Those are simply *sell* statements and do nothing to increase your knowledge of detectors. The manufacturer who says his detectors are the best, above all others, should be asked to prove it. After all, HE made the statement, its up to HIM to prove it! And, while he is trying to do the impossible, go buy the best detector for you.

To achieve the greatest depth in detecting large objects use the Depth Multiplier attachment, which can double detection depth, ignore minerals and small objects and pinpoint precisely.

201

How do you find this detector? Get your hands on one or more, and *try them out.*

There is no one particular brand or type of detector that is "just perfect" and that will do every job perfectly with total capabilities. There are, however, many types of detectors in all price ranges that will perform admirably in many situations and under extreme environmental conditions, and a few detectors that will do most jobs quite satisfactorily.

If possible, rent a detector of the type you wish to buy. Spend as many hours as possible using that detector to learn its characteristics and capabilities. There is no better way to find out for yourself if a detector is suited for you, than to use one. Many dealers do have rental programs, and the few dollars that you spend on rental fees can often be repaid by the detector many times over. Some rental contracts specify that a portion of, or all, rental fees can be used toward the purchase of a new detector.

Concerning dollars and cents, please don't make the very common mistake of thinking that if you look around and choose the highest priced detector, you will be getting the best instrument. Instead, determine a price *range* that fits your pocketbook. Then, diligently analyze all detectors priced within that range before buying the one that suits you best.

Let's say that you've decided to spend from $600 to $800 on a new detector. Analyze and use the various models in that range. Compare them and judge their versatility, capability, quality and the ability to do the specific jobs you require. Then, purchase the detector that you find best suited to your metal detection wants and needs.

Above all, you must depend upon the reputation of the manufacturer...the record a company has achieved over the years. It has happened many times that a detector with a square foot of printed circuit board was out-performed by a detector with a board the size of a playing card. And, think of what it may cost you to have that one square foot of printed circuit board repaired! Don't fall for the gimmick that this detector has transistors in it that are the equivalent of a microprocessor or has x-many more transistors than any competitive instrument. Someone may be trying to dump an engineering nightmare on you that wears out batteries every 30 minutes.

Knowledgeable and conscientious engineers continually strive to design circuitry with minimum components. The more components there are, the less reliable the product. And, *nothing* does the work of a microprocessor in a detector except a microprocessor.

Be sure to take a look at the detector. Does it look like quality? Does it have jagged edges or unfinished parts? Is it ruggedly built or does the control housing flop on its handle? Pick up the detector and feel it. Does it feel like quality? Grasp the control housing and rock it back and forth. Is it solid or loose? Switch on the detector and put it through its paces by adjusting all the controls.

Speaking of controls, just how many are there? You go into the field to find treasure, not to prove your expertise by manipulating controls on an electronic instrument. Are all controls absolutely necessary? Are they smooth to operate? When you put the detector through its paces over various targets, does it respond smoothly or are there sudden changes and squawks and squeals in the audio?

Compare Several Brands

Match different against each other and check them out. The searchcoil should be extremely well made and the components mated together properly. If there is a visible bonding seam, it should be a uniform bead properly applied. The stem mounting brackets on the searchcoil should be correctly aligned, and there should be two upright brackets, not just one. The method used for mounting the stem to the searchcoil should be simple, yet strong and functional, with only a reasonable twist of the wing nut or locking nut to hold the searchcoil securely in position...despite the bumps it is sure to take against the ground, stumps and bushes. Quality construction should be demanded! If you suspect less-than-the-best construction in any single one of a detector's components, it may pay you to double-check everything else associated with this particular instrument.

Is the detector reasonably stable, or does the audio and meter indicator seem to change (drift) so that you have to continually make adjustments?

Please don't rely too much on the results of so-called "air tests'" i.e., checking the distance that a detector will detect various small and large targets with nothing but air between the searchcoil and target. Of course, you'll probably want to check a detector's sensitivity for yourself in such a test. If so, try to measure detection distance with a small coin like a penny. Don't use a silver dollar! The smaller coin is a better test target. If a detector will pick up a penny to a good distance, it will surely detect a silver dollar to an even greater one.

Let me point out, however, that the new computerized detectors have made "air tests" completely invalid.

Remember that microprocessor-controlled circuitry enables a detector to analyze simultaneously all soil conditions as well as the target(s) beneath its searchcoil. Thus, computerized detectors with microprocessor controls, when properly designed, can sometimes detect objects at greater distances (depths) in the ground than in the air! It's a fact.

Selection Checkpoints

When selecting a metal detector, here are a few specific points to consider:

● **Portability.**

– When not in use, the equipment may be quickly and easily disassembled, without tools, for storage in a protective case.

204

- **Ease of Operation.**

  – The equipment should be lightweight and engineered for comfortable use over extended periods of time. Remember, however, that the lightest equipment may not be sufficiently durable.

  – The equipment should have only the controls and functions necessary to do the job intended.

  – Extra controls and functions require extra circuitry which can degrade reliability.

  – Extra controls and functions can confuse an operator, especially one who uses the equipment only occasionally. Improper adjustment or improper use, if only temporarily, can decrease the effectiveness of a search...and make a hunt less enjoyable.

  – The equipment must have certain controls and functions to be effective.

  1. Circuit or means to check the batteries.

  2. Push button or automatic controls to switch easily between different hunting modes (All Metal and Discriminate, for example).

  3. Circuitry to eliminate (ground balance) the effects of iron minerals in the soil and/or ocean beach salt if you are a beachcomber.

  4. Audio controls that can be adjusted easily.

  5. Headphone jack for this essential accessory.

  6. Compatibility with different sizes and types of searchcoils. No matter what you are told, one "standard" searchcoil will not be sufficient as you gain expertise. Make certain your detector will accept other sizes and types...and that they are available!

  – Access to batteries (if not rechargeable) should be easy. Are the batteries readily available and reasonably priced?

- **Capability.**

  – The detector should be capable of performing, with good efficiency, all the tasks you intend for it to perform.

– Necessary searchcoils (see above) and other accessories should be standard equipment or available for optional purchase.

● **Depth Detection.**

– When evaluating a metal detector, depth detection – the ability to detect an object at a given distance – is sometimes the only point a purchaser considers. True, this is vitally important. But, a quality detector should also have excellent sensitivity, mechanical and electrical stability, plus the ability to operate at great efficiency over *any type of mineralized ground.* Without all these characteristics, you may have an inadequate metal detector.

– When evaluating sensitivity, evaluate different types of objects. Some instruments are more sensitive to iron, some are less sensitive to coins. Detection depth on coins, however, can be reduced when operated in the Discriminate mode. So, make sure that not much detection depth is lost when discrimination is dialed in.

● **Stability**

– No detector, regardless of features, is worthy unless it is electronically stable and not subject to erroneous signals from...

1. Changes in battery voltage.
2. Minor temperature changes in circuit components.
3. Current leakage on printed circuit boards because of moisture.
4. Poor quality components.
5. Poorly designed searchcoils.

– Mechanical stability is the ability of the detector to produce no erroneous signals or changes in control adjustments because of normal scanning movement of the detector. Such problems can be caused by...

1. Movement of the searchcoil connector.
2. Movement of improperly secured internal wiring and connectors.
3. Movement of improperly secured batteries.

4. Movement of the printed circuit board caused by flexing of the detector housing when the detector is lifted or moved by its handle.

5. Flexing of the searchcoil as it is moved back and forth over the ground.

6. Movement of internal searchcoil components when the searchcoil is bumped against an object, such as a large rock or tree trunk.

The most sensitive equipment may not have the stability to be effective.

• **Durability** is important because a metal detector will often be used many hours in rugged environments. Since electronic circuits can be expected to be functional for many years, a strong mechanical package is important. Points to consider are...

– Metal structural components should be strong enough to prevent excessive flexing. Flexing can cause metal fatigue and breakage and also can be a source of mechanical instability.

An important measure of a detector's quality is its capability of detecting at great depths small targets such as this gold nugget that Jack Lowry found at a depth of several inches.

207

– Rivets, screws and other fastening devices must do their job dependably to prevent loosening of the mechanical package due to use.

– Parts made of plastic must be properly designed and manufactured from the materials that prevent breakage, warping, melting and cracking from heat and cold.

– Properly designed carrying cases should be available to protect the equipment during transportation and storage.

● **Environmental Considerations** are important in selecting a detector. Some examples of problems due to environment are...

– To operate at temperatures below freezing, use of alkaline or nickel cadmium (NiCad) batteries must be possible.

– Moisture protection is important to enable the equipment to be used in light rain or among wet vegetation.

– Submersible searchcoils allow searches in shallow water as well as under conditions listed above.

– If the equipment is to be used under water or is to be used extensively in shallow water, a guaranteed seal is absolutely necessary.

– If the equipment is to be used a great deal in a salt beach environment, a sealed underwater detector may be necessary (it's certainly desirable) to eliminate the effects of sand, moisture and the corrosive atmosphere on the circuitry, controls, and metal surfaces.

Evaluation Summation

When evaluating a specific detector, here is a summary of things to look for...questions you *should* ask...

● Is the detector easy to operate? How much "adjustment" is *really* necessary?

● Are the instrument and its components well protected for storage, transportation and use?

● Is the detector easily assembled and are the batteries and all controls readily accessible and properly located?

• Is the equipment designed so that weight is always properly balanced?

• Is the equipment constructed with strength and durability? Look for areas that are mechanically weak and flex easily. Look for controls, meters or other items that protrude which could be broken off. Are there sufficient fastening devices, locking nuts, etc., to keep the handle and stems from working loose?

• Is plastic used properly in the equipment? Are the searchcoils made of heavy gauge ABS for long wear and abrasion resistance? Are the searchcoils solid filled with urethane foam for mechanical stability and long life? Is the plastic stem or stem extension made of strong materials that will not be expected to crack or break?

• Are desired operational features such as a battery check, detection depth (sensitivity) control, discrimination, ground balance and earphone jack included?

• Are desired accessory searchcoils available? Can all searchcoils be submerged?

• Are controls clearly marked? Is the instruction manual adequate, yet easy to understand?

• Is the equipment designed to do the jobs intended? Is it suitable for the operating environments in which it will be used?

Bench Test

Bench test the equipment indoors. Be sure the searchcoil is not on a metal table or near metal table supports or any other kind of metal.

– Turn the equipment on, regulate audio level and listen for a smooth sound.

– Listen to the sound and watch the meter. The sound and meter should remain reasonably constant. If the detector is not already at room temperature, a small change can be expected due to the temperature stabilization of the circuit components and the searchcoil.

– Check the detection depth (distance) and sensitivity

to a representative group of targets, i.e. coins, guns, knives, etc. If the detector has more than one operating mode, check them all.

– Check sound for loudness and tone quality.

Field Test

Take the equipment outside, away from metal in walls, floors, furniture, etc., and test for mechanical stability. Turn the detector on and set the audio threshold before making the following tests...

– Grasp the searchcoil with one hand, and squeeze and flex the coil. Normally the sound will change, the less the better, but it must return to the starting point when the coil is released. No pops or crackles should be heard. (Be sure the wire is wrapped lightly around the stem and you do not change the angle of the coil on the stem during the test. Either of these can cause a faulty test). Also, be sure to remove your rings and watch before making the test.

– Take the detector and bump it from all sides with your hand. No pops or crackles should be heard. The batteries should not jar loose.

– While holding the detector by the handle, lightly bump the searchcoil against a large rock or wall. Audio and meter should not change.

– While holding the detector by the handle, raise the searchcoil above your head and lower to two feet off the ground. The sound should not change significantly.

Facing

Seeking a large metal box believed to be deeply buried, this treasure hunter on the Mexican border used a Depth Multiplier that would ignore mineralization to find his target.

Over

A convenient hand-held detector such as the Pocket Probe is ideal for scanning walls of old buildings to search places where a conventional coil will not reach.

– In an area with grass or vegetation more than three inches high, moisten the vegetation with a hose. Now test the Faraday shielding of the coil. Movement of the searchcoil through the vegetation should produce no, or very minor, audio responses.

– Check balance, ease of operation, sound level, detection depth (by searching for representative targets you have buried), mechanical and electrical stability.

How to Determine Capability

This is a basic selection guide to help you choose the correct, or optimum detector. Various detector characteristics, including ground balance and discrimination for the type of searching you will be doing, are discussed. It is divided into three categories:

- Treasure Hunting for coin, cache and relics (see also Chapters 26, 27 and 28),
- Underwater Hunting (see also Chapter 30),
- Gold Hunting (see also Chapter 29).

There are numerous books written which describe the various facets of metal detecting in much greater detail than space allows in this book. *Modern Treasure Hunting, The New Successful Coin Hunting, Treasure Recovery from Sand and Sea* and *Modern Electronic Prospecting,* all published by Ram Publishing Company, are recommended. To improve your expertise with the instrument and to learn how to become more efficient in all phases of detec-

Facing

Dual detection modes such as those offered by this Freedom Two Plus is an ideal feature to look for in selecting an easy-to-use detector for hunting coins.

Over

An electronic prospector must be demanding in choosing a metal detector with the proper features for finding gold in nugget, ore or other forms.

tor use you should read all of these books, as well as others on the hobby, to acquire their valuable knowledge.

Your selection and purchase of a metal detector ought to have the same careful consideration that goes with anything you buy. Shopping has become very much a part of life, and you must depend upon yourself to make the right choice. The more clearly you understand what you want, the more likely you are to be correct in your choice. Choosing a metal detector should take no less time and consideration than buying any other valuable and expensive item. Buying the correct instrument depends both on whether you understand all the important facts about the different types and what your requirements really are.

In this chapter, I list most of the facets of metal detector usage; and I recommend the type instrument or instruments and searchcoils to use. I describe operational aspects so that you can compare the features and capabilities of the various brands and types. This information is designed to recommend a specific type of detector. Instructions on using that detector will be found in Section V. I hope this information will help you decide if the metal detector you are thinking of buying will, indeed, do the job you intend for it to do.

Coin Hunting

At Garrett we recognize that every detector that we manufacture will be used, at least part of the time, to hunt coins...and, many detectors will be used for nothing else! Thus, every detector should be manufactured with coin hunting in mind. Discrimination control is a must for coin hunting detectors. Also, the instruments must be ground balanced. Ideally, you should have your choice between Automatic and Manual Ground Balancing types with good discrimination control. Locating the maximum number and deepest targets will require an All Metal mode, while the Discriminate mode can eliminate digging many junk targets.

Round searchcoils eight to nine inches in diameter have traditionally been preferred for coin hunting. This size is lightweight and has good depth detection and scanning width. Something new, however, has come into the picture...the new elliptical searchcoils. These newly designed coils provide good scanning width and have proved especially effective in areas where trash metal targets abound.

For deeper penetration, use the 10 or 12-inch sizes. Pinpointing will be a little more difficult with larger searchcoils, but you can expect to get the deeper coins. For operation in tight places adjacent to sidewalks, metal buildings and fences, and for Super-Sniping, use a three-inch to four-inch diameter searchcoil.

Cache or Money Hunting

Ground balancing is essential, and you should choose a *manual-adjust* instrument that is capable of using a large searchcoil and/or the Depth Multiplier. The Bloodhound Depth Multiplier should be used whenever possible, as it detects deeply and ignores small objects like nails, etc.

Large, deepseeking searchcoils are usually necessary to enable even a sensitive detector to find classic Civil War relics such as these projectiles and handsome belt buckles.

Since you are not looking for small objects, forget small coils. A ten-inch size might be good, but a 12-inch size would be even better. When using large searchcoils, an armrest or hipmount configuration is recommended. (See Chapter 22 for discussion of the hipmount accessory).

Relic Hunting

Relic hunting calls for the same type of equipment that cache hunting requires. You definitely need large searchcoils. You will need a good hipmount configuration, and headphones. Most relic hunters do not use any form of discrimination because they don't want to take the chance of missing valuable iron relics. Some use a small amount of discrimination only when searching for brass and lead objects.

Ghost Town Searching

If you are outdoors and looking for coins, rings and jewelry, an automatic ground balanced type with good discrimination will give the best results. Since most ghost towns contain many junk metal targets, discrimination will be important. Oftentimes, a great amount of junk may necessitate your reducing the detection depth of your detector.

If you are searching for ghost town relics or money caches, use a Manual-Adjust instrument in the All Metal detection mode. It would be best to use the largest searchcoil you have available. Large money caches may be quite deep, so you should consider using the Bloodhound Depth Multiplier attachment. This multiplies the depth capability of VLF detectors, producing great depth on objects larger than quart size while almost completely ignoring nails and other small metal trash.

Indoors, the same rules apply in ghost towns as in all other forms of indoor searching.

Beachcombing

Several good new detectors have been developed primarily for beach hunting. These instruments feature

218

automatic ground balance and offer excellent discrimination capabilities. Still another type of detector to use when searching ocean beaches is a pulse induction type with discrimination. To search fresh water beaches, all types of detectors are more or less suitable.

Manual-Adjust detectors cannot ignore both salt water and black magnetic sand simultaneously, but Pulse Induction detectors can. Automatic Ground Balancing types can be adjusted to ignore salt water and magnetic sand simultaneously.

There is a phenomenon that causes Pulse Induction detectors to detect coins and rings extremely deep in salt water. Consequently, immediately after they were first placed on the market, they became a favorite among beach coin hunters, especially those who search ocean beaches.

When hunting on any beach, be sure to wear headphones for maximum depth detection and elimination of surf noise.

Underwater Detectors

There are two basic mechanical configurations. One is designed primarily for underwater searching. This type has the searchcoil, handle, and stem, all permanently attached to a short stem. The stem is too short to use above water, but accessories are available for conversion. Long-stem land units are easily convertible to the short stem for underwater use. The only detectors now manufactured with a guaranteed seal for underwater use are pulse induction instruments.

Headphones are essential for maximum sensitivity and depth. Some underwater detectors use meters and lights. Indicator lights are not as sensitive as meter indicators, which are very sensitive but are difficult to watch at all times and, in all but clear water, become difficult to see.

Gold Hunting

The recommended type detector for gold hunting will have excellent ground balance and precise calibrated discrimination. The ideal type is a Manual Adjust Ground Balancing instrument that has been proven in the field. Not all detectors are the same. Some are more versatile and sensitive than others and some are more capable of operating over highly mineralized ground. You should select a model that has a wide range of searchcoils from which to choose. Selection of the right searchcoil depends, to a great extent, upon you. How well you have mastered your detector and how well you apply your experiences and observations will in large measure determine your success.

The Bloodhound Depth Multiplier attachment will give you multiplied depth on large ore veins, even those containing iron ore. Iron ore, when in association with gold and silver, can enhance the detection characteristics of veins.

Searchcoils

Think of the searchcoil on your detector as having the same functions as the wheels on your automobile. Wheels take power from the motor and interface between the automobile and the ground. They roll along, take the bumps, grinds and shocks to get you to your destination. Searchcoils take power from the oscillator via the searchcoil cable. They are the interface between the metal detector and the ground. They scan along and take the bumps, grinds and shocks. They get you to your destination...the target.

Most searchcoils have electromagnetic transmitter and receiver antennas. These antennas are embedded within the searchcoil. The searchcoil is mounted on the lower end of the metal detector stem to be scanned over the ground or a specific object. An invisible electromagnetic field generated by the transmitter winding flows out into the surrounding medium...air, wood, rock or whatever.

Because a metal detector without a searchcoil simply would not function, coils constitute a vital element in its operation. They come in many sizes and shapes, ranging from about four inches in diameter to the very large, deepseeking depth multiplier. Generally speaking, the smaller searchcoils detect smaller objects, and larger searchcoils find larger and deeper targets. Of course, this is not altogether true since I have found tiny coins with a large searchcoil and also detected quite deeply with the little 4 1/2-inch Super Sniper.

For hunting large objects at great depths, the most popular cache hunting searchcoils are those 12 to 14 inches in diameter. These are large enough to give excellent depth, yet small enough to be reasonably light in weight. Larger searchcoils obviously make it more difficult to maneuver around obstacles. Under water, however, the extra weight is no problem.

Searchcoil Diameters

Generally, the "standard-diameter" searchcoil accompanying most metal detectors is the one that gives the best general purpose results. The chart on Searchcoil Sizes on Page 225 will guide you in your understanding of the characteristics and capabilities of the various sizes of searchcoils. It should be noted, however, that there truly can be no "standard" size since the size searchcoil preferred for one particular type of hunting might not be especially satisfactory for another.

For most general treasure hunting, however, you should select a searchcoil that ranges in diameter from about seven or eight inches to ten inches. Searchcoils that size will scan a wide swath and give good detection depth. As searchcoils increase in size, however, it becomes more difficult for them to pinpoint detected objects.

When working in high trash areas, you should consider using a smaller searchcoil, usually about four inches in diameter. These Super Sniper-class searchcoils offer an extra measure of success by "helping" the detector to read individual targets. This increased capability is especially valuable when the discrimination mode is being used. Larger searchcoils obviously can cover more objects at any given time. Consequently, the detector's circuitry has greater difficulty identifying these objects simply because there are so many of them. Small Super Sniper coils eliminate this problem for the most part. They usually won't detect as deeply as larger coils, but can often be far more efficient, especially in trashy areas. You can learn more about the smaller coils by reading my *Garrett Guide* entitled *Use the Super Sniper to Find More Treasure*.

A size of searchcoil developed by Garrett many years ago is called an *elliptical coil*. As its name implies, this coil has an elliptical shape. Garrett now manufactures two sizes, 5x10 inches and 3x7 inches. This coil was originally developed to give extra wide scanning width yet good gold-hunting depth.

Special 2D windings on the new Garrett models have increased their capabilities for all types of treasure hunting. Because of these new windings, the new Garrett elliptical coils are intensely sensitive along a narrow strip down the center of the search coil, which makes them detect deeper and find targets that other types of searchcoils might miss.

No matter how effective its circuitry, no metal detector can do more than process the information relayed to it by its searchcoil!

Reviewing the Diameters

3 to 4 Inches: This size is referred to by Garrett as a Super Sniper. It projects an intense electromagnetic field which gives good detection of small objects. The narrow detection pattern permits excellent target isolation and precise pinpointing. This size scans a more narrow width than larger searchcoils, and it will not detect as deeply. The ability for close scanning of metal objects such as fences and concrete with reinforcing bars is an added plus.

Treasure hunters rate these searchcoils highly, but not all detectors are capable of using them, nor do all manufacturers provide them. The purchase and use of one is suggested, especially if you hunt in worked-out or high junk areas.

7 to 9 Inches: Most detector types and brands are sold with searchcoils about eight inches in diameter (Garrett offers 8 1/2-inch models.) as standard equipment. These are the best general purpose sizes because they generally are lightweight, have good scanning width and are sensitive to a wide range of target sizes. Objects as small as BB shot can be detected. Good ground coverage can be obtained with scanning width at shallow levels equal to the approximate diameter of the searchcoil. Scanning width becomes less toward the bottom of the detection pattern as shown in the previous chapter. Since the detection pattern of all round searchcoils is somewhat cone-shaped, overlapping of each detector sweep is necessary to lessen the possibility of missing targets. Pinpointing is good but can be made even better by electronic pinpointing and proper use of target center.

10 to 12 Inches: Searchcoils of this size while still able to detect small coin-size objects at great depths are classified as the smallest searchcoils to be used for cache and relic hunting. Precise pinpointing is more difficult with these larger sizes, and the extra weight usually necessitates use of an arm rest or hip-mounted control housing. This is especially true when the detector is used for long periods of time.

When do you use a larger searchcoil? Reason it out for yourself. Suppose you find a target in the fringe area of detection with your 8 1/2-inch searchcoil. Weak audio signals indicate you're reaching the outer detection limits of the searchcoil. By using the next larger size you will detect deeper. Of course, there are limitations. You may not find tiny targets as easily with a large searchcoil. You'll stand a much better chance using a Super Sniper. Practically speaking, when you're hunting on the beach or in the surf, a 10-inch coil is generally the largest size you should use. Only if you're looking for a specific large or deeply buried object should you use a larger coil. On the other hand, you'll find many uses for a Super Sniper on the beach. How about hunting among rocks...near metal...or, in areas with lots of metal trash?

The chart on the facing page illustrates recommended searchcoil sizes for optimum results. Note the overlapping capability of all searchcoils. The wide dynamic range of several searchcoils is obvious.

Depth Multiplier Attachment: Just as its name implies this valuable attachment can multiply the depth that your detector can search effectively. A Depth Multiplier can double or triple the depth to which your detector can find a large target, such as a large cannon or safe.

The depth multiplier is easy to use. It can be attached to your detector in a matter of minutes. No adjustments are required. Simply turn your detector on and select the All Metal mode. Adjust your threshold sound and begin searching. More information on this important accessory can be found in my *Garrett Guide* entitled *Money Caches Are Waiting to be Found.*

The depth multiplier is recommended when searching for money caches, large relics, safes, cannons, ore veins

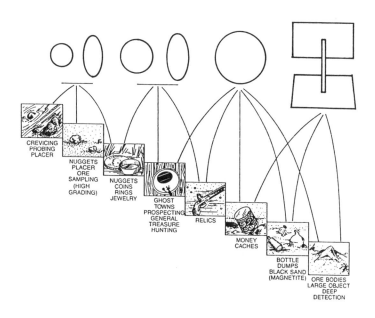

This chart illustrates the various sizes of circular and elliptical searchcoils and identifies all of the types of treasure hunting for which they are usually most suited.

and mineral structures. It's not an accessory normally required in routine coin or beach hunting, but it's one with which every detector operator should be familiar.

Electronic Shielding

There are two types of electronic field potential, electromagnetic and electrostatic. Electromagnetic field potentials are the radiated power field that illuminate the matrix being scanned. When the electromagnetic field penetrates metal, eddy currents are generated on the metal's surface. Power is drawn from the electromagnetic field, alerting the operator to the presence of the metal.

An electrostatic field potential is of a constant voltage nature. This electrical phenomenon occurs whenever two objects come in close proximity to one another. When wet grass, for instance, comes close to the searchcoil, a "false" detector signal may occur. Fortunately, well engineered detectors have solved the electrostatic potential problem. Quality manufacturers construct what is called a Faraday Shield to shield the windings from nearby objects.

You are advised not to purchase a detector without an electrostatic shield on each of its searchcoils. To test a searchcoil pull a handful of weeds and wet them with water. Turn your detector on and adjust its threshold. When you drag the weeds across the bottom of your searchcoil, very little change should occur in the threshold sound. If there is a noticeable change, the searchcoil does not have effective shielding. Slight audio changes are not objectionable when grass is passed over the top of the coil.

Determining Target Center

Any given searchcoil may or may not produce maximum audio when small coin-size targets are directly beneath its exact *physical* center. To determine *target* center of detection, set your detector's audio at its threshold level and place a small coin directly on the bottom of the searchcoil near its center. Slide this coin around and listen closely to the sound from your detector.

The target center is the spot where you hear maximum audio sound. Mark an "X" with a felt tip pin at this point on the searchcoil both on top and bottom. Knowing this target center enables you to pinpoint targets precisely. Since, pulse induction searchcoils are generally constructed with an open center, it is not possible (nor necessary) to mark the center of these coils.

Dynamic Detection Range

As used by detector manufacturers this term indicates various target sizes a searchcoil can detect to a practical depth. Examples of dynamic detection range:

— A *12-inch searchcoil* can detect objects from BB shot size to very large targets and detect this wide range of objects to practical depths. It functions most effectively on larger targets at greater depths.

— A *4 1/2-inch searchcoil* can often surprise you with the depth it can achieve on all target sizes. For the most part, however, it works best on smaller targets at relatively shallow depths.

— An *8 1/2-inch searchcoil* is selected for most "general" searching because it offers a wide range of both target detection and depth. It detects objects from BB shot size to very large targets. In addition, its size and weight insure good maneuverability

A few minutes study of the searchcoil charts in this chapter will reveal the relative dynamic detection ranges of the various types and sizes of searchcoils.

Specific Gravity

When manufacturers produce searchcoils for use both on land and under water, they must achieve a happy medium. The searchcoil must be light enough for practical land use yet have slightly negative buoyancy for use under water. An example is the special Crossfire searchcoil now used on Garrett's AT4 Beach Hunter. It is a few ounces heaver than the normal 8 1/2-inch coil and requires no extra weights for use in the surf or elsewhere under water.

Hobbyists who formerly had to devise various means of weighting their searchcoils used sand bags on the coil or lead weights on the stem. Of course, there was a problem here since the lead could not be too close to the searchcoil.

Searchcoils with slightly negative buoyancy require considerably less effort to use under water than coils that try to rise to the surface. When in doubt about equipment for surf or underwater use, contact your dealer and/or factory for specific information.

Waterproofing Designations

Searchcoils are built with varying degrees of waterproofing. *Splashproof* indicates that operation will not be affected if a small amount of water gets on the searchcoil, such as moisture from wet grass. *Waterproof* means the searchcoil can be operated in a heavy rain and operation will not be affected. *Submersible* means that the searchcoil can be submerged beneath the water as deep as the cable connector without affecting the detector's operation. Standard configuration metal detectors, generally, have searchcoils that can be submerged about 30 inches under water (to the connector on the detector housing). Hip-mount models have searchcoils that can be submerged about four to five feet. *Underwater* metal detectors have searchcoils designed to withstand great depths, even down to 200 feet.

Searchcoil Skid Plates, also called coil covers, are popular items, available for most size searchcoils. They are simply a round, plastic disk-shaped cover that fits over the bottom of the searchcoil. They are held in place by friction, and generally utilize no mounting brackets or screws. Skid plates provide protection to the searchcoil against scraping, bumping, and gouging when it is slid over the ground or scanned over rocky areas. They prevent holes from being worn in the searchcoil. By providing protection they keep searchcoils in good condition, adding to their resale value.

Attachments and Accessories

There are many different kinds of attachments manufacturers make available for users of their equipment. Some of them are very important; others, not so important. Not everyone will use all the attachments that are available. Some will perhaps use only one or two; others, as many as a dozen. The most popular attachments are described so you will have an understanding of them and can select those you can put to good use.

Headphones

You should *always* use headphones whenever you search with a detector. They are especially useful in noisy areas, such as the beach and near traffic (when you are looking for dropped coins around parking meters). Headphones enhance audio perception by bringing the sound directly into your ears while masking "outside" noise interference. If you own a detector, you should own one or more headphone sets.

There is no question that most people can hear weaker sounds and detect deeper targets when quality headphones are used. As proof, bury a coin at a depth that produces a faint speaker signal. Then, use headphones and scan over the spot. You'll be amazed at how much better you can hear the detector signals with headphones than you can with the speaker alone.

Headphones come in many sizes, shapes and configurations, the most popular being stereo types that cover the ears. Many fine detectors do not have volume controls since they are not particularly necessary. Headphones equipped with volume controls allow a wide degree of loudness adjustment while not degrading detector sounds.

Manufacturers know that reducing sound volume of the detector's signals is accompanied by loss of detection depth and sensitivity. Reducing circuit "gain" reduces the sharp, quick audio turn-on necessary for good operation. Even on detectors with volume control, the manufacturer usually recommends that these controls be used to set volume to maximum. Most detectors are operated at full volume with the tuning (audio) control adjusted so that a faint sound (threshold) is coming from the speaker. When a target is detected, the sound volume increases quickly from threshold to maximum loudness. Headphones allow this threshold to be set even lower, giving improved performance. Modern detectors can be operated "silent" or with slight threshold sound.

A mono/stereo switch on the headphone set is desirable. If you want to use both headphone pieces, flip the switch to mono to let sound come through both earphones. If you want to use only one headpiece, perhaps to leave the unused headpiece resting off your ear to enable you to hear sounds around you, flip the switch to stereo and only one headpiece will be operative. Some detectors have an internal connection, however, that sends audio into both headpieces. In that case, a mono/stereo headphone switch would be non-functional.

Dual, miniature headphones are sometimes used. While satisfactory, they do not block as much external sound as the large padded kind. They are, however, lightweight and comfortable and a quality pair will usually

Because this THer (with headphones) does not want the detector's weight on her arm, she uses a hipmount kit to carry the detector housing at her waist.

produce good sound. A coiled extension cord is desirable to keep the cord out of the way.

Headphones help you keep others from knowing what you are doing. In most cases, a person standing within a few feet will not be able to hear the headphone signals unless the sound is very loud.

Since headphone plugs are usually either one-eighth or one-fourth inch in diameter, make sure which size you require. Right-angle plugs are highly desirable because they minimize the possibility of broken plugs, which often occurs with plugs that extend straight out.

The recommended type of headphones are those that have an extra-heavy-duty coiled cord, because the cord is the source of most wear. They should have adequate mufflers or cushions to mask most of the outside noises. And, as stated, headphones should have adjustable volume controls on each individual earphone to set sound levels to suit the operator's own hearing requirements. I recommend that you purchase one or more sets of head-phones and use them. You'll soon see that headphones pay for themselves many times over.

There are various types of cordless headphones on the market. Some of them are modifications of existing AM/FM radio headsets. Generally, there is a great amount of undesirable static generated. If you are near a radio station transmitter, you may have difficulty in keep-ing the radio station from serenading you while you work. There may be snaps, and pops in your headset. You may find that the detector threshold signal changes as you swing the searchcoil from side to side. Swing the searchcoil to the left and the audio threshold will be at one level; swing the searchcoil to the right, and it will change to yet

Treasure hunter at left wears a coin hunting kit on his belt, and the one on the right use a handsome carrying case for both convenience and to protect his instrument.

another. That can be annoying! Before you buy, try to get a money-back guarantee. When you receive the headphones, if you do not like them, return them immediately, in new condition, for a refund. If you use and abuse them and get them dirty, don't expect a refund.

Physical Aids

Hipmount Kit is a popular accessory. A typical hipmount kit includes brackets, screws, and other hardware to convert a standard configuration detector to the hip- or sling-mount configuration. The hipmount configuration attaches most of the control housing's weight to the operator's belt. The searchcoil is attached to the handle, and its cable provides a flexible link between the control housing and the searchcoil. It reduces operator fatigue, especially if larger than seven-inch to eight-inch searchcoils are used. Larger searchcoils are heavier, consequently, the more difficult and tiring they are to scan for hours on end. When the sling mount is used, the person slings the detector around his neck and shoulders. One belt suspends the control housing while another securely fastens it around the person's waist so it does not swing about, especially when the person kneels or stoops to dig.

Because of the popularity of hip mount kits, some detectors come equipped only for this configuration. One example is Garrett's AT4 Beach Hunter, which is hip-mounted for ease of use in choppy surf waters or on rough terrain. Other detectors such as models of Garrett's new Ultra GTA computerized detectors include a detachable battery pack which enables the detector to convert instantly to a hip-mount configuration.

An *armrest* is usually not needed for balance with small, lightweight searchcoils, it is used only with larger ones. This accessory attaches to the detector handle. The balance and ease of operation achieved with an armrest makes the cost a worthwhile expenditure. Like the built-in hip mount of Garrett's new Ultra GTA detectors, the latest types of detector feature an armrest as an integral part of the detector design. This built-on feature improves the balance and ease of operation, providing much less tiring operation, even during long periods of scanning.

Other Accessories

Speaker Cover. When it comes to operating in the rain, the most vulnerable component may be the speaker. Some speakers use waterproof mylar cones, others use paper. Should the paper cone in your detector become wet, the sound will become muffled; you will be unable to hear high sounds or the whispers of sound so vitally important to detection. When your speaker cone dries, it may or may not recover its full sound reproduction characteristics. To protect your speaker, some manufacturers offer optional speaker covers. Always remember that while speaker covers can prevent water damage, they will also reduce speaker volume.

Audio/Video Cassette Instructions. Some manufacturers provide both video and audio instruction tapes covering the basics of detector operation. Video tapes are especially recommended. They are relatively inexpensive, yet combine both sight and sound to show how a detector should be used. Audio cassettes are even less expensive; if they do no more than teach you to adjust your detector correctly, they are easily worth many times their cost.

Carrying bags and suitcases are optional pieces of equipment that a person may wish to buy. There are many different types and styles on the market. Some are made of flexible vinyl plastic and others are rigid like a suitcase. The latter provides maximum protection for your detector regardless of whether it is stored or transported.

Flexible bags come in several kinds. Some have a single long pocket into which the detector can be slipped. Others have draw strings, zippers, and snaps, and some have pockets for carrying various items like headphones, shovels, finds and spare batteries. Suitcases are available in several styles, but most look like enlarged briefcases or equipment cases. Locks may be desirable.

A *coin apron* is certainly a must in any kind of coin hunting or any other kind of light treasure seeking activity. They are generally constructed of waterproof material with at least two pockets, one for good finds, the other for junk. All junk items, of course, should be collected for later discarding. Never leave trash lying about!

Coin probes should be considered a must! They are inexpensive and provide an accurate means for pinpointing your finds and locating them precisely. Be sure the one you make or buy has a rounded, smooth point that will not damage your discoveries. Just as important is making certain that it stays that way! You don't want to scratch a valuable coin...especially before you even dig it up!

There are various *extension arm* designs which, true to their name, extend the reach of your arm. These generally extend your searchcoil reach to about six to eight feet. They allow searching in deep water, up in trees, across overhead ceilings, and in other, hard-to-reach inaccessible places. The use of an extension arm allows you to scan an extra wide sweep path; consequently, you can cover more territory with each scan sweep. Generally, extra-length searchcoil cables are needed when a detector is to be equipped with an extension arm. If you are planning to search in water, you may wish to purchase submersible searchcoils designed specifically for that job.

Helper handles provide a greater ease in swinging the searchcoil. Most people who have hand or wrist injuries, tennis elbow or other various muscle or joint problems, will find the speed handle a joy to use. You simply guide and direct the searchcoil along with your left hand. Maneuverability is precise, and many people find they actually enjoy using speed handles. Among minor inconveniences are the additional weight added to the detector, and each time you lay it down you have to "do something" with the speed handle. In other words, it must be moved out of the way in order to dig, etc., but it is considered an asset by many people.

Rechargeable batteries are now reasonably reliable and long lasting. The user can save money, especially if the detector is used often.

Follow manufacturer's recommendations on keeping batteries in a recharged condition. Called NiCads (from their nickel/cadmium composition) these batteries are notorious for taking a "'set," or in other words, limiting themselves internally to the time for which they are regularly used. If the rechargeable battery is discharged for one hour and recharged; then, discharged one hour and recharged again; the battery will soon take a one-hour set, and you will only be able to get one hour's life from what otherwise might be a ten-hour battery. So, vary the time which you use your detector. Recharge the batteries promptly, and do not charge longer than manufacturer's recommended length. Battery manufacturers recommend

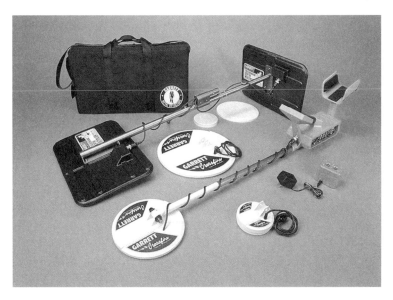

Illustrated above are a veritable plethora of detector accessories, including an armrest, carrying case, various searchcoils and skid plates, NiCad recharge kit and a Depth Multiplier.

237

that NiCads be completely discharged and then fully recharged once every three months or more often. Chapter 9 contains additional information on NiCad batteries. There are various kinds of *NiCad Recharge Adaptors* available for NiCad batteries. Two United States models are the 110V, 60 Hz and 12V cigarette lighter rechargers. In foreign and overseas countries, voltages are generally higher, with the frequency slightly lower than U. S. ratings. Adaptor kits are available that let U. S. rechargers operate on other voltages. If you are traveling abroad, make sure you have the correct recharge adaptor kit. Plan ahead since it's usually much cheaper to buy them in the U. S. than to wait until you get to your destination, where you may not even be able to find the correct adaptor.

Miscellaneous Accessories. There are various other miscellaneous accessories such as battery trays, touch-up paint, extra battery doors, foreign language instruction manuals, etc. One miscellaneous accessory deserves comment because it is quite desirable...especially when you regularly change searchcoils. This is an extra lower stem attached to the searchcoil. To change searchcoils, you normally loosen the wing nut, remove the screw, remove the searchcoil, place another searchcoil on the lower stem, realign the holes, insert the screw, mount all the hardware, and tighten the wing nut, wrap the cord around, etc. You can purchase extra lower stems, screws, and wing nut hardware. This allows you to keep a lower stem attached to each coil to make changing them easier and faster.

Miscellaneous Clothing, Hats, Caps, etc. Caps, coats, patches, bumper stickers and different kinds of paraphernalia usually include a company's name and logo in an attractive design. There's nothing wrong in using any of these. In fact, many people like the sense of belonging. They are proud of their hobby and the equipment they use. When you see a jacket, tee shirt or cap that you like, buy it! Caps and tee shirts designed in good taste can do a great deal toward promoting the use of metal detectors.

Metal Detector Dealers

The majority of detectors are sold through dealers, most of whom are honest and knowledgeable and will correctly guide you in the selection of a detector. We hope that after reading this chapter you will be able to find a good dealer and will stick with him. The rewards will be yours.

All dealers must make a profit to stay in business. Yet, most dealers rarely place sole priority on making money. These dealers understand that customers are their reason for existence. They know that a satisfied, well-trained customer will be the main reason they will still be in business tomorrow. The greatest number of sales result from customer referrals and word of mouth. It's just human nature to want to deal with a store or company that treated you or someone you know well and provided proper service.

It gives a person a good feeling to know that he has been truthfully advised about a product. It is equally disheartening to learn that, after you have just spent several hundred dollars, you didn't get the best detector possible, or you find it about one-half as capable of performing as you were told it was. Select your dealer wisely and reap the rewards.

You will probably benefit from buying from a factory-trained metal detector dealer. You may not get what you want if you buy from a mass merchandising outlet. I'm not saying these people aren't factory-authorized and absolutely honest. What I am saying is that the salesmen may not be sufficiently knowledgeable about detectors. They may barely know one end of the detector from another.

Certainly there are good metal detectors being sold in merchandising stores, but if you want to learn about a product, go to a professional for advice. You may save a lot of money purchasing a detector through a bargain outlet, but the amount you save will be long forgotten as you try to use an inadequate detector over the years...without the adequate training and advice you would have received from a good dealer.

If you have a local dealer, he's the man you should start with. If there is more than one detector dealer in your area, visit them all. Contact detector manufacturers and ask them to recommend one or more dealers in your area.

As a rule, when you find a good dealer, in all probability he will fit a certain "mold" and will have many credits to his name. Select a dealer who is factory or seminar-trained and who has one or more graduation certificates posted on his wall. It's true that no one can learn all there is to know about metal detectors by simply attending seminars. If a dealer goes to the time and expense of attending factory seminars, however, it is a good indication that this dealer cares about his business and his customers. Generally, the trained dealer is more closely attuned to the factory and will be more knowledgeable about the latest detectors, accessories and detector techniques. Detectors are improving at a dramatic rate and only the conscientious dealer, who makes an effort through study, can keep up with the advances.

Many small dealers cannot afford to travel great distances to attend factory seminars. These same dealers, however, can be as well-trained as those who visit the factory. They train themselves by spending lots of time in the field searching and experimenting with their equipment. They are determined to acquire the knowledge to teach you. Try to select, first and foremost, the dealer who is field-knowledgeable and can (and will) teach you the basic "how-to-use" skills about the detector you are purchasing. The dealer who gets into the field and uses his equipment is the man who knows more about that equipment and how to use it. Of course, there are many aspects of treasure hunting such as coin hunting, gold hunting relic hunting, etc. If a dealer specializes in beach hunting, he may not have a lot of experience in land coin hunting but at least he has some field experience and can guide you better than one who has no field training.

Perhaps the greatest problem concerning the first-time detector buyer is lack of adequate initial training. If a dealer takes the time to train you in the use of your equipment, he's concerned about you and wants you to be successful. Time is money for you and the dealer. If he takes his time to train you, in all likelihood he will be a full, or near full, retail-priced dealer. In order to stay in business a dealer must make money. He cannot show a profit if he discounts his equipment and then spends hours training his customers.

Some dealers offer free training for detector owners,

Progressive detector manufacturers provide seminar training for dealers on developments within the industry and to make certain they understand all features of new company instruments.

241

while other dealers charge up to $50 or more for training seminars. If a dealer charges for a training seminar, ask him for information about it. Find out how long the seminar lasts, how many total hours of instruction there are and the percentage of hands-on training that you will get. Seminars should provide up to fifty percent hands-on training. Then get the names of half a dozen people who have taken the seminar, call them and get their opinion.

A good dealer is one who won't destructively criticize another brand or another man's product. He may be very quick to point out the good features of the product that he recommends and he may be very quick to give you reasons why he believes his brand is the best for you.

Keep in mind that there is no "one-best" detector. There are a number of good detectors and a few very good ones. Listen closely and ask lots of questions...especially when a dealer seems to be touting you on one that just happens to be hanging in a his showroom. The detector you want is the one best suited for your current needs.

The dealer who downgrades another brand, or another man's detector, is the dealer you should avoid. It's all a dealer can do to learn everything possible about one or two brands of detectors. No dealer has time to evaluate every brand. To adequately and completely analyze a given detector under all environmental conditions and under all situations requires countless hours of testing. Few have that kind of time.

Even when it is possible to find fault with a competitive detector, it could be quite simply the fault of that one particular instrument. It is also possible that the manufacturer has learned of a particular fault and has taken steps to correct it in future production. When a fault is spotted on a new detector and criticism is heard, it could seriously and unjustly damage the reputation of that manufacturer and/or that particular product unless remedial action is taken immediately.

For this reason you'll never see the various treasure

hunting magazines report negatively or be super-critical in their analysis of the detectors they field test. In product reviews they point out the detector's good features and highlights, leaving a final judgment up to the person who buys the product. For them to criticize the product harshly would be wrong and certainly an unjust thing to do. When a dealer begins to destructively criticize another man's product, perhaps you should walk out the door and leave him talking.

A good brand...high quality product sells itself. Word of mouth is a key thing for which to listen.

The dealer who says that the brand he is pushing is the best and that all others are no good, may be the man who either owns part of the manufacturing company or is a distributor and gets a kickback on each detector sold in his area. Perhaps he makes more money when he sells the particular brand of detector he is promoting. There is nothing wrong with making money, but when it comes to telling untruths to sell you a detector, *you are the loser*... that dealer is *stealing* from you..

Authorized Dealers

An authorized dealer is an individual or retail outlet authorized by a manufacturer to sell that manufacturer's metal detectors.

Check your local dealer's bulletin board for his Authorized Dealer certificate. Each manufacturer should supply its dealers with such a certificate. A dealer may be an *authorized* dealer for several brands of detectors but may "bootleg" other brands into the store. You should expect authorized dealers to be better trained than un-authorized ones. Plus, when you deal with an authorized dealer, you have the full protection of the manufacturer if a product ever needs repair or if you need a particular service. The authorized dealer may also sell fresher stock. Even a manufacturer's warranty could be limited when it concerns products purchased from unauthorized dealers.

Most manufacturers feel that the dealer is the strongest link between them and the customer. Some dealers will place their customers on manufacturers' mailing lists. This regular contact keeps customers alert about what is going on in the field, including new products and accessories, and it provides new operating tips and procedures that could be of benefit to that manufacturer's product users.

Basic Guidelines for Asking

Don't be afraid to ask questions. Definitely expect good answers.

Be open with the dealer you visit. Explain as best you can what you intend to do with the detector...how you plan to use it.

Tell the dealer how much you prefer to spend.

Don't pretend to know more about detectors than you really do.

When you ask a question, listen to the answer; if you don't understand it, say so.

Ask the dealer what detector or detectors he or she hunts with personally.

Ask why.

Ask about the limitations of the detector recommended...what it *can't* do.

Ask about warranties and guarantees.

And, ask about training and service after the purchase.

After Your Purchase

Make it a habit of staying in contact with your dealer...even after you buy a detector. Stop by occasionally and talk with him. Let him know what you are doing, if you are having problems, etc. Keep in mind that a satisfied customer is the best advertising a dealer can have.

Product Warranties

Before you purchase a metal detector, you want to know all about the warranty that supports this product. It is certainly true that the Federal Trade Commission regulates certain aspects of warranties, but there are some claims made by certain manufacturers that can't be regulated.

Consider a "lifetime guarantee," for example. What would one actually mean as it relates to a metal detector? Obviously, no manufacturer, wholesaler or dealer can unconditionally guarantee a product as complex as an electronic metal detector...especially for life...unless there are provisions that protect the manufacturer or seller. What are these provisions? What will they mean to your detector? What will it *cost* you? When you study warranties, read the fine print!

Does the warranty protect only you, the initial purchaser, for example? Is it voided if you sell the instrument? If a warranty is not transferable during its stated protection period, the value of your detector is reduced. Who pays shipping costs on detectors returned to the factory for warranty repairs? Is there any service charge in addition to shipping? When a detector is returned to the manufacturer for warranty repair(s), are there any charges or does the manufacturer pay for *all* parts and labor?

What exactly is the value of your warranty if it requires that you pay expensive service and shipping charges?

Some warranties specify that repairs will be made for a period of time after which the owner will be charged for certain repairs and components. For instance, a five-year warranty might protect you for only 90 days against most failures, then require a surcharge for labor and payment for all parts after this initial period. Do you have a 90-day or a five-year warranty?

Some warranties state that if the detector malfunctions during the warranty period, you must take it to the dealer from whom you purchased it. This dealer then ships the detector to the factory after you pay him several dollars for shipping charges both ways. Returning to this dealer may be inconvenient for you, but unless he is a large-volume operator it is more inconvenient for this dealer to have to pack and ship your detector, plus keep all records on its status.

Some manufacturers, and rightly so, will charge a fee when a detector needing only fresh batteries is submitted for warranty repair. Don't laugh! This happens. Be sure you check your batteries *whenever* your detector is "broken." Worn-out batteries are the primary cause of detector "failure."

Does the warranty say anything about guarantees on replaced parts? Some companies give reduced-time warranties on replaced components. In other words, if a searchcoil malfunctions with nine months remaining on an initial two-year warranty, will the new searchcoil carry a nine-month warranty or will it be guaranteed for only 90 days...or guaranteed at all?

You will find some dealers who make a concerted effort to repair their customers' detectors in their own shops. If a detector malfunctions, this dealer encourages the owner to return it to him. The dealer then makes every possible attempt to repair the detector himself. Sometimes a dealer can spot the problem, correct it and/or call the factory for quick shipment of a new replacement part.

Man-made products are prone to failure. Such failures please nobody...the maker of the product, the dealer who sold it, its purchaser who bought it in good faith. When this happens, however, necessary steps must be taken to have the product repaired as quickly as possible and under terms stated in a warranty given the purchaser when the product was bought. The manufacturer fully understands the problems and inconveniences created for his customer when a product fails. You can be assured that any ethical manufacturer wants your detector properly repaired and back in your hands as soon as possible!

A copy of each manufacturer's warranty that covers the products a dealer is selling should be prominently displayed in the dealer's store. Ask to see it *before* you buy a detector. If necessary, write to the manufacturer to get a copy of the current warranty.

This chapter on warranties should not be understood to mean that detector buyers use them very often. *They*

This veteran technician who has been repairing Garrett detectors for more than 20 years benefits from experience ranging from BFO circuitry to microprocessor-controlled computerized instruments.

don't. Any quality detector will usually provide years of trouble-free service...even when the instrument is subjected to rugged use at regular intervals. Still, some detectors will fail...no matter how much care is given them...in their manufacture or by their owners. If this occurs with your detector, you want to be protected properly with a good warranty.

Make certain of this *before* you buy a detector.

Facing

One of the "old pros" of treasure hunting, mentioned time and again in this book, was the late L. L. "Abe" Lincoln of Arkansas, whose like will not be seen again soon.

Over

Treasures found with Garrett metal detectors include these two horses discovered in Turkey and the gold and ivory locket dug from a beach on Florida's Atlantic coast.

Know Your Detector

Provided that it performs basic functions, a poorly built detector will produce more in the hands of a professional than will a high quality detector in the hands of a person who does not understand the instrument or know how to use it. There are various grades of detectors being sold. Some detectors will barely detect a coin one inch deep, yet others will detect that same coin at extreme depths. A most important factor, however, in successful detector operation is the expertise and ability of the operator.

This chapter contains practical methods, tips and procedures recommended to all who use a metal detector. It is my sincere hope that study of this chapter along with others in this book will enable you to increase your abilities. The success you obtain will be in direct proportion to the amount of time and study that you devote to learning how to use your instrument.

Metal detector manufacturers get letters from customers who complain they cannot find anything but bottlecaps with their detector. Yet, other letters seem to bubble over with enthusiasm and joy because their writers are finding coins, rings, jewelry and other valuables. Accompanying photographs often illustrate the tremendous quantities of treasure they have found.

This newcomer to the hobby is already finding treasure with her new Ultra GTA 500 detector because she learned the *right* way to hunt as pointed out in this book.

253

What is the difference? Certainly, it does not lie in the capability of the detector. One can take identical instruments and place them in the hands of two different people and the results may be entirely different.

The best advice I can give you about any metal detector is perhaps the most obvious. *Read your instruction manual!* Yes, that's right...carefully read and study the operator's manual that accompanied your detector. In fact, we at Garrett recommend that you study this manual *before* you purchase a detector. If the manufacturer has "skimped" on providing instructions and advice, you might find yourself shorted in other areas of an instrument.

On the other hand, an extremely detailed manual that you find hard to understand could well indicate a detector that's going to prove complicated and difficult to learn how to use. At Garrett we believe that computerized, microprocessor-controlled detectors are *simple to use*, not difficult. Our Owner's Manuals will tell you this. If some other manual indicates otherwise, be wary of the detector it describes.

Getting Started

If you buy through the mail, or from someone who won't or can't offer instruction, you must work especially hard to learn about your detector. If not, you will probably miss far more treasure than the dollars you saved by ordering from the cheapest source. Your goal should be to find treasure, not a metal detector bargain!

Getting hands-on instructions from the dealer from whom you purchased your new detector is the first step. This step cannot be stressed too greatly. Learn all you can from your dealer, then — after you have studied your Owner's Manual (and audio/video tapes) thoroughly — go into the field with a notebook and carefully write down all questions you have and the problems that have arisen. Return to the dealer for your answers. Don't neglect this vital first step!

254

Assuming that you have made a careful study of the metal detector market to select an instrument you feel is the best for you, the next step is to make up your mind that you are going to learn how to use this detector properly, regardless of the time and effort it takes. Never deviate from your decision! A detector will remove the blindfold and permit you to "see" coins, jewelry and other buried and concealed metal. But you have to trust your detector. You have to learn the correct methods of operating it. You have to learn its idiosyncrasies. You have to learn what makes it tick! In other words, *learn your metal detector* and don't worry, at least at first, about what you are finding!

As you put miles behind your searchcoil, you will find yourself getting better and better with your detector. You will find you are more at ease in using it, and there are fewer and fewer "problems" that bother you. The quantity of found items will be growing at an accelerated rate.

All through your learning and training period and even on down through the years, you must develop persistence. Never give up! Persistence, Persistence, **Persistence**! These are the words of a successful operator, the late L.L. "Abe" Lincoln. You must stay with it and never give up.

When you begin your home study, don't immediately assemble the detector and run outside to begin looking for treasure. First, read your instruction manual...not once, but several times. The first time through, read it as you would a novel...from front to back without stopping. You should pay no attention to the metal detector or its controls. Simply read the instruction manual. If video or audio instruction tapes are available on your detector, watch or listen to these several times. Then, assemble your instrument according to the instructions on the tapes or in the manual. Take the time to do it right.

Once you have assembled your detector properly, you should become familiar with its various controls. The instruction manual should explain each switch and each control, describing to you its function and basic operation.

The next step is to begin to operate your detector in its various modes and functions. The instruction manual and tape(s) should guide you through this learning process and enable you to start practicing with your detector.

Lay it on a wooden bench or table. Do not use a table with metal legs and braces because the metal could interfere with your testing. Begin with the part of your instruction manual that describes the operation of each control. Go through the procedures! If your detector is equipped with a sensitivity or detection depth control, test the detector at several levels. Reduce it all the way. When you have adjusted each control, and have a general understanding of how they all work, you can begin to test the instrument with various metal targets. After you have become familiar with the sounds of your instrument, its meter and its response to various targets in various modes, it is time to go out into the field.

You'll now be *so* grateful for all the knowledge you gained indoors. When you worked with your detector on a table, operation was probably very simple. Now that you are outside, the situation has changed. If you set your threshold with the searchcoil held in the air, when you lower the searchcoil to the ground, you may be in for a surprise. As you lower the coil, the audio sound may begin to change with the meter deflecting up or down because of minerals or metal targets in the ground where you are standing. It will be necessary for you to learn exactly what is causing any signal changes.

On many metal detector models there are "set and forget" controls. Controls like TONE, AUDIO (TUNING) and MANUAL and AUTOMATIC TUNING are just that; once you set them, you rarely have to change or reset them. If you set them when you followed your preliminary inside instructions, you don't have to worry about them outside. So, you are now left with Ground Balance (if your detector has this control) and Discrimination (trash elimination). The beginner should initially consider the Discrimination dial as a "set and forget" control. Set it to zero discrimination (all-metal detection) and leave it there until you have at least 10 hours operating time. In other words, dig everything!

We have developed "Starter Phases" for our new computerized Garrett detectors. These instruments are so simple to operate that you can press just one touchpad and begin hunting successfully. We urge all customers to follow the instructions of the "Starter Phase," no matter how much experience they have with a metal detector.

During the learning phase with your own detector, keep in mind that you should work smarter, not harder. As you scan along, each time you receive a signal…before you dig or do anything else…try to guess what the target is, what size it is, its shape and its depth. Analyze the audio and/or meter signals. Say to yourself, "This is a coin," or "This is a bottlecap. It is about three inches deep." Then pay careful attention when you dig the object. Try to determine exactly how deep it is and how it was lying in the ground.

Did you guess right? Great! If not, try to determine why. The more you do this, the greater your success will be. You will quickly learn how to use and actually "read" your instrument and understand everything it is telling you.

As you scan the searchcoil over the ground, use the "straight- line" sweep method recommended in this chapter. You should hold the searchcoil slightly above the ground and scan at a rate of about one foot per second. Don't get in a hurry, and don't try to cover an acre in 10 minutes. Always remember that what you are looking for is buried just below the sweep you are now making with your searchcoil. It's not across the field.

After you used your detector for several hours, you can begin to test its discrimination. Study your owner's manual. But, whatever you do, don't use too much discrimination…just enough to eliminate from detection the junk you have been digging. Do not try to set the control to eliminate pulltabs. That can come later when you know

257

more about your detector and only when you feel such discrimination is absolutely necessary.

If you haven't started using headphones, now is the time to do so. You'll learn how important they really are. You'll dig coins that you couldn't detect from just listening to a detector's speaker. You'll hear sounds you didn't hear before. Headphones may get hot and the cord may get in the way but your rewards will make it all worthwhile.

After you have even more experience and are beginning to get comfortable with your detector, it's time to go back over the same areas you searched before you learned how to use your machine. You'll surprised at the quantity of coins and other objects you missed. In fact, each time you come back to these places you'll find more coins and other treasures, especially at greater depths.

Begin to learn about other forms of treasure hunting such as ghost towning, relic and cache hunting and searching for gold nuggets. Learn about the various optional accessories and searchcoils that are available for your detector. Prepare now for other treasure hunting opportunities. Be ready when they come along.

Always remember that well designed detectors are not complicated or difficult to learn to use. The first time you drove a car it was difficult, but now you drive without thinking about it. The same will be true with your detector. Take it easy, and don't give up if you think it is not performing as it should. Just keep working with your detector, restudy your manual, contact your dealer or manufacturer, and ask for more information. Quite often, problems are cleared up with just one simple demonstration by your dealer or someone who knows how to use detectors. Remember, keep the Detection Depth (Sensitivity) control turned to a low level and certainly not above its "Initial Set Point." Scan with the searchcoil about two inches above the ground and scan at a moderate speed. Even in areas with large amounts of "junk" metal, which are very difficult to work, reduced detection depth and moderate scanning speed let you hear individual target signals rather than just a jumbled mass of sounds.

Success stories are written every day. A lot of treasure is being found and a lot of treasure is waiting to be found where you live. Detectors are not magic wands, but when used correctly they will locate buried and concealed treasure. Keep your faith in your detector, have patience and continue using your instrument until you have it mastered. Success will be yours!

Make Your Own Test Plot

One of the first things a new detector owner does is bury a few coins to see how deeply they can be detected. The usual result...*disappointment.* You see, newly buried coins are quite difficult to detect. The longer an object has been buried, the easier it can be detected. Not only is a "barrier" to electromagnetic field penetration created when a coin is first buried, but no "halo effect" has been developed. As time passes, coins become more closely associated, electrically, with surrounding earth materials and the molecules of metal begin to leave and move out into the surrounding soil. Also, it is theorized that in some cases (especially in salt water) the coin's surface becomes a better conductor. In some areas it is believed that coins buried for some time can be detected at twice the depth compared with coins that have just been buried.

Select an area for your own test plot. First, scan the area very thoroughly in the All Metal mode and remove all metal from the ground. Select targets such as various coins, a bottlecap, a nail and a pulltab. Select also a pint jar filled with scrap copper and/or aluminum metal, a long object such as a foot-long pipe and a large object such as a gallon can. Bury all these objects about three feet apart, in rows, and make a map showing where each item is buried and note its depth.

Bury pennies at varying depths, beginning at one inch. Continue, with the deepest buried about six inches deep.

Bury one at about two inches but stand it on edge. Bury a penny at about two inches with a bottlecap about four inches off to one side. Bury the bottlecap, nail and pulltab separately about two inches deep. Bury the jar at twelve inches to the top of its lid. Bury the pipe horizontally three or four inches deep. Bury the gallon can with the lid two feet below the surface.

The purpose of the buried coins is to familiarize you with the sound of money. If you can't detect the deeper coins, don't worry. After a while, you'll be able to detect them quickly. If you can detect everything in your test plot, rebury some items deeper. The penny buried next to the bottle cap can give you experience in Super Sniping with a smaller searchcoil and will help you learn to distinguish individual objects. The jar and gallon can will help you learn to recognize "dull" sounds of large, deeply buried objects. The pipe will help you learn to contour. Check the targets with and without headphones. You'll be amazed at the difference headphones make.

The test plot is important. Don't neglect it. From time to time expand it, rebury the targets deeper and add new ones. Your test plot is important because your success in scanning over it will be a measure of how well you are progressing and how well you have learned your equipment. Remember, however, that you must make an accurate map and keep it up to date when you change and/or add to your test plot.

Miscellaneous Tips

When searching areas adjacent to wire fences, metal buildings, metal parking meter posts, etc., reduce detection depth and scan the searchcoil parallel to the structure.

Learn to use a probe to locate the exact point where coins are buried. This will help you retrieve coins with minimum damage to grass.

Why not join with thousands of other individuals and organizations throughout the world who have endeavored to preserve their lands and heritage and create good will by following these basic rules:

Metal Detector Operators Code of Ethics

- I will respect private and public property, all historical and archaeological sites and will do no metal detecting on these lands without proper permission.
- I will keep informed on and obey all laws, regulations, and rules governing federal, state, and local public lands.
- I will aid law enforcement officials whenever possible.
- I will cause no willful damage to property of any kind, including fences, signs and buildings, and will always fill the holes I dig.
- I will not destroy property, buildings, or the remains of ghost towns and other deserted structures.
- I will not leave litter or uncovered items lying around. I will carry all trash and dug targets with me when I leave each search area.
- I will observe the Golden Rule, using good outdoor manners and conducting myself at all times in a manner which will add to the stature and public image of all people engaged in the field of metal detection.

More Tips

Coins lying in the ground at an angle may be missed on one searchcoil pass but detected when the searchcoil approaches from a different angle. If your detector has a volume control, keep it set at maximum. Don't confuse volume control with audio (threshold) control. You should use earphones that have individual earphone volume adjustment and set each one to suit yourself.

Never dial in more Discrimination than you absolutely need. Too much may reduce detector efficiency.

If you are working on the beach, set discrimination at about bottlecap rejection. A slight amount of adjusting may be necessary but you can set the detector to ignore salt water. Pulse Induction detectors and others designed for beach hunting ignore salt water automatically.

Use your common sense. *Think* your way through perplexing situations. Remember, success comes from detector expertise, research, patience, enthusiasm and using common sense.

Don't expect to find tons of treasure every time you go out! In fact, there may be times when you don't find anything. But the fun and reward of metal detecting is never knowing what you'll dig up next!

Be sure to check your batteries before you venture out. Check them often. Carry spare batteries with you every time you go hunting.

Always keep the searchcoil level when you scan (as shown on the facing page) and scan slowly and methodically. Be sure to scan the searchcoil from side to side in a straight line in front of you. Do not scan the searchcoil in an arc unless the arc width is narrow (about two feet) or unless you are scanning extremely slowly. The straight-line scan method allows you to cover more ground width in each sweep and permits you to keep the searchcoil level throughout each sweep. This method reduces skipping and helps you overlap more uniformly. Overlap by advancing the searchcoil as much as 50% of the coil's diameter at the end of each sweep path. Occasionally scan an area from a different angle. Do not raise the searchcoil above scanning level at the end of each sweep. When the searchcoil begins to reach the extremes of each sweep, you will find yourself rotating your upper body to stretch out for an even wider sweep. This gives the double benefit of scanning a wider sweep and gaining additional exercise. To insure that you completely scan any given area, use string or cord to mark scan paths three to six feet wide.

When you dig a target, always scan back over the hole to make sure you recovered everything.

Fill your holes. Pick up and carry off all trash. Don't destroy property.

Beginner's Short Course

These instructions are for a modern manual adjust (non motion) detector. They are also applicable for motion instruments with automatic ground balance.

1. Assemble your detector according to the Owner's Manual, using the smallest diameter searchcoil you have.

2. Go outdoors away from all metal and hold the detector with the searchcoil about four feet in the air.

3. Turn the detector on and reduce Detection Depth (Sensitivity) to minimum.

4. Adjust the Audio to a very low sound. This is your threshold level. Depending upon your detector, you may have to depress a switch while you make this adjustment.

As demonstrated here, the straight-line, side-to-side method of scanning covers ground more thoroughly and helps keep the searchcoil at a constant height.

5. Select the All Metal detection (no discrimination) mode.

6. Lower the detector and listen carefully. If the sound increases or decreases, it will be necessary for you to follow the instructions in your manual for ground balancing your detector. This will be done automatically by *Fast Track* with the new Grand Master Hunter CX II and Master Hunter CX. No ground balancing is ever necessary with the Ultra GTA detectors.

7. Continue to raise and lower the searchcoil until there is no change in sound and your detector is ground balanced properly.

(Earlier editions of this book had several paragraphs devoted to techniques for ground balancing. I have eliminated these instructions since ground balancing of modern detectors is so simple.)

8. Lower the searchcoil to a height of about two inches above the ground when your detector is ground balanced and begin scanning the searchcoil slowly over the ground, keeping a constant height.

9. At the spot the audio increases, a target is buried in the ground.

Preset "Initial Setting " Points

If your detector control panel has initial preset points, it will be easier for you to learn to use the instrument. Set all knobs and switches to these preset points. Adjustments are for average soil and operating conditions. Any controls that do not have initial preset points may then be set according to instructions given above.

Health Safeguards

Over the past 25 years metal detecting has become a very popular activity. People of all ages roam parks, ghost towns, beaches and gold mining areas in search of treasure. Occasionally, but not often, some individuals complain of pains after they have used metal detectors for long periods of time. Most often, these complaints come from persons who are just beginning the hobby and after their first day out. They spend, perhaps, 10 or 12 hours swinging their detector and wake up the next day with a good case of sore muscles.

Of course, after a short time, the soreness has gone and off they go again. Although the incidence is rare, some may suffer from tennis elbow. Tennis elbow is a perfectly real condition...injury to the tendons of the elbow, whose medical name is epicondylitis. Characterized by mild to sharp pain at the side of the elbow, it is believed to be caused by a gradual weakening of muscle tissue. Repeated muscle strain without adequate time for the muscles to repair themselves, causes the problem.

I have been using metal detectors for most of my adult life and have never had tennis elbow or any serious problem. I develop more problems from using my gym equipment. Over the years, I have developed four ways to lessen the dangers of strained muscles.

– Select the proper equipment including accessories.

– Strengthen the hand, arm, back and shoulder muscles through an exercise program.

– Before beginning each day's detecting activity, spend a few minutes doing warmup exercises.

– During metal detector activity, use the correct scanning techniques and take intermittent break periods.

Proper stem length and balance are the key to correct scanning techniques. Adjust your stem to a comfortable, not necessarily shortest, length. If it is too long, you cannot balance yourself properly, and your swing will be awkward. If it is too short, you'll have to search stooped over. If large searchcoils do not give proper balance, use a hipmount kit or armrest.

There are many books written on the subject of muscle strengthening. You should select a program that will strengthen your fingers, hand, arm, shoulder and back muscles. Not much strengthening is really required, not even bar bell and dumbbell workouts. Toning up is of primary importance. As you use your metal detector you'll develop the correct muscles. It's just that at the beginning, and after periods of inactivity, you should protect against strained muscles and ligaments.

For this reason warmup exercises are recommended before each day's metal detecting activity. A few minutes of stretching and using your muscles will loosen them and prepare you for the day's pleasure. Observe how a cat stretches itself and try to do likewise.

A brisk walk, a few toe touches, a few arm and wrist curls with a one or two pound weight held in the hands, a few body twists at the waist standing erect and perhaps a minute or two running in place...these will get the job done. You can develop your own warmup exercises.

Now, to proper scanning methods. First, don't try to scan while balancing on one foot. Keep a firm footing and don't scan in awkward positions that may force muscles to make unnatural movements. Keep all movements as natural as possible. When scanning on steep hills, in gullies or other unlevel places, keep good balance, take shorter swings and don't place yourself in awkward positions.

Grasp the metal detector handle lightly. Slight wrist and arm movements will be necessary, but make your searchcoil swing from side to side short. If you must swing the detector widely from side to side, use a method that is natural and one that causes the least unnecessary wrist movements. Let the entire arm "swing" with the detector. Occasionally, change hands and use the other arm to swing the detector. If you feel yourself tightening up, stop and rest. Most likely, however, each time you stop to dig a target, you will get the rest you need. Actually, you should think of your next detected target as a blessing. You'll get to stop, stoop down and dig the target. This activity gives other muscles a workout, which will help prevent sore muscles that come from long periods of continuous metal detector swinging without a break.

All Kinds of Treasures

This chapter will lead into those that follow by discussing the various facets of treasure hunting. All of this should be read in conjunction with Chapter 20 in which recommendations were given to help you select the best type of detector for every task you undertake.

Now let's consider each of those tasks...

Coin hunting is the searching for and retrieving of lost coins. Countless millions of coins have been lost and await recovery by the metal detector hobbyist. Thousands of Indianhead and Wheat pennies, Buffalo nickels, Barber dimes, Liberty and Washington quarters, Liberty Walking half-dollars, silver dollars, early colonial coins, gold coins and many other types are being recovered every day. People are losing more coins today than the coin hunter is finding! Coins are lost everywhere people go, and coins are being found everywhere people have been. Coin hunting is one of the most active family hobbies in America.

The person not familiar with this hobby finds it difficult to believe that coins can be found. "Who loses coins?" they ask. "Surely, there are not enough lost coins to make it worthwhile to buy a metal detector or spend time looking for them!" I have said many times that "any active and experienced coin hunter can find five thousand coins each year." This is only an average of 100 coins found each weekend for 50 weeks...a reasonable and attainable goal. If you'll apply the principles set forth in my book, *The New Successful Coin Hunting,* you'll easily find 5,000 coins each year and more!

Don't make the mistake of believing there are no coins

267

to be found where you live. If you don't have the experience now, you soon will gain the knowledge to convince yourself that coins are truly found everywhere. The first place every person should start searching is right in his own backyard before branching out from there. Many people erroneously believe there is nothing in their areas worth searching for. The truth is, all the good coin hunting sites will never be cleaned out.

Exploring a ghost town is a popular and rewarding hobby which includes a number of activities. In ghost towns you may discover old coins, perhaps a buried treasure cache, relics or antiques dating back to the earliest settlers, or lost items from only yesterday. Any place people have gathered will produce relics and coins. There are thousands of abandoned town sites, old forts, homesteads and farmhouse locations. The list is endless. Finding a place to search will never be your problem! Finding the time needed to pursue and enjoy your hobby is often more of a challenge. You will need a good metal detector since most surface items have already been picked up and those remaining will lie below the surface.

A 100-year-old rifle was found in Athens, TX, by a treasure hunter who was curious enough to search the attic of an old house. Karl von Mueller tells of a straw-encased bottle filled with 773 dimes found with a metal detector over the doorway of an old shack near Maitland, FL. All the coins were dated prior to 1918. There were 46 of the rare 1916-D's, worth more than $100 each, two 1895-O's, worth more than $50, and 10 1904-S's, worth more than $10 apiece. The numismatic value of the other coins brought the total value of the cache to over $5,000, with today's valuation many times more than that amount. The

A universal detector such as the Garrett Master Hunter CX is the ideal choice for the hobbyist who wants an instrument that will find all of the different kinds of treasure.

most significant aspect of the find, however, is that when the coins were hidden they were probably worth little more than their face value of $77.30. In other words, they were probably not hidden by a wealthy person but rather, as the modest shack would indicate, by someone relatively poor. This bears out the old cliche that, "treasure is where you find it."

Cache hunting is seeking money or valuables that have been put away or cached by someone, the little old lady's "hard times" coins she buried in a jar in the garden 50 or 100 years ago, the old man's "bank" jar he kept hidden in the bottom of a fence post hole or, the washtub filled with gold coins. These are all "caches!" There are many, many thousands of these treasures waiting for the detector operator who seeks them out. Buried only a few inches deep or at arm's length below ground surface, they will stay buried forever if they are not dug up by the treasure hunter. These treasures can be found anywhere...in an old chicken coop, halfway between the well and a tree, between two trees, in the ground under the horse stall, in the walls of houses and barns, etc.

Collecting and studying *battlefield relics* constitutes an interesting pastime for many people. Of course, the great war in this country was the Civil War, and values placed on artifacts and other items from this time are often astronomical. Simple buttons from Union and Confederate uniforms have been sold at open and private auctions for as much as $1,000. Buckles, a favorite item with most collectors, are highly sought and often demand prices beginning as low as $25 for common buckles in poor condition to more than $2,000 for the more rare or ornate

THing choice of most metal detector hobbyists, coins are among the easiest of treasures to be found and are often discovered by beginners their first time out hunting.

ones. The finding of battlefield relics brings history so close that one can visualize it in the making.

The numerous battle and skirmish sites of the eastern and western campaigns and naval operations abound in relics and artifacts valued by war buffs and professional collectors. All types of weapons or instruments of the war are being located by the persistent metal detector operator. There are many "known" battle areas in the country, however, protected by state and federal governments. There areas, rightfully so, are protected and strictly "off limits" to all metal detector operators.

There's Treasure on the Beach!

On some beaches there are roped-off areas designed for swimming. Search these places first! Strike up a conversation with the lifeguard or concession stand operators. It may be that the swimming areas of bygone days were located elsewhere on the beach. You would certainly want to search those sites. Also, lifeguards may know where rings and valuables are reported to have been lost. Try working along the water's edge at both low and high tides as both could be profitable. You will encounter much less trash near the water, but remember, some very valuable coins and jewelry have been found back away from the beach in the heavy traffic areas. There are thousands of swimming beaches no longer used. Visit your library and do a little research to locate these resort and health spa swimming areas where much treasure awaits discovery.

My recently revised *Treasure Recovery from Sand and Sea* presents valuable information on beach and underwater hunting for the novice and expert alike.

Rocks, Gems and Minerals

The most important and useful tool of the rockhound (besides his rock hammer and patience) can be a metal detector. If it is properly understood and operated, its use can be very rewarding and interesting, but it should not be used as the ultimate answer to the positive identification

272

of all detectable specimens. The metal detector should be used as an accessory to the rockhound's field equipment, which will aid in locating conductive metallic specimens that the human eye cannot distinguish or identify. Check known samples and become acquainted with the metal detector. You cannot see inside an ore specimen but a good quality modern detector can.

For our purposes "metal" is defined as any metallic substance of a conductive nature in sufficient quantity to disturb the electromagnetic field of the searchcoil. If your detector responds to a target as "metallic," collect it for future inspection; it contains conductive metal in some form. If the detector responds as "mineral," it means only that the specimen contains more iron mineral than it does metal in a detectable form. In just a few minutes you might find some high-grade metallic sample that has been passed over for years by fellow rockhounds.

These Spanish weapons — guns, cannon and sabre, dating from the 17th and 18th centuries — are typical of those that have been found with metal detectors on shipwrecks in the Caribbean.

273

When searching for high grade specimens of metallic ore, pay close attention to old mine tailings. You may find that a "worked out" area isn't so barren after all. Certain gems, such as the thunder-egg, have a covering of outside magnetic iron. Some forms of jade and even garnet respond to a good detector.

NOTE: Ore sampling can only be accomplished with a detector that is designed for prospecting and is correctly calibrated to give exacting ore sample identification. To learn about, select and correctly use calibrated instruments, read the new book Roy Lagal and I wrote, *Modern Electronic Prospecting,* published by Ram Publishing Company.

The Pocket Probe metal detector is the rockhound's perfect field companion.

Laws of Treasure Hunting

While this book does not attempt to give legal advice, you need to become aware that there are laws applicable to various treasure hunting situations. Each state has its own laws concerning where you can hunt for treasure and whether you may keep treasure when it is found. You should learn these laws.

All states have laws against trespassing. If a sign says, "Keep Out," do just that. It is always best to seek permission. With the proper attitude and a true explanation of your purpose, you will be surprised at the cooperation you will receive from most landowners. The majority of them will be curious enough about your metal detector and what you hope to find, to agree to let you search. Offer to split, giving them 25% (or less) of all you find and they will be more willing. If large amounts of treasure are believed to be hidden or buried on another's property, a properly drawn, legal agreement is a *must!* Such an agreement between both you and all landowners (husband and wife, etc.) will eliminate any later disagreements which might otherwise arise.

In most cases, public property is open to you. Do not destroy the grass or leave trash or holes. Most park superintendents know that conscientious coin hunters pick up trash and leave the grounds in better shape than they found them. There are several ways to properly remove coins from the ground. You should read Chapter 11 "Digging Coins" in my new *The New Successful Coin Hunting* from Ram.

All treasure hunters must become aware of their responsibility to protect the property of others and to keep public property fit for all. Persons who destroy property, dig large holes and leave them unfilled, or tear down buildings in search of valuables, should not to be called treasure hunters—but, more properly, looters and scavengers.

All treasure that you find must be declared as income during the year in which you receive a monetary gain from that treasure. If you find $1,000 in coins, which you spend at once because they have no numismatic value, then you must declare the face value of those coins in the current

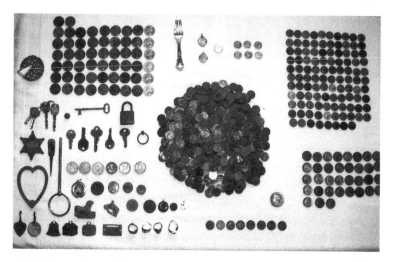

All of these items, including 980 coins, were found in just the first few months that a newcomer to treasure hunting in Illinois used a Garrett Master Hunter CX metal detector.

year's income tax report. If, however, you discover a valuable coin—or, say, an antique pistol—you do not make a declaration until you sell the item(s) and then only for the amount you received. If you decide to donate some of your finds to historical societies or museums, you may be able to deduct the fair market price of the items as charitable contributions. Simply stated, the tax laws require you to declare all income from treasure hunting.

You may be allowed to deduct some or all of your expenses but you must have good records. You are advised to check with a tax accountant, especially if you plan to become a full-time treasure hunter. An accountant will advise you as to what type records you are required to keep.

Join a Club!

There are approximately 350 treasure hunting clubs in the United States with a total of over 500 clubs located throughout the world. Why not join one and take an active part? Clubs are an invaluable source of information. You can learn about metal detectors and treasure hunting from those who are active in the field. You will meet people, share their success stories, and perhaps gain a few hunting partners. You will be encouraged by found treasure, and you can swap some of your treasure and build up your collection.

The hobby and sport of metal detecting has been kept clean and dignified by people who care about their hobby, themselves and their fellow men. Most detector owners go out of their way to protect a most rewarding and enjoyable hobby and to share their enjoyment with others. Keeping the hobby clean takes the effort and dedication of everyone...not just a few. So, as you go about enjoying your leisure, or perhaps full-time activity, be professional! Be worthy of your calling!

Coin Hunting

Hunting for coins is the heart and soul of the metal detecting hobby. Literally everybody hunts for coins...they are certainly the initial target that most first-time detector owners seek.

And, at Garrett we know that every detector we design and build will be used at one time or another to search for coins. We also suspect that many of our detectors will be used for no other purpose. Oh, jewelry and other valuable items will certainly be sought, but it will be coins that are the thrust of the search for most hobbyists, no matter what their intentions.

Thus, it is essential that you master techniques for this phase of the hobby. You'll use them in all other hunting.

As noted in Chapter 20, the recommended detector for hunting coins is a modern instrument with automatic ground balancing and good discrimination. The best instruments, however, are the new computerized detectors with microprocessor controls that give you the alternatives between several modes and discrimination levels. Of course, any detector with an All Metal mode will find more and deeper coins, but every target will have to be dug. This can be a blessing in disguise since valuable metal objects are sometimes rejected when discrimination is used.

Another equipment tip is one we've already discussed. Let me urge you again, however, always to use headphones. Get a quality set and you'll be amazed at how much more you can hear from your detector. With a modern instrument that tries to tell you such a great deal, you really want to be able to listen to it.

When using headphones (or, even the speaker, if you must) we urge that you operate with audio threshold at a very slight level of sound. Adjust it for the faintest sound you can hear.

Silent operation has enabled treasure hunters to find many targets, true, but it has also been proven that silent operation results in a slight loss of depth. With silent operation you will also lose some ability to read all targets properly, especially in trashy areas.

There will be times when you get a coin tone while scanning over a spot in one direction and a standard audio blip when scanning from another angle. This is most likely a junk target; however, we advise you not just to walk away from it. Continue scanning back and forth across it from numerous angles. Draw your imaginary "X;" slide your searchcoil from side to side. Even push it forward and backward. Listen to the sound carefully. (Here's where headphones are a real help!) If you ever get the coin tone in both directions, dig the target.

You'll probably find a coin in close proximity to some sort of junk.

We know how much will power it takes to resist the blips coming over your headphones or from the audio speaker beneath the handle of your Grand Master Hunter. You know a target exists, and it's human nature to want to dig them all! Remember, however, that a quality modern detector will never lie to you. Its meter and audible sounds will properly identify all objects being detected beneath the searchcoil at any given instant.

Scanning speed is very important. Your detector will operate and analyze targets no matter what speed you swing the searchcoil. We recommend that you operate at a speed of between one to two feet per second. Go even slower, and you might be surprised at your increased success, especially in high junk areas. We suggest that you try a test. Slow down and scan with your searchcoil very deliberately. You may reap great benefits.

Some of you prefer to scan with a searchcoil lightly skimming the ground. This is fine; don't worry about it. Our only recommendation about such activity is that you use the appropriate skid plate (coil cover) to protect your searchcoil against unnecessary abrasion and wear.

We recommend that you use the standard, 8 1/2-inch searchcoil for scanning most parks, playgrounds, beaches and other conventional coin hunting areas. It is the best general purpose, all-around searchcoil. Numerous letters and personal inquiries regularly ask me about use of the larger coils. My answer is a definite YES...the reason being that larger coils can detect even the smallest coins.

Now, those of you to whom this is a new idea may be asking just when should you use the larger searchcoil. Good question!

After you scan an area with the 8 1/2-inch coil, you may suspect that you are detecting deep targets since they give

There is no thrill in the hobby of treasure hunting that can match the exhilaration that comes from examining a batch of coins that your skill has helped you find with a new model metal detector.

you only a faint signal, even with headphones. If so, you're detecting at the outer limits of that all-purpose searchcoil, and you may be missing deeper coins. You need the additional detection depth that's available with the 12 1/2-inch searchcoil. After scanning such an area thoroughly with the 8 1/2-inch searchcoil, go over it again with the larger coil, scanning very slowly and using headphones. If there are deeper coins to be found, you'll detect them!

There are many books on the subject of coin hunting. It seems that I can learn "something" from every one I pick up.

New Successful Coin Hunting replacing my book *Successful Coin Hunting* that has been the top seller on this subject since 1974 presents a comprehensive review of the latest in coin hunting techniques with computerized metal detectors. We urge that you read this new book and apply its principles. Other *Treasure Hunting Texts* from Ram that might help you are *Modern Metal Detectors* and *Treasure Recovery from Sand and Sea*, which I also wrote. Incidentally, Ram's new edition of *Treasure Recovery from Sand and Sea* represents a significant improvement over the earlier edition.

All of these books are available from Ram Publishing Co. An order blank is included in the back of this manual.

Coins can be detected to extreme depths with just about any modern detector. Those with specialized features like coin tone, coin-depth measuring, electronic pinpointing and specialized meters and indicators enhance the operator's capability. Searchcoils in a wide variety are available.

Smaller searchcoils will make you more efficient in your coin hunting efforts. You will dig a higher ratio of coins to trash, but detection depth will not be as great as with 10 to 12-inch sizes. These searchcoils should be weapons in your normal coin hunting arsenal.

For instance, if a park is known as a good coin producer, but has been overworked, you may want to consider the larger searchcoils. Adjust the Discrimination controls to reject the typical trash found in the area or set it to "zero." Adjust the detector to ignore iron mineralization and use one or more of the pinpointing methods explained in this book. As you retrieve coins and trash, notice their depth. If mostly junk is found in the first few inches, you may want to dig only the deeper targets.

If your detector is equipped with a depth measuring meter, dig only the targets beyond a predetermined depth. If yours is equipped with a detection depth control, try setting it to maximum. When you have pinpointed an object, rotate the control to minimum and recheck the target. If you don't detect it now, dig. It will be deep. (*Note:* When you change detection depth with older detectors, it may be necessary to press the retune switch or button.) You should analyze detector operation using various detection depth control settings to find the optimum setting for any particular coin area.

Coin Hunting in Junk Areas

Some of the most troublesome places over which to search are those that contain a large amount of metal "junk." It doesn't matter what type detector you have, you'll have some erratic operational problems because of the presence of all this metal. In effect, the detector just cannot decide what's beneath its searchcoil. Consequently, when scanning high junk areas you may find it necessary to reduce detection depth. You will actually gain efficiency. You'll find the detector will be easier to operate and you'll be able to dig more good targets. The reduced detection depth allows the detector to more easily isolate and identify individual targets.

Another excellent method to use when searching these high junk areas is the Super Sniper method described below. Also, certain modern detectors have classifier meters and audio systems that continue to classify detected targets accurately even when the discrimination control is set to "zero." Oftentimes, using these meters properly will prevent the loss of good targets, even in trashy areas.

Be especially alert to your detector's signals. If you hear a single good "beep" amongst trash "blip" sounds, investigate the spot carefully. It may be a coin *hiding* alongside or under the trash. Carefully and slowly scan the area, moving toward the spot from several directions. You may also eliminate some of the "blips" by reducing detection depth. The Super Sniper searchcoils and the new 2D elliptical coils do an excellent job of isolating coins out of trash.

A very efficient method of scanning "worked out" areas or those with numerous junk metal targets is Super-Sniping, the use of small (four-inch diameter) searchcoils. The new 2D elliptical searchcoils are also very effective. Super Sniping is a good way to have a successful coin hunting day!

The four-and-one-half-inch "Super Sniper" is the most popular optional detector searchcoil. It can be operated extremely close to sidewalks, fences, etc. It efficiently permits the working of high trash areas (Super Sniping) to recover coins that larger searchcoils cannot locate in the trash elimination mode.

Seven-inch to eight-inch diameter searchcoils are the most popular coin hunting sizes. As 10 to 12-inch sizes became more popular, many professionals began using the 10-inch for general coin hunting. Larger coils give greater depth and cover a wider sweep path, although their extra weight makes them more tiring to use. Pinpointing was also found to be slightly more difficult.

New elliptical coils are now becoming increasingly popular for several reasons. A 5x10-inch coils offers an effective 10-inch scanning path, yet is lighter than a normal 10-inch coil. The new 2D elliptical coils also offer additional depth and are useful in trashy areas since they scan only in the small area down the center of the searchcoil.

Fourteen-inch searchcoils can be used for coin hunting and are surprisingly sensitive to small coins. Pinpointing is difficult, but extra depth can be achieved.

Computerized Hunting

Coin hunting is a field in which you can excel with an Ultra GTA, the Grand Master Hunter CX II or the Master Hunter CX...Garrett's computerized detectors with microprocessor controls! Any of these versatile instruments will be found especially fitted for coin hunting. Consider the Ultra GTA

Although it has universal capabilities, the Ultra GTA was designed primarily as a coin hunting detector. The greater depth and precise discrimination possible with microprocessor-controlled circuitry combine with the Ultra's light weight and ease of handling to make it a superb instrument for finding coins.

Whether you choose to hunt for them in a park or on a beach, the Ultra's factory-set operating modes will offer

All found with metal detectors, this impressive collection of Roman relics and coins, along with old coins from Great Britain, was exhibited at a hobby show in England.

283

discrimination that responds ideally to conditions normally encountered. Discrimination preset in the Ultra for its *Coins* mode is designed to eliminate detection of lower conductivity trash targets normally encountered in coin hunting, such as bottlecaps and most pulltabs. Bent pulltabs and pulltab pieces may not be eliminated from detection. Successful treasure hunters, however, must *expect* to dig some junk occasionally.

From time to time you may discover quantities of specific trash targets that are not being eliminated from detection by factory- set discrimination. You can then use the **REJECT** touchpad to eliminate these pesky pieces of junk, no matter which operating mode you are using. Just move your searchcoil across a junk target and watch the Ultra's Upper Scale for its response and push the **REJECT** touchpad. You'll have no more trouble from that type of trash metal. You'll spend less time digging trash and more time digging coins!

There are numerous reasons why you would want to accept or reject specific targets:

• You may be looking for *only one item...* a certain lost piece of jewelry, for example. You can program the Ultra to reject *all other* types of metal targets.

• You may be hunting in an area where you are plagued with a specific type of trash. You can reject *just this type* of trash metal and continue to hunt in all metal.

• You may have your own *special* ideas for designing a mode of detection. The Ultra gives you unlimited opportunities to try out any and all of your ideas.

You will want to hunt in the Ultra's *All Metal* detection mode when greatest depth is sought, such as when searching for caches or deep relics. You may also wish to hunt in this mode when hunting in areas with many targets spaced closely together. This will help to identify individual targets and improve discrimination. Because *no discrimination* is programmed in the this mode, your detector will give an audible signal announcing every piece of metal it scans over. Remember, the Ultra offers another special feature: you can always return to any discrimination mode by pressing **LAST MODE**.

Hunting with the CX II and CX

The Grand Master Hunter CX II and the Master Hunter CX are truly unlimited in their capabilities for finding coins or any other treasures. When hunting for coins, here's a tip on setting the discrimination controls that will result in your finding more of them. Turn both discrimination controls all the way counterclockwise...as far to the left as they will go...to the LOWEST setting. Scan any area you have chosen for a few minutes or until you have dug a couple of dozen targets. Analyze these targets...study them carefully! Determine exactly WHAT trash you are recovering.

Then, set your discrimination controls absolutely no higher than necessary to reject the most troublesome of the little pests.

For instance, if you have located a dozen bottlecaps but only two pulltabs, set your detector to reject only bottlecaps. Do not set the controls to reject pulltabs; be content to dig a few of them for the greatest success. One axiom of treasure hunting you must learn: *To have the greatest success, you must dig some trash!*

Here's another tip that many professional treasure hunters have learned to use: For achieving absolute maximum depth while scanning, operate your detector in the All Metal mode.

The *Fast Track* system of automatic and continuous ground balancing on both the Grand Master Hunter CX II and the Master Hunter CX will completely eliminate any problem with minerals in the soil.

Remember, also, that the target identification meters on these detectors correctly read all detected targets whether you are operating in the Discriminate or the All Metal mode. Therefore, you can scan in the All Metal

285

mode and detect all targets, both junk and treasure, at maximum depth. Once you have detected an object, simply glance at the meter to determine if you wish to dig or not. If the pointer falls in the extreme left hand side of the scale, the out-of-range section, by all means dig the target. It could be a valuable object that is simply too deep to be read properly by the discrimination circuitry.

When scanning in the All Metal mode, there are other methods you can employ to increase your coin-hunting success.

After you get a signal and have the target pinpointed, press the Discriminate touchpad. If the audio signal increases in loudness or does not change, dig the target. It will probably worthwhile. If the signal decreases or you hear a junk blip, don't bother to dig.

One of the greatest coin-hunting tips that many treasure hunters use every day is to search with the 4 1/2-inch Super Sniper searchcoil. Many areas that you will want to search contain a tremendous amount of junk...small bits and pieces of trash of all kinds, both ferrous and non-ferrous. Remember that your Grand Master Hunter, like any other detector, is continually analyzing *all targets* beneath its searchcoil. When there are several targets at detectable depths beneath a Crossfire searchcoil, they are read simultaneously. Thus, you may occasionally hear numerous little blips along with, perhaps, even an occasional single coin tone in some areas.

To work these locations proficiently, we encourage you to use the Super Sniper. Its narrow diameter lets you scan a much smaller area at any specific instant but offers excellent detection depth.

Identifying and studying old coins that have been found with a metal detector can open the door to still another new and exciting phase of the treasure hunting hobby.

286

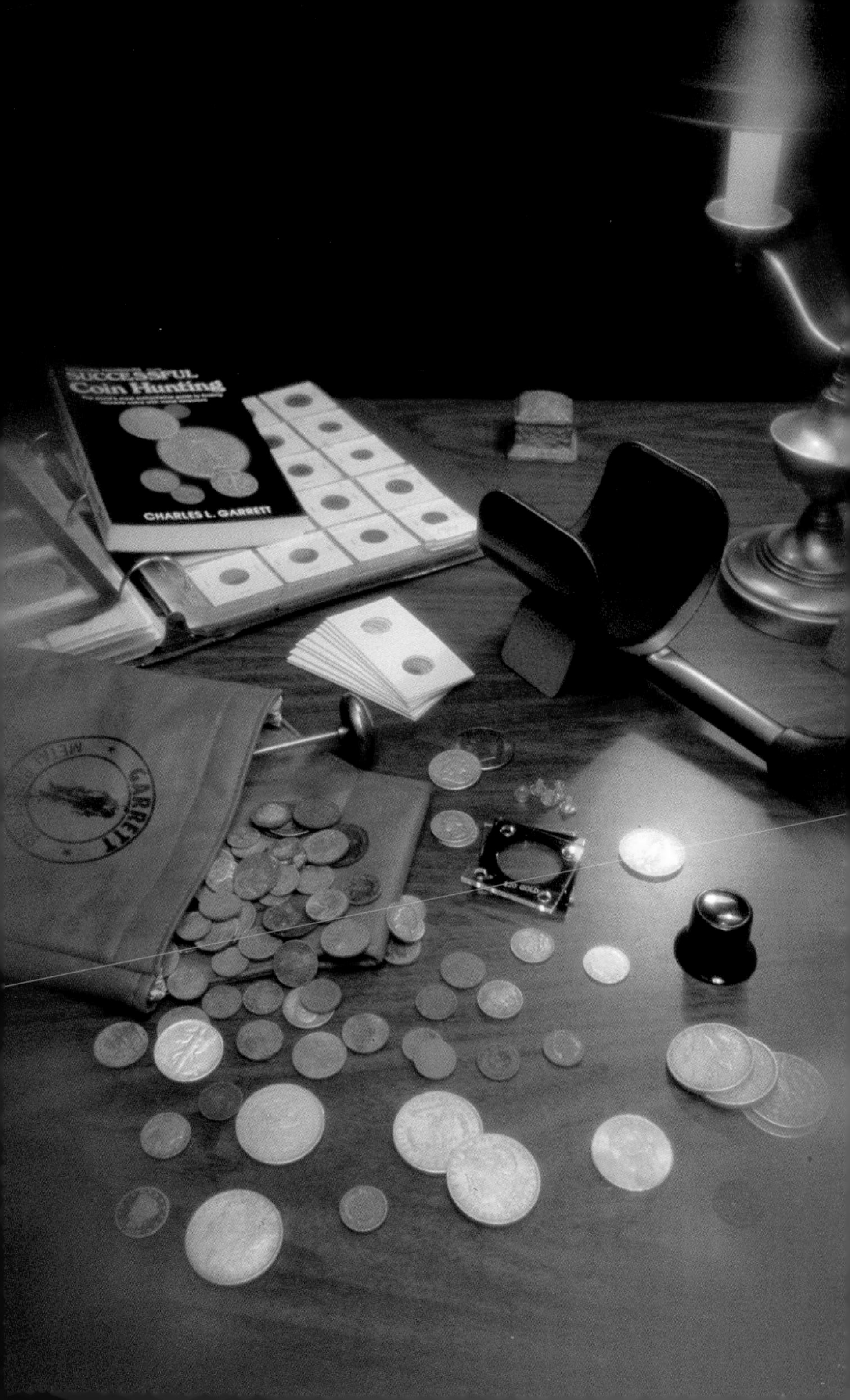
SUCCESSFUL
Coin Hunting
CHARLES L. GARRETT
GARRETT

When the items detected in a smaller area of ground are considered by the intricate circuitry of the CX II, your detector's built-in computer can do a much better job of analyzing individual targets, letting you pick out the good coins amongst the junk trash. Try this small searchcoil! You'll be convinced after only a short time of its great value.

Dual Discrimination

The Grand Master Hunter CX II and Master Hunter CX feature a new and innovative dual discrimination system that is unique with Garrett. It offers both a ferrous target range and a non-ferrous range to provide multiple selectivity and the ability to reject and accept targets in both the ferrous — iron, or course — and non-ferrous ranges. These controls can be found on the extreme left of the side control panel.

The two controls split the full range of discrimination between ferrous and non-ferrous. Detection of iron objects such as nails, some foil, iron bottlecaps and small pieces of junk is controlled by the left knob. The control on the right governs discrimination of such non-ferrous items as aluminum pulltabs and aluminum screwtops.

Each of these controls operates independently of the other. The setting of one has no effect whatsoever on the other control. If you wish to detect all ferrous materials, rotate the left control fully counterclockwise. As you advance it back to the right to higher numbers, you will reject more and more ferrous materials. The control operates cumulatively; that is, if you have it set at bottlecap rejection (about 2), most nails and some foil will be rejected

Although having universal capabilities, Garrett's Ultra GTA detectors were designed primarily as coin hunting instruments, and discoveries made with them are impressive.

along with bottlecaps. We urge that you advance this control *no farther clockwise* than necessary to eliminate the troublesome ferrous junk material in the ground you are searching.

Operate your non-ferrous control in the same manner. When it is turned fully to the left, few of the non-ferrous materials will be rejected. To eliminate, say, pulltabs, rotate the control clockwise to approximately 5 or the Initial Setting (>). Keep in mind, however, that there seem to be as many different kind of pulltabs as there are bottling companies. Some few pulltabs, especially those that are bent or broken, seem to be acceptable to any detector at any setting. Set your controls for those you are finding just in the area where you are hunting.

Here's how to set these dual discrimination controls precisely. Collect examples of that junk you want to reject—a nail, bottlecap, pulltab and, perhaps, small pieces of iron trash. Place your Grand Master Hunter on a non-metallic, preferably wooden, surface with the searchcoil at least three feet away from all metal. Make certain you are wearing no rings or jewelry on your hands or arms that could be detected. Rotate the two control knobs fully counterclockwise to their lowest settings. Turn the detector on and listen for the beep that tells you it is ready to operate. Adjust your audio for minimal threshold sound.

Pass the iron bottlecap across the bottom of your searchcoil about two inches away from it. Your detector will probably make a signal. Rotate the ferrous control to the approximate bottlecap reject position (Initial Setting) and pass the cap across the searchcoil's bottom again. You should hear nothing more than, perhaps, a slight blip. You may be able to rotate the control counterclockwise back to a lower number and still not detect the bottlecap. Practice so that you can set your control as far to the left as possible because you always want to use the lowest setting that is absolutely necessary.

Using the same technique, adjust the non-ferrous control just far enough clockwise that you do not detect the aluminum pulltab. This should be between 4 and 5 at the Pulltab setting. Advance the control as needed from here to eliminate those pulltabs you are finding. Again, let me stress that you should rotate these controls no higher than necessary to reject the junk items in the ground where you are searching.

Dual discrimination controls such as those on your Grand Master Hunter CX II, Master Hunter CX and other Garrett detectors offer a greater dynamic adjustment range than single controls. You have more resolution which allows you to set the controls precisely to reject specific junk targets. A most important feature is that you can reject most aluminum pulltabs while accepting the majority of gold and silver rings. When searching for rings on a pulltab-infested area such as a beach, set your non-ferrous control no farther clockwise than necessary to eliminate most of the pulltabs. Rings with a higher conductivity and — especially — mass than pulltabs will be accepted.

Remember, however, that some rings will fall into the lower, or ferrous, range. Thus, Garrett's dual discrimination lets you select rings that register both "above" and "below" pulltab rejection. So, don't advance either control any farther clockwise than you absolutely must.

There is another important reason for setting your discrimination controls conservatively. When a modern detector detects a junk target that you have asked it to discriminates against, it cancels out this junk target with a negative audio response that you normally cannot even hear. As you know, however, good targets generate a positive response which you *love* to hear.

If both positive and negative targets are beneath your searchcoil simultaneously, the two responses tend to cancel one another, and you may miss a good find. Of course, the situation is rarely this simple. Depth of targets, their metallic content, size and many other factors must be considered. So, simply remember this: never use more discrimination than you absolutely need.

The Grand Master Hunter CX II and Ultra GTA 1000 are equipped with three different audible methods for signaling detection of acceptable targets. These are determined by pressing one of the three touchpads on the extreme right of the side panel of the CX II or by using the **SELECT** touchpad of the GTA 1000.

If the **BELLTONE** sound is selected, the Grand Master Hunter and GTA 1000 will signal an acceptable target in the ferrous range with an increase in its audio volume. When it detects a coin or other highly conductive non-ferrous target, you hear the exclusive Garrett Belltone™, *The Sound of Money!* These different audio responses were designed to help you determine what kind of target you've discovered before you dig. Occasionally a ring will generate the Belltone, but they usually respond with an increase in volume. Because any metal with high conductivity can generate the Belltone, that sound doesn't necessarily mean you've found a coin. While it is true that just about any United States coin will generate a Belltone, it can also result from detection of some other object composed of such high conductivity metal as brass, copper or aluminum.

Press the **STANDARD** touchpad, (or rotate to it with the **SELECT** touchpad) and all accepted targets will produce the same audible response.

When you choose the **BI-LEVEL** setting, your CX II or GTA 1000 will signal targets accepted in the non-ferrous range with an increase in audible sound. Those targets accepted in the ferrous range will be identified with a sound pitched slightly lower.

Whenever either detector is turned off, its memory will retain the audio setting that has been selected, and it will return to this same audio mode whenever it is turned on again.

All Metal Mode

When hunting in this mode with either detector, your instrument will report finding all metals with no discrimination. It also detects to the greatest depths possible. This mode is used extensively by cache and relic hunters and by prospectors. Of course, it can be used by coin hunters or anyone who seeks extreme depth and is willing to forego discrimination — except for *metered discrimination which is discussed elsewhere in this book.*

To activate the All Metal Mode on a Grand Master Hunter, press the touchpad marked **ALL METAL.** An audible tone will indicate that the instrument has responded to your command. *Fast Track* ground balancing is accomplished in this mode by pressing and holding the **ALL METAL** touchpad while scanning the searchcoil for only a few seconds in a normal manner. Release the touchpad, and *Ground Track* will continue to track ground minerals continuously and make necessary precise adjustments simultaneously as they are required by changing ground conditions.

On the GTA 1000 use the **SELECT** touchpad to rotate to the *Mode* selection and use the $+$ and $-$ touchpads to choose the *All Metal* setting. The GTA 500 in its *A Mode* offers discrimination set at the factory for an All Metal mode.

If you find while searching in the All Metal mode that movement of the searchcoil over the ground causes a noticeable increase or decrease in the sound coming from your Grand Master Hunter CX II or Master Hunter CX, you may readjust the ground balance of the detector by pressing and holding the **ALL METAL/FAST TRACK** touchpad while moving the searchcoil from side to side three or four times about one to three inches from the ground. When the sound becomes constant again, release the pad and your ground balancing is completed.

Under unusual conditions, if your audio signal continues to increase or decrease to any degree, more precise manual ground balancing is possible on the CX II and the CX. You can make this adjustment using the plus + and minus — touchpads below the GB under the Secondary Functions heading on the side panel controls of the CX II and by using the + and — pads on the console of the CX.

Remember that you must press and hold the **ALL METAL** touchpad to make these manual ground balancing adjustments on either detector.

Ground balancing of GTA detectors is preset at the factory.

On those rare occasions when you determine that manual ground balancing is necessary while you are coin hunting with the Grand Master Hunter CX II or Master Hunter CX, follow these instructions. Raise and lower your searchcoil and listen closely to the audio signal. If the audio signal grows louder, press the touchpad marked minus (—) several times. You will notice the meter pointer move down slightly with each touch. Lift your searchcoil again and lower it to operating height.If the sound level now decreases, you have made too great a negative adjustment. Press the touchpad marked plus (+) a few times.

Repeat these procedures until the audio does not change or changes only slightly when the searchcoil is lowered to operating height.

Notice that as you continue pressing down either the plus or minus touchpad, your meter indicator shows that you are moving up and down the scale rather quickly. This feature of the Grand Master Hunter CX II greatly speeds up precise ground balancing. When searching extremely mineralized ground, we recommend that you operate the searchcoil two inches or more above the ground. You will not lose depth, but will actually detect deeper because ground mineral influence is greatly reduced.

Caches, Ghost Towns And Relics

The three types of treasure hunting discussed in this chapter are somewhat related. When engaged in any one of these three types of searching, you can suddenly find yourself deep into one of the other two phases. This is especially true in exploring ghost towns, where both caches and relics abound. Of course, the metal detecting techniques you have already learned will apply to these more specialized phases of treasure hunting. This chapter is designed to introduce you to new ideas that will prove useful when looking for any one of these three types of hidden wealth.

Cache Hunting

Looking for money caches means searching for a large quantity of buried treasure. Your cache can be an iron kettle filled with gold or silver coins. It can be a cache of gold or silver bars or even guns. When cache hunting, you are generally looking for objects much larger than single coins...though smaller money caches in tobacco cans are sometimes found in old buildings.

Techniques necessary for successful cache hunting differ somewhat from those used by coin hunters. In searching for coins, you generally used the Discriminate mode with occasional ventures into All Metal. For cache hunting, we suggest the opposite. In fact, to find caches most effectively, we recommend that you use the All Metal mode almost exclusively. In this mode the electromagnetic field of your detector will penetrate even an iron pot to detect the coins concealed inside.

In such a situation your instrument is actually signaling to you about the big pot, not all those coins inside it. If you were scanning with the Discriminate mode, the detector might reject the iron pot, and you'd never dig it. What a disaster! Use the All Metal mode, but remember what you've learned earlier and so many other times: If you seek *real* success, you must be prepared to dig lots of junk!

Unless you're searching for a cache in a building — where you know that it cannot possibly be too far away — always use the largest searchcoil possible. Remember that larger searchcoils can detect larger objects and detect them at greater depths. Money caches have been found at all depths (arm's length seems to be popular), but you want to be prepared for extremes. In some areas, where washing has occurred and drainage patterns have redesigned the landscape, caches have been found that were covered far more deeply than when they were originally buried.

All the more reason to use the larger searchcoils — even the Depth Multiplier Bloodhound!

When searching a farmyard for a money cache, look closely at specific objects and obstacles in that yard, such as a well, the corners of the farmhouse and its chimney. Search inside the chimney and all outbuildings...especially those that contained animals.

Never fail to search an old garden area. Here's where the farmer's wife may have hidden some "rainy day" savings in a fruit jar. Remember that when people buried caches, they didn't want to be observed. It would be quite normal for a farm wife to hide a jar of money in her apron, carry it to the farthest part of the garden and "plant" it secretly.

When you are using the 12 1/2-inch searchcoil, and certainly the 8 1/2-inch size, these coils will detect objects far smaller than caches.

296

Therefore...expect some junk! When you suspect that the cache you are seeking is larger than a small fruit jar, we recommend that you use the Depth Multiplier, called the Bloodhound. This attachment multiplies by several times the depth detecting capability of any detector with which it is compatible. An important feature of the Depth Multiplier is that it will not detect small objects. In an old farmyard you won't ever be bothered by trash certain to be littering the soil, which will permit you to dig only larger targets.

It's easy to use the Depth Multiplier attachment with a compatible detector. Just get into a basic All Metal mode and forget about trying to adjust your ground balance. Wear headphones and set your audio threshold for faint sound. Be sure you aren't carrying a large metal object such as a shovel or large knife even though a few coins in your pocket may not matter. Hold the detector and fully extend your arm. Let the detector cradle in your fingers. Slowly walk across the area you wish to search.

Listen carefully for an increase in the audio level. When you hear the louder sound, stop and scratch a mark on the ground with your shoe. Continue walking without adjusting any of the detector's controls. When you have walked across the object you have just detected, the audio will return to its threshold level. Walk a few more feet before turning around and walking a return path. At the point where the audio increases as you are walking from this direction, make another mark on the ground. Your target will lie at the center point between your two marks on the ground.

Successful searching for caches requires considerable experience...and thinking. You must learn to put yourself right in the shoes of the person who hid that cache for which you are searching. You can understand why no person would just run out into his yard haphazardly and dig a hole to bury a jar full of gold coins. No, siree! If you were burying a cache, you'd select a secret place and a secret time to bury it...perhaps, at night during a thunderstorm. And, your "secret place" would be one that you could find in a hurry!

Practice this yourself. Put some money (or something similar) in a mason jar. Go outside your house and bury it.

Would you do it in broad daylight? Would you just walk out into the yard and start digging? Probably not, because you wouldn't want anyone to see what you were doing. So, choose the right time and the right place to bury your cache. After you've done this, you'll be able to ask yourself the questions that should have come to that person who hid the cache you are seeking. Can I find it quickly? Could it be discovered accidentally? Will it be safe? Many other questions will come into your mind as you recover your own cache and relocate it a time or two. This is good experience. Believe me when I tell you that doing this will make you a better cache hunter.

Be especially careful not to hurry when searching for money caches. Scan your searchcoil very slowly and walk slowly with the Depth Multiplier. Do not be in a hurry, for that may cheat you out of a valuable find.

When searching for a money cache behind or inside a wall in a house, use either the All Metal or Discriminate mode. But, even when using the Discriminate mode, we recommend that you turn the discrimination controls to their lowest settings...just enough discrimination to eliminate nails from detection.

In either mode you'll have more than enough sensitivity to detect almost any size money cache in all walls, despite their thickness or type of construction.

When your treasure map leads you to a stucco wall containing a wire mesh, here are some tips to help you detect through that mesh. Place your searchcoil against the wall, set your detector in its Discriminate mode and rotate the discrimination control(s) to the lowest setting. By carefully sliding the searchcoil across the wall you can lessen interference from the mesh. You may hear a jumbled mass of sound, but you should always listen for significant changes that could indicate you have located your cache.

Some prefer to search walls with a mesh by holding the searchcoil several inches or even a foot away from the wall.

Getting the searchcoil this far away should take care of the jumbled sound, yet still let your detector detect large masses of metal such as a money cache.

These are just a few of the tricks that can help you become proficient in searching for and discovering caches.

You can learn more from the *Garrett Guide: Money Caches Are Waiting to be Found.* Of course, there are many other techniques, and you'll doubtlessly develop a few of them yourself. We could describe these at length, but that's not the purpose of this book. It is intended to be your basic introduction to achieving the most from any metal detector. We want to give you the basics to start out right. Then, it will be your challenge to master your instrument fully, just as you master a new camera or automobile.

Relic Hunting/Battlefield Searching

Searching battlefield and other areas for lost relics is not considerably different from cache hunting. Perhaps one difference is that the targets you are seeking are usually quite smaller, such as a single button or spent projectile.

Techniques of scanning and locating, however, remain the same.

What size searchcoil should you use? You may be thinking that if you seek a small bullet, you shouldn't use the large 12 1/2-inch searchcoil. Wrong! The large searchcoil will detect almost any tiny projectile, button or coin that you might find in an old battlefield. Because you will need all the depth possible when searching battlefields, especially when the battles were fought years ago, we urge you to use the 12 1/2-inch searchcoil. If, even with a light and easy-to-handle detector, you find this large coil too heavy for a full day's scanning, use an arm rest. This accessory provides counter-balance for the detector and enables you to use your instrument with less muscle fatigue.

We recommend that you operate in the All Metal mode for greatest depth. Precise ground balancing circuitry on modern detectors, such as *Fast Track* on the Grand Master Hunter CX II and Master Hunter CX will solve all your mineralization problems. Of course, large amounts of trash in the ground may cause you to think still further. If you're really not concerned about losing just an occasional target, operate in the Discriminate mode – but, with only a slight amount of discrimination dialed by your controls. You'll miss small iron objects (including trash!), but will detect other objects such as lead, brass, bronze and, of course, coins to great depth.

Now, most professional relic hunters would be aghast at reading that last statement. They use absolutely NO discrimination. Here's one reason why: If a valuable coin is lying right next to an iron object and you are using discrimination, the iron object may cancel out the coin, causing you to miss it.

In relic hunting and battlefield searching, it is of the utmost importance that your detector be precisely ground balanced. As you have learned, *Fast Track* circuitry makes this an easy matter with the CX II and CX. Even when extreme mineralization causes an excessive amount of audio change, you can use the manual controls to ground balance the instrument as precisely as you wish. When you do this, you'll know that signals you receive from your detector come from targets and not from ground mineralization.

You perceptive treasure hunters already know what comes next, but I'll repeat, anyway: For maximum depth and sensitivity, use headphones and set your audio controls for the faintest threshold you can hear. This advice has been proven worthwhile over the years.

As the following advice...scan slowly. Your goal will be to cover an area methodically, completely and thoroughly. Grid search an area if you can by tying lengths of ropes to create grid squares and carefully searching each square before moving on to the next.

Another seemingly obvious tip is to double-check your hole always...no matter what kind of target you uncover. Just because you've dug up one relic doesn't mean that there can't be another in the exact spot! Of course, you should always double check every hole no matter what kind of hunting you are engaged in. If, for example, you're seeking large objects with the Depth Multiplier, always check your holes with a smaller searchcoil (or pocket scanner) to make certain that no smaller valuables are hiding in them...or that some other target isn't buried just an inch or two deeper.

Because any battlefield might contain explosives, take all necessary precautions. Any time you dig into an object and you suspect it might be an explosive, consult an authority...quickly! Remember that many guns are lost while still loaded and that even old guns that have been in the ground a number of years can still be fired. Don't get into arguments with explosives of any kind. It might prove dangerous to your health!

A military historian recently told me the story of how he owed his life to a Garrett detector. While scanning in Korea, he often found remains of Chinese soldiers still bearing live hand grenades. The advance warning provided by his Garrett permitted him to call in a bomb squad to dispose of the explosives.

The same need for precaution holds true for underground power cables. If you're detecting to great depths with the Bloodhound, you might occasionally find an underground cable.

Stop digging immediately! Contact the appropriate authorities, and inform them fully so that they can inspect your site and cover it properly.

Searching Ghost Towns

Hunting in and around ghost towns...ghost towning, we sometimes call it...is quite similar to general treasure hunting. When searching ghost towns, you may one day be scanning over a field that contains only a few relics. Then, the next day, you might encounter an entire town; that is, structures still intact with buildings and rooms in them just as they were when people—for some reason—left, perhaps decades ago.

To search ghost towns properly you must learn the techniques of scanning both ground areas and structures of all kinds. Remember that incredible treasure caches have been located in walls, floors and ceilings.

When you're searching a building, also keep in mind that most wooden structures contain a truly countless number of nails.

You can expect your metal detector to respond with multiple target signals. Of course, you don't want to tear into a wall just to locate a nail. We recommend, therefore, that you search in the Discriminate mode, using only enough discrimination dialed in to reject troublesome small nails.

You'll not be likely to overlook a large money cache!

When scanning around window and door frames, be alert for signals you receive from the iron sashes used to suspend the window frames. Don't rip open a wall looking for treasure until you have exhausted all techniques for peering into that wall by other means. Most wall areas can be visually inspected simply by pulling slightly back on a single board and shining a flashlight into the cavity. Never tear down or otherwise destroy old buildings. In fact, you should let all structures remain just as you found them...without harm or defacement of any kind. Walk away leaving all ghost town sites in such condition that no one can really tell whether you found treasure there or not.

Brick chimneys are familiar occurrences in many ghost towns, and treasures have been found behind their loose bricks. Remember, however, that most bricks are made of highly mineralized clay with iron in the conductive soil from which they were baked. Is this an impossible problem? Not for the detectors like the CX II and CX with their unique *Fast Track* system of ground balancing. Simply use *Fast Track* or the ground balancing circuitry on your detector to ground balance it against a chimney as you would against the ground. Most likely you'll find no chimney stones or bricks that you cannot properly ground balance. Be alert, of course, to nearby metal or pipes within the chimney. You cannot ground balance your detector if metal is too close.

Ghost towns will present you with a seemingly endless amount of junk iron of all shapes and sizes. If you are looking for coins, brass objects or other similar targets, therefore, use the Discriminate mode and dial in a small amount of discrimination. It would take weeks or months — perhaps, even years — to dig every target to be found in a ghost town. This makes discrimination mandatory. But, let me urge that you employ all techniques we have already considered...the Super Sniper searchcoil, minimum discrimination, slow scanning, careful study of questionable targets, etc.

When looking for money caches, use a larger searchcoil or the Depth Multiplier. All ghost towns had a trash dump, and these sources of potential prizes can be located quite easily through methodical use of a Depth Multiplier.

All the junk you are certain to find makes it mandatory that you develop techniques for properly identifying targets before you dig. Rely heavily on your detector's meter or visual target display to do this for you. And, remember how your detector identifies targets both audibly and visually. Especially when searching ghost towns should you pay close attention to both audio and ID meter/graphic readout signals. Try to correlate the audible and visual signals before making a decision on digging a specific target.

If available on your detector, the Belltone mode of sound will be helpful here because most iron objects will then simply increase your sound level while objects of conductive metal such as coins and objects of brass and bronze will respond with the distinctive Belltone.

Simply hearing a signal will often let you know in which range your target falls. Always inspect the meter to see if it agrees with the audio, which will usually be the case. There will be times, however, when only a faint blip might cause you to suspect a target should be rejected, yet your meter indicates it to made of metal with high conductivity. Dig to determine if the target is junk such as a large stove lid or something that has simply overridden the electromagnetic field of the searchcoil.

In areas with lots of junk targets your audio may sound often with blips and other sharp signals as well as an occasional coin tone. If using one of the new computerized instruments, remember that your detector is hunting deeper than other detectors. Consequently, it will give you more signals over a given spot of ground than another instrument that is not detecting as deeply. You have several options that will cut down on these sounds. First, you can reduce detection depth to 50% or below and still probably have sufficient depth for most targets in a ghost town. Also, you can reduce threshold to silent to reduce spurious signals. Try various combinations of adjustments such as these to achieve optimum audio for any difficult ground you encounter.

Do your research homework to locate lost and forgotten ghost towns. Find them, and then search thoroughly. It will pay financial dividends as well as enable you to relive history.

This religious relic discovered with a metal detector by California treasure hunter George Mroczkowski is typical of the excitement that can lie in store for hobbyists.

Gold Hunting

Gold can be found!

Just as I began final editing of this chapter for the First Edition I received a letter from an electronic prospector who, during the past summer, had found one hundred nineteen (119) ounces of gold! One nugget alone weighed in at a whopping ninety-one (91) ounces! He and his partner found the gold in a well-known gold area of the United States.

Such letters, accompanied by photographs, often come to me from electronic prospectors who have found gold. The value of the gold being discovered with metal detectors, that I am aware of, totals in the tens of millions of dollars. The people who write are bubbling over with joy as they share their "sudden wealth" stories with me.

Gold and silver is being found *right now* with metal detectors. Sure, you don't just run out, turn on your detector and start finding gold. If that's the way it worked, I'd have never even written that First Edition. Instead, I'd have just headed out with MY metal detector (which I do a great deal of the time, anyway).

I have found gold and silver with my metal detectors...just about every time that I have gone electronic prospecting. Sometimes I have found only a small amount...sometimes, I have found several thousand dol-

The old U. S. Cavalry post in West Texas, above, is an ideal place to search for all types of treasure such as relics, gold nuggets or the cache of coins shown at bottom.

lars worth. Searching for precious metals with an electronic detector is profitable, but it takes time, energy and patience. You can find your share of gold, silver, platinum and copper if you will put forth the effort. Precious metals can be found!

Many people claim that gold cannot be found with a metal detector. These people believe, erroneously, that since you cannot attract gold with a magnet, a metal detector cannot detect gold! A magnet will not attract gold simply because gold is non-ferrous. Magnets attract only ferrous (iron) objects. When a magnetic field penetrates iron, the molecular structure becomes polarized in such a way that the iron is attracted to the magnet. This polarization does not occur in gold, nor do metal detectors work on the attraction principle (see Chapter 3). Some people do not believe that gold can be found because they have tested their instrument with gold *dust* and failed to detect it. Certainly, extremely fine gold cannot be detected because it presents insufficient surface areas for electrical (eddy) currents to flow.

This chapter discusses gold hunting (electronic prospecting) primarily through the use of modern metal detectors with precise, manually adjustable ground balance controls. Other older detectors have been used successfully in many forms of electronic prospecting, but in all situations the modern, computerized detector is greatly superior.

If you are interested in prospecting, I recommend you obtain a copy of the Ram book, *Modern Electronic Prospecting,* a complete guide to finding gold by using all types of detectors. Also, you should view Garrett Electronics' video presentation, "Weekend Prospecting" and read Roy Lagal's book by the same name. These will guide you in the various forms of gold hunting. (Look for the book order form and video listings at the end of this book.)

Nugget Hunting

Nugget hunting is the most popular form of electronic prospecting and offers immediate rewards when you are searching the proper areas. Look for nuggets where they have previously been found. That is the key!

If you are a good coin hunter, you already know how to search for nuggets. Use the same techniques. Only use them in gold country instead of in the park or schoolyard. Novice electronic prospectors are often concerned about *all* the signals they expect to receive from trash while operating in the All Metal mode. We urge that you rely heavily on the target identification meter or visual readout of your detector to help you identify *any* detected target.

We recommend that you use the 8 1/2-inch searchcoil or the 4 1/2-inch Super Sniper when searching for nuggets. Of course, the 12 1/2-inch searchcoil can be used because it will certainly find small nuggets. Whether you use it or not depends on the area and upon the types of nuggets that have been found there.

Nuggets at extreme depths, for instance, may require the large searchcoil.

Headphones are an absolute must in nugget hunting. Because of their extremely small size, many nuggets produce only faint audio signals,

The most troublesome aspect of searching for nuggets — depending upon your search area, of course — is the detection of junk and mineralized pebbles... known as *hot rocks.* These mineralized pebbles are really just geologic freaks. Because they are "mislocated" for one reason or another, no ground balancing circuitry can ever be set for them. Therefore, they produce an audio signal just like a metal target. Since we do not recommend the use of discrimination while searching, you should learn other techniques for determining if you have detected a possible nugget or just some type of iron ore.

First of all, be prepared to dig some trash metal. You'll be working, most likely, in or near old mining camps where

309

countless pieces of junk iron were discarded. Just imagine how many boot nails may have been lost here! Unfortunately, boot nails all too often sound just like a good target. Luckily, boot nails are usually shallow, and you can spot them rather easily once you learn how.

Another way to determine quickly if you've detected an iron object is to carry along a strong magnet. At your point of detection, rub this magnet in the dirt. Lift up the magnet and your target will be stuck to it if it is, indeed, iron.

Several good digging tools and rakes are available that contain a strong magnet in the end of the handle for quick recovery of iron objects.

Be sure to carry a pouch with you to carry out all detected objects. Other hobbyists will follow, and there is no need for them to encounter your trash. Who knows? You may search the area again, and you certainly don't want to have to bother with the same junk targets.

Use those techniques you have mastered while coin hunting with the CX, CX II or GTA detectors. Yes, I said *coin hunting!* Coin and gold nugget hunting, you see, are nearly identical. Adjust your audio for faint sound. Use a good set of high quality headphones. Scan slowly and methodically to cover all areas of the ground. Be certain to move large boulders aside so that you can scan under them.

Scan up against brush and other obstacles. If you find the ground extremely uneven and cannot maintain a constant searchcoil height, you'll probably encounter problems with mineralization, especially when it is so extreme that manual ground balancing is necessary. If so, simply elevate your searchcoil a few inches, make certain that your detector is ground balance precisely and continue scanning. You will not lose depth. In fact, because of the better quality of your audio, you may even detect nuggets more deeply and more accurately.

If the area you are searching is so littered with iron junk that it is really troublesome, experiment with small amounts of discrimination. Dig quite a few targets you detect at zero discrimination and study what you have found. Then use the discrimination techniques discussed earlier in this manual, but advance your controls no farther clockwise than necessary to reject the most troublesome of your pests. True, you may lose a nugget. Your choice may be to chance this rather than digging hundreds and hundreds of worthless nails. Who knows...the time that you save by not digging this junk may let you search that extra bit of ground where a real beauty of a nugget awaits you.

Others of you will continue to dig *everything* that signals. You don't want to miss even the tiniest sub-gram nugget.

Author, foreground, and Roy Lagal use modern Garrett detectors to look for veins of precious metal that might have been overlooked by the pioneers who originally worked this Idaho mine.

311

There are vast areas in the world where nuggets can be found with a detector and there are numerous ways of finding potential hot spots, including word of mouth, study of governmental records and early-day histories of mining camps, as well as other sources. You need to learn where nuggets have been found previously. For instance, in Northern California there are numerous areas where early-day miners located gold nuggets by sight. The nuggets simply lay on the ground! When you find areas such as this, go to work with your detector! Incidentally, many of those early-day nuggets, especially the larger ones, are on display in some Northern California and Oregon banks.

In Australia, Peter Bridge of P.O. Box 317, Victoria Park 6100, Western Australia did a study of governmental records dating back to about 1850. These published reports gave the size, depth and location of all reported gold nuggets found. In analyzing these records, he came to the astonishing realization that a large percentage of the nuggets were at such shallow depths they could have been found easily with a detector. If, he reasoned, miners found tremendous quantities of gold simply by visual search, just imagine the multiplied quantities of gold that must be within range of a good detector! The research information coupled with Peter's determination to select the right detectors to find this gold led to the modern-day gold rush that began in Australia in the late 1970s.

No one can tell you where all the world's gold-bearing regions are located. Even if they knew, they wouldn't tell you. They'd go find all the gold for themselves. To achieve success, you must carry out research. This same reasoning, of course, holds true in any form of detecting. Whether it be cache hunting or looking for coins, you must do your research to find the best places to go searching.

Gold nuggets found in water will usually be rounded, but occasionally flattened nuggets are found. Rounded nuggets are more difficult to detect. The more surface area of the metal that is facing toward the bottom of the searchcoil, the stronger will be the signal. The rounded covering of most nuggets reduces the amount of flat surface that is "looking" at a detector's searchcoil, thus reducing the chances of detection.

Gold nuggets ranging from pinhead size to nuggets weighing nearly one thousand ounces, have been found with metal detectors. There are various techniques to learn in order to become efficient in gold nugget hunting, but these can be acquired through study and field work.

Incidentally, the largest reported gold nugget found in the United States weighed 161 pounds. The largest reported gold nugget found in the world, was found in Australia. It weighed 248 pounds.

There is no magic to locating nuggets! Believe me. Finding them just requires patient application of all the skills you have learned with your detector. Nugget hunters are successful because they are willing to work hard and hunt for long hours in areas where nuggets can be found. Try it. It will pay you dividends!

Vein Locating (Mine Searching)

Locating veins actually uses the same techniques of scanning that you learned in nugget hunting. You are, in most cases, simply scanning vertical or elevated wall surfaces. Use the larger size coils, such as the 12 1/2-inch Crossfire.

Make certain that your detector is ground balanced precisely. You can accomplish this either with automatic circuitry or manually. You will want to balance it against mineralization in a the wall and methodically scan your searchcoil over that wall, carefully covering all its area. If the surface of the wall you are scanning is uneven (as it will be in most mines), you may have to hold your searchcoil as much as a foot away from it to smooth out the irregularities caused by mineral disturbances. Regardless, any object that causes an increase in the audio level should be investigated immediately.

313

When you study additional books such as *Modern Electronic Prospecting* or *Weekend Prospecting,* you will learn how conductive metals such as gold, silver and copper can be easily detected. Often, however, iron minerals of some sort are associated with these conductive metals. More likely than not, the iron content enhances detection, enabling you to locate the vein more easily and from a greater distance than if it did not contain any iron!

All news of iron isn't pleasant when broadcast by your detector. Occasionally you will find that your signal came from an iron spike, nail or candle holder embedded in a wall. This object might prove to be a welcome addition to your collection of relics.

Above all, observe all safety precautions when entering mines; in fact, never enter a mine alone. And, never enter a mine whose shoring appears to be rotted or otherwise unsafe.

Cave-ins and poisonous gases are an ever present threat once you get inside a mine. It is best to avoid such dangers by entering mines only in the company of an expert.

To learn more about mine searching—as well as all other areas of electronic prospecting—let me strongly urge that you read the two books mentioned previously. Roy Lagal, who wrote *Weekend Prospecting* and joined with me to produce *Modern Electronic Prospecting* has spent a lifetime searching mines for veins and ore-bearing deposits. He can tell you far more about them this subject than is possible in the limited space of this manual.

One final note...you can use the Depth Multiplier when searching for veins in mines. It is most likely, however, that the 12 1/2-inch searchcoil will provide all the power you require for whatever detection depth is necessary.

For centuries miners have worked unknowingly to bring precious metal ore veins to within range of modern metal detectors. Countless miles of tunnels have narrowly missed rich ore, now hidden from eyesight behind tunnel walls by only inches...or even fractions of an inch. The electronic prospector, through patient searching, can find these mines where such tunnels are present. A thorough scan with a modern detector will discover these over-looked veins.

In Mexico, I located two silver veins and one pocket, in an old Spanish mine. The pocket and one vein were small, but the second vein turned out to be large. At eye level my detector gave an obvious audio indication. My friend, Javier Castellanos, owner of the mine lease, placed a stick of dynamite at the location, and lit the fuse. We heard a deafening sound as we waited at the mine entrance. A short while later, after the dust had settled, we returned to the location. A large chunk of rock had been blown out of the wall. We saw a one-half-inch wide native silver vein shining in the dim light of our carbide lamps. A beautiful sight it was! As we hacked away this wall, following the vein as it snaked downward, the vein grew larger. When, finally, we reached floor level, the vein of silver was one foot wide.

Searching Mine Dumps/Tailings

You can locate mine dumps in all shapes and sizes and in varying conditions. Each one probably contains *some* material of value. Essentially, a mine dump is nothing more than a storage, waste or holding area for rocks that have been removed from a mine. They can be small piles or huge mountains of rock. Most mine dumps were meant to contain waste, the rock that surrounded ore material destined for the crusher. Many times, however, miners unknowingly discarded precious ore. The use of a metal detector offers the only practical means of discovering the ore. The naked eye is useless for such a task, but the probing electromagnetic field of the Grand Master Hunter's deepseeking circuitry can look within rocks to find those that are valuable.

How do you search mine dumps? One method is to conduct general scanning over a large area of rock surface. The second is to select a specific spot and test likely looking rock specimens from that area.

When scanning mine waste, remember what lies beneath you...a jumbled mass of rocks that have been removed from their natural geological locations and thrown together. Perhaps each rock contains a different amount of iron mineral. Because the proper modern metal detector will analyze all conductive matter beneath its searchcoil at any time, it will have difficulty with such non-uniform minerals. Your challenge will lie in proper ground balancing, but there are tricks we will recommend.

First of all, let your instrument's circuitry ground balance your detector automatically before you scan any immediate area of rocks. If your audio changes significantly, watch your meter and try to determine an "average" reading. Then, use manual controls for more precise ground balance at your "average" reading. If that fails, either switch to a larger searchcoil or scan with the searchcoil held a greater distance away from the rocks. Try all of these techniques, even reducing your audio down to silent to cut down the chattering effect of this mass of uneven minerals.

Use your All Metal mode and scan as you normally would for metal objects. Wear headphones and scan methodically. Be thorough in analyzing each signal from your detector. It could come from a manmade object or a piece of gold or silver ore. Be careful not to lose your specimen, especially in a pile of loose rock. When digging for the object that caused a signal, you could dislodge it to fall farther down into the pile. Your recovery then becomes more difficult, if not impossible.

Use a plastic gold pan. When you get a signal, rake the top layers of rock into your pan, then scan the pan to see if you have recovered that object causing the signal. If it is still in the pile, discard those rocks in the pan and keep trying until you know exactly what caused the signal from your detector. Using the gold pan, you will stand a better chance of not losing your target, and you will probably recover it more quickly.

When scanning in the All Metal mode, listen for even the faintest signal through headphones. This is important because it takes only a little gold to make a valuable ore specimen. After you have searched an area and received no signals, shovel away a layer of rocks and continue searching. By removing this top layer you are placing your detector's searchcoil closer to possible paydirt.

No one specific location — the top, sides or lower levels — in a mine dump can be said to be consistently better as a place to recover nuggets and/or ore. As you gain experience and train yourself to analyze rock and rock structures, you will be able to pick out the best locations more easily. Remember that the early day miners did little more than follow a vein into a mountain. They piled the associated rock in a cart and dumped it. Careful study will indicate the type rocks that require scanning.

When you find some of these rocks together, lay your detector flat on the ground away from any metal and conduct a little in-the-field bench testing. Switch to your Discriminate mode. Make certain that discrimination controls are at their lowest settings. Pick up individual rocks and bring each quickly to the center of the searchcoil's bottom. Bring them in and back out immediately. Do not scan across. If any rock causes a signal increase, keep that specimen for further study.

Another way to sample ore specimens is to press the appropriate ground balance manual override controls until your detector's meter pointer is aligned with its Ore Test calibration point.

This test point has been precisely calibrated at the factory to enable you to test ore samples properly. Evaluate rocks using this method just as you did in the Discriminate mode — if a sample causes a signal increase, save it for study; if the signal decreases, discard the rock.

Once again, use caution in digging and climbing, especially on steep piles. You could easily create a rock slide and injure yourself and others.

Do not expect to sample ore properly unless you use a modern detector that is factory calibrated to locate the true metal/mineral zero null point.

Dredge Pile Searching

In their efforts to recover precious metal, prospectors came into gold country with huge earth-moving devices and scooped out streams down to bedrock, literally turning the land inside out. Countless tons of rock were removed in a relentless search for gold. Since gold is one of nature's heavier elements, the actions of wind and water work with gravity to pull it down to the lowest possible level. This is especially true in stream beds where the gold finally reaches bedrock. There it may lie for eons, awaiting the prospector...whether he has a huge dredge or a sophisticated modern metal detector.

Prospectors with dredges scooped up vast quantities of rocks which they immediately began processing, first by classifying according to size. Huge conveyor belts transported waste material and large rocks to locations on the banks of the stream where they lie today, often in unsightly heaps.

These are the dredge piles that have been successfully searched by so many electronic prospectors. Not all of the materials in these piles is worthless. Occasionally, large nuggets escaped the eyes of the dredgers and their sorting equipment and went into the dredge piles. Small nuggets passed through in mud balls. They are still there awaiting your detector.

Scan these piles as you learned to scan mine dumps. Make certain that your detector is precisely ground balanced, and listen closely for increases in sound. From time to time, dig down into the pile to expose your

318

searchcoil to a different layer of material. Searching individual samples with the ore test method is not effective here since you will not be able to find any accumulations from one specific area in the earth.

Your dredge piles are truly just piles of individual rocks that were tumbled from many different locations...first by nature and later by the dredgers.

High Grading/Ore Sampling

While this is presented as a distinctly different type of gold hunting, it has been discussed thoroughly in the section on Mine Dumps. You learned the method for determining if any individual rock samples contain a predominant amount of conductive metal, such as gold, silver or copper. As discussed earlier, test rocks one at a time as in the Discriminate mode or at the Ore Test calibration point.

Where can you find individual samples for testing? One good place is from the floors of deserted mines. As ore was brought from a mine on carts, good pieces were occasionally dropped and overlooked. Miners sometimes set aside good pieces for themselves, and these were sometimes forgotten. As you walk through old mines, seek out likely looking rock specimens and test them with your detector, using the techniques we have discussed.

You know that gold was found in and around the old mining camps. Some of it is still there awaiting today's electronic prospectors.

Locating Black Sand

Black sand is generally sought in hopes that gold will also be found. For such hunting it's best to use the largest possible searchcoil.

Use your detector's All Metal mode and adjust its ground balance as precisely as possible, using manual controls when available. Black sand concentrations, more "dense" than the ground matrix to which your ground balance controls are adjusted, will respond with an audible signal. Walk slowly forward with the searchcoil held in front of you. Do not try to scan it from side to side. Always use headphones so that you can hear even the slightest variations in sound level. When this volume of the signal changes, however slightly, keep walking straight ahead until it returns to its normal threshold level. These distinct changes will mark the limits of your black sand (or placer) deposit.

These methods are not infallible, of course, since you may also locate iron ore deposits and veins. A rule of thumb holds that black sand concentrations can be found only to a depth equal to the diameter of the searchcoil you are using. Thus, whenever you are digging to test for black sand, it is only necessary to dig down to a depth slightly deeper than the diameter of your searchcoil. If your signal occurs over a large area, and you don't find black sand at the shallow depth, the detector may have detected a deeper ore deposit or metal target.

Searching for "Float"

Float is ore that has broken away from the mother lode and worked its way down a mountainside, coming to rest, perhaps slightly buried beneath soil and rock. Float can be found on mountain slopes and on flat ground. Perhaps, ground that is now flat, was once a mountain that slowly eroded over eons of time. There is much disagreement as to how the vast quantities of gold came to be in the flat ground in Australia's gold regions. Some believe the country was once very mountainous.

Searching for float is the same as nugget hunting and vein searching. Use large searchcoils. You should seriously consider using the Depth Multiplier attachment in regions, such as Canada's Cobalt mining district, where monstrous silver chunks have been found. This detector is discussed in the previous chapter. Patience is required in this form of searching, but the rewards often make it all worthwhile.

Searching for Placer

Placer (pronounced plaster with the "t" removed) is gold that has become trapped, or has accumulated in cracks, fissures and low spots in stream beds (or where streams once flowed). Placer also accumulates downstream behind boulders and other obstructions. Placer can usually be expected to accumulate in those places in rivers and streams where the water action changes its characteristics.

Gold placer, in the form of nuggets, flakes, dust, etc., becomes concentrated because it is heavier than sand and rock. The gold becomes permanently trapped because there is nothing heavier that can come along and force the gold out.

Placer in sufficient quantity can be located with a modern metal detector. Various sizes of submersible searchcoils are necessary, depending upon the places to be searched. Because quantities of black magnetic sand are most often found present with gold, discovering black sand can aid in the search for gold placer.

If you will study Roy Lagal's books, *Gold Panning is Easy* and *Weekend Prospecting,* you will learn how, and where, to locate placer gold. A modern metal detector, equipped with the correct searchcoils, can find this gold so much more easily than the old prospectors who had to use only their eyesight and instinct.

Three-inch to eight-inch diameter searchcoils are good sizes to use in confined places. Use scanning techniques similar to those for nugget hunting or vein searching. In very rocky areas of locations with irregular surfaces you may do more probing and "sticking" of the searchcoil than scanning. It is necessary that your detector be ground balanced accurately to eliminate the effects of ground minerals. Research is necessary to locate the correct places. Then, patience is required in order to achieve maximum success.

Searching Ancient Stream Beds

Placer can be located in present-day rivers and streams, or in dry, ancient stream beds. In the gold country, often near rivers and streams, you can find these ancient stream beds by searching for deposits of sand and rounded, smooth rock. The rocks were rounded eons ago by the action of water, sand and other rock. Perhaps, earth upheavals caused the stream beds to be thrust above water level. Placer deposits formed when water was flowing can still be found in the same locations, and some good finds have been made in these ancient river beds. Scan using the same techniques described above for wet searching. Learn to identify sand and rock deposits that point to the location of old stream beds. It might pay off!

You Need Patience!

It is quite possible that many of those who claim that no one can find gold with a detector have simply not had the patience to stay with gold hunting long enough to be successful. You see, the successful electronic prospector *must have patience to spare.* You must be willing to search all day...for days at a time...perhaps even in the very same location. Do not expect to stumble into a gold prospecting area accidentally, turn on your detector, scan around for a few minutes and find nuggets. It just doesn't happen that way! Finding gold takes time and intense study of the area.

Facing

He may resemble a "grizzled sourdough," but Rattlesnake John is a sophisticated electronic prospector who relies on metal detectors to find nuggets like the one he is displaying.

Over

At right is the $1 million Hand of Faith gold nugget found with a Garrett detector in Australia. The beautiful nugget at left was also found in Australia near Kalgoorlie.

It takes a lot of searching and, oftentimes, a lot of digging to be successful. When you are using the proper equipment, your success will be in direct proportion to your efforts.

The main thing to do now is to get the right kind of detector, head for the gold fields and practice. Plan to spend many hours and many days scanning your detector. That is the only way that you can hope to dig gold targets.

You may decide to travel to different areas and search for different elements. The more you search, the more you study, the more you learn the capabilities of your detector and what it is telling you...*the more successful you will be!*

Computerized Detectors

All Garrett's **Grand Master Hunters** and the **Master Hunter CX** bring *Fast Track* to gold hunting! These detectors will adapt themselves automatically to changing conditions of ground mineralization. And, the detector adaptations will be made continually and simultaneously, even as the prospector continues searching. Only when erratic signals from extreme ground conditions indicate that manual ground balancing will be required will any specific ground balancing action be required by the electronic prospector.

Fast Track ground balancing, therefore, makes these instruments easier to use that any other detectors ever designed for prospecting. Combine this ease with the deeper seeking circuitry made possible by microprocessor controls, and you have an instrument that is truly second to none in the gold fields!

Let me emphasize that the unique *Fast Track* circuitry may make it unnecessary for you ever to have to ground

Developing an effective instrument for finding gold requires both lab work and field study, such as that being undertaken by Charles Garrett and Bob Podhrasky.

balance the detector manually. Only when you can hear the audio change by an amount that you feel is too great, will manual ground balancing be required. Never hesitate to make these adjustments. Extreme mineralization of certain gold area soils make manual ground balancing necessary. In addition, you may wish to ground balance to a slightly negative or slightly positive condition for certain hunting situations. The precise adjustment of ground balance available with Garrett's computerized CX detectors will enable you to deal with these specific situations.

Even though the **Ultra GTA** detectors do not offer manual ground balancing, they will be an excellent instrument for gold hunting. The factory preset *All Metal* mode of the GTA 1000 (*Mode A* on the GTA 500) should enable you to hunt satisfactorily over even the most severe ground conditions.

Precise discrimination capabilities of the GTAs provide distinct advantages in gold country. What if you are hunting in All Metal mode and continue to discover a particular item of junk metal. A boot nail would be a typical example since literally thousands of them are always present. When this occurs while you are hunting with either Ultra GTA, simply use the **REJECT** touchpad to discriminate against *this particular type of junk metal* and continue hunting. You won't be troubled by boot nails again, but you will detect all other metallic objects outside this specific "zone" of conductivity.

The special discrimination capabilities of the Ultra GTA will permit you to design your own special modes of hunting for any area, and storage capabilities of the detector let you retain the mode for use at a later date.

Hunting Under Water

The water's edge...and beyond...has been called the *new frontier* of treasure hunting. Coins in the sands of popular beaches and gold in mountain streams have long lured both the casual hobbyist and professional treasure hunter alike. As the number of treasure hunters in parks and playgrounds has multiplied...and as restrictions on land hunting have increased...more and more treasure hunters are heading to the oceans, lakes and streams for what is already proving to be a never-ending source of coins, jewelry and countless other valuable items.

This chapter will discuss the various types of hunting activities now being carried out under water with traditional and computerized detectors.

Only one type of metal detector is now being commercially manufactured for underwater use. It is the pulse induction type, which can be used in both fresh and salt water.

Although several new detectors especially designed for beach hunting have recently introduced, certain other modern metal detectors can be used for hunting on the beach, regardless of the type of sand or the amount of salt present. Many types of older detectors are unsuitable for ocean beaches because of salt that is present there.

This chapter is designed to improve your understanding of metal detection near and under the water, but you should always study the Owner's Manual that accompanies your detector. If you are truly interested in searching the new frontier, I urge you to read my new and totally revised *Treasure Recovery from Sand and Sea,* in which hundreds of pages and dozens of color pictures are all devoted to in-depth discussion of all forms of water hunting.

Some beach and underwater detector models have interchangeable searchcoils and discrimination similar to conventional land detectors. Most of the underwater pulse detectors are convertible. They can be used on land, in the surf and submerged to 200 feet. Some have land headphones while others come standard with submersible (consequently, totally environmentally protected) ones. Some use standard batteries; others, rechargeables.

An important consideration when selecting a beach detector is its environmental protection. Some beach detectors are designed for shallow (six feet or so) submersion, while others are just protected against "splashing" waters. *Never* submerge any part of a control housing in any water unless you are certain that its manufacturer guarantees it.

On dry ocean beaches that contain no magnetic black sand, even the old BFO and TR models will operate adequately (as adequately as they *ever* operate). To operate in wetted sand or in the surf, however, you must use a modern instrument or a pulse detector.

Modern beach hunting detectors are designed with automatic ground balance because of the difficulty of eliminating from simultaneous detection both iron mineral (black sand or magnetite) and salt water. The automatic ground balance permits excellent discrimination of wetted ocean beach sand and salt water, while the automatic circuitry ground balances the detector against iron minerals and black sand.

Modern beach hunting detectors give excellent detection depth on coins, rings and other metals with good discrimination available against such normal beach pests as poptops and bottlecaps. Modern detectors that are designed properly with all of the necessary discrimination capabilities can also be used very successfully in highly mineralized good hunting zones. These detectors work just the same above water as below, and can be used when searching for nuggets in dry areas.

Pulse Induction Detectors

Because the pulse induction detector simultaneously ignores both black magnetic sand and salt water, it is now the only type of underwater detector being produced. Pulse detectors are easy to use. Simply turn the detector on, adjust audio for faint threshold sound and commence scanning. Quality pulse detectors like the Garrett Sea Hunter will operate with perfect stability and with the utmost precision, almost regardless of environmental conditions. If there is an adjustable sensitivity control, select the amount you want. If the detector features discrimination, select the degree of rejection you desire. Coins, rings, relics and other metals can be detected to extreme depths.

Pulse detectors are not recommended for prospecting. Gold nugget detection may be poor and "hot rocks" are difficult to identify before digging.

Construction of Underwater Detectors

Underwater detectors are considerably more difficult to manufacture than land models. A great amount of skill, planning, design, bench and field testing and retesting, and extremely exacting production methods must be followed to build quality underwater detectors. The housing must be water tight and able to withstand great pressure. Salt environments will quickly damage ferrous metals.

In order to regulate detector power and to control the detector's various functions, control shafts must be brought out through the housing. These must then be sealed against not only water but also the contamination that is always present in underwater environments. The most common method of sealing the shafts that penetrate through bulkheads is the use of single or dual O-ring seals. O-rings are extremely efficient and when properly constructed will provide perfect seals.

Since salt is very corrosive and will ruin electronic components, moisture-absorbing desiccant should be installed in the control housing.

Underwater Detector Discrimination

Elimination of trash metals can be achieved in all types of underwater detectors. Pulse detectors were the last ones in which the problems of rejecting trash metals were solved. They do an excellent job of rejecting foil, iron bottlecaps and small "junk" metals, including aluminum pulltabs. Some rings and nickels may not be detected at the pulltab setting, and depending upon the amount of rust present, nails may not be rejected.

A selectable *detection depth control* expands the versatility of an underwater detector. Objects that have just recently been lost in water can be found more readily when the control is set to minimum depth detection. Deeper metal objects are ignored while only surface or shallow objects are detected. In a situation where an extreme amount of junk is present, lower settings will eliminate most erratic responses. Individual metal targets are more readily detected at the lower depth setting.

Detection depth selection gives the operator a marked degree of ability to determine object depth. For example, when the operator is operating with full detection depth and detects a target, a quick switch to a lower setting will allow the operator to compare detection signal levels which, when interpreted, give target depth.

Mechanical Configurations

Mechanical configurations are mainly of two types. One built primarily for underwater searching is usually constructed compactly with a short stem and suitable gripping handle and armrest. The operator scans with the searchcoil and whenever a metal object is encountered, needs only to extend his free hand to the point of detection to recover the object. Long stem detectors are not practical for underwater scanning.

The second type of construction is sometimes called the universal or convertible type and can be used either on land or underwater. This instrument is usually built with a control housing that is mounted on a person's body with a suitable quick release belt strap. A cable connects the control housing to the searchcoil. The searchcoil is mounted on a long, adjustable-length stem suitable for land searching. The operator simply walks along scanning the searchcoil over the ground the same as when using conventional land detectors. If wished, the operator can walk right out into the surf and continue scanning for surf treasure.

A suitable means of underwater scanning with the convertible type is with a short stem or handle about one foot in length. The searchcoil is attached to one end. The connecting cable connects the searchcoil to the control

Author uses a pulse induction underwater detector to examine a veritable "wall" of coral-encrusted cannon discovered in a 16th century Spanish shipwreck in the Caribbean.

housing, which is mounted on the operator's waist, arm or leg. The operator then swims in a horizontal position, grasping the handle grip, scanning the searchcoil along the bottom. To recover detected targets, the operator merely extends his free hand forward to the point of detection. It is not efficient for a diver to use a long stem because it is a waste of time and energy to have to extend the free hand so far forward to retrieve detected targets.

Searchcoil Selection

The selection of underwater detector searchcoils follows the same rules as given for selection of land detector searchcoils. Smaller searchcoils are generally used to detect smaller objects. Larger searchcoils will detect objects at a greater distance, but the objects must be larger in size for detection at these distances.

Small three-to-four-inch diameter searchcoils scan a more narrow path than larger ones and can pinpoint targets easier, detect extremely small metal targets and operate effectively in confined areas such as between large rocks, boulders, coral and bottom growth. Also, small searchcoils are well suited for operation in areas with large amounts of metal trash.

General purpose searchcoils range in diameter from seven to ten inches. Within this searchcoil range, target response is roughly equal, but pinpointing is more difficult with the larger sizes.

Searchcoils with larger diameters give slightly greater depth, but pinpointing is even more difficult. Of course, if the bottom is primarily loose sand, then pinpointing, digging and retrieving is not nearly the problem it would be if the bottom were hard packed clay or coral. Consider that when surf hunting, you may be standing in water up to your waist or deeper, recovering targets with a long handled scoop, precise pinpointing becomes important!

Larger searchcoils are desirable during preliminary shipwreck and other site searches. When it comes to the actual search of these sites, if Target Elimination is used, smaller searchcoils can identify individual targets more readily. Thus, items such as gold, silver and copper coins can be more readily identified even if lots of junk targets are present. As discussed under Super Sniping good and "trash" targets have the effect of canceling one another when trash elimination is used. Consequently, the smaller the searchcoil, the more good items you should recover. Of course, keep in mind, smaller diameter searchcoils will not penetrate as deeply as larger searchcoils. In cases where there is a lot of junk mixed in with good targets, it may be necessary for you to scan a given site with two or more searchcoil sizes. In loose sand areas, scan the area first with the largest searchcoil. This allows fast coverage

Some metal detectors, designed especially for beach and surf hunters to use in shallow water, can be taken into a lake or the ocean with no fear of damage from an occasional dunking.

of a site and deeper "good" targets will be detected. Then rework the area with smaller searchcoils. "Good" targets "lost" among the trash will now be more correctly identified. In difficult digging and recovery areas (hard-packed clay, "concrete" coral, etc.) use the smaller searchcoils first for quicker recovery of shallow, individual objects.

In shipwreck areas where valuable gold coins and other objects may be present amid large quantities of junk metal, it may be desirable to use "zero" or rusty iron elimination only. You'll dig more junk, but you may also dig more silver and gold.

Batteries

Some underwater detectors are equipped with standard batteries that need to be replaced periodically while others are equipped with rechargeables. Good design dictates that underwater detectors should be manufactured with rechargeable batteries with the instrument sealed at the factory. Underwater detectors with conventional, non-rechargeable batteries which must be periodically replaced may lead to grave problems, great expense and lost time for the operator. Unless extreme caution is used when replacing batteries, the circuitry can be destroyed. A single drop of salt water on a printed circuit board can cause an instant short circuit and destruction of electronic circuitry. Any moisture that is left inside a housing will cause rust, thus slowly deteriorating metal components. Of course, it is more expensive and difficult to produce detectors with rechargeable batteries, but in the long run is far cheaper and certainly results in better detectors.

Garrett's Sea Hunter has a unique system for recharging its batteries. The recharge connector is the same one to which the headphones are attached. Whenever the detector batteries are to be recharged, the operator simply unscrews the head phones and screws the battery recharger into the same connector.

Underwater Headphones

There are two types of underwater audio signaling apparatus: headphones and bone conductors. Because of the stringent design specifications of underwater headphones, less audio power is produced for a given power expenditure from the battery. Consequently, underwater headphones and bone conductors tend to produce less volume than land units. Properly designed underwater headphones produce more audio power than bone conductors.

Dual piece underwater headphones offer the same advantages, basically, as land detectors: the sound being channeled into both ears, and a reduction of outside noise interference. The major sources of outside noise are the scuba diver's exhaust air bubbles when the operator is submerged and surf noises when the operator is working on ocean beaches or in the surf.

There is not a lot that can be done to overcome the air bubble problem. Some divers have learned to breathe at a slower, more controlled rate with longer breath spacing. Since scuba schools warn against skip breathing, each individual must work out his own procedure if air bubbles are a bother. Some divers are not bothered by air exhaust noise and lose no detection capability.

Bone conductors are held against an ear or a temple area by the mask strap. Bone conductors, of course, are smaller and don't get in the way as much as headphones. Their convenience, however, may be offset by the outside noises that can come into the ears. Which a person uses, is a matter of preference. Obviously, bone conductors cannot be worn when ground searching above water; the audio will not be as loud outside the water as when submerged.

Maintenance

Because of extremely hostile underwater environments, it is recommended that underwater detector

337

O-rings and other seals be replaced and lubricated at least every other year by the manufacturer, and that the detector be cleaned, retested and recertified. Foreign matter is present in most bodies of water. Sand and microscopic particles can filter down into the control shafts and become lodged between the O-rings and the shafts thus creating a potential problem. The cost of regular maintenance is certainly less than the cost of a complete overhaul if salt water should seep into a detector through a seal. Like your automobile, your underwater detector should be given regular maintenance.

Before purchasing an underwater detector, you should determine when and where the instrument will be used. Are you going to use the detector both underwater and on land, in fresh and/or salt water? Do you need interchangeable searchcoils? Will you be searching for gold nuggets in water where iron minerals are present? Will you be searching for gold and silver coins among iron trash?

Features like target elimination, interchangeable searchcoils, selectable depth, rechargeable batteries, land/sea conversion stems and ground elimination capability should be considered and perhaps required in the detector you purchase. There are countless millions of dollars' worth of treasure lost in the water; give thought to finding a share for yourself!

Archaeology

No book on modern metal detectors would be complete without presenting the relationship of metal detectors to modern archaeology and historical field research. Only a few years ago, a student of archaeology would not have heard of the metal detector and its connection with archaeology. Today, many colleges are not only presenting the metal detector as a valuable tool but are using them at their archaeological sites.

The role of the metal detector in archaeology is analogous to the role that it plays in law enforcement. In proceeding with the search (or, "dig") the collection of evidence (or, artifacts) with screening/digging tools and metal detectors is similar.

Of course, the two professions do not utilize all the same equipment. Law enforcement crime scene managers use fingerprinting equipment which archaeologists do not use. Archaeologists use vertical aerial surveying to obtain a plain "view" of the ground. They use electrical resistance surveying, which makes use of variations in the humidity of the soil, to obtain a "map" of underground ditches, pits, walls and other structures. Vertical aerial surveying and electrical resistance surveying equipment and metal detectors are all valuable tools. The metal detector can be the eyes that "see" into the ground to locate metal objects that are of interest to archaeologists.

In 1988 several others and I spent more than a month following the route Moses and the Jews took in their Exodus from Egypt about 1400 B.C. Team leader Dick Ewing devoted years to planning this expedition. Members of this team included Astronaut Jim Erwin, Dr. Roy Knuteson and I, who each participated by bringing equipment knowledge and/or expertise into play during the various searches. Irwin's responsibility was to man various aircraft deploying photography, infrared and other specialized airborne equipment. My responsibility was to handle land and underwater metal detection equipment at the various sites. Our many discoveries will be the subject of future books and videos.

Case Histories

Egyptian archaeologists believed recently that a second burial vault was located beneath an existing vault discovered 30 years earlier. Rather than destroy the floor of the existing vault on the basis of this theory alone, a metal detector was brought into the vault. Metal detector signals indicated that there was metal beneath the floor. A portion of the stone floor was removed, below which was discovered the second vault containing priceless artifacts.

At Custer's famed battlefield on the Little Big Horn in Montana, archaeologists, historians and war buffs undertook a new type of research and documentation to further their knowledge about the events that took place on that fateful day of June 25, 1876. Believing the ground would yield clues to solve many mysteries about the battle, modern-day archaeologists used metal detectors in a foot-by-foot survey of the historic site.

Hundreds of shells from the troopers' Springfield carbines and the Indians' Henry .44-caliber rifles were located, numbered, bagged and plotted on maps. The shells established previously unknown skirmish lines and indicated that by the end of the battle, Indians were using Army ammunition taken from dead soldiers. Because of the success of the metal detector surveys, the work will continue.

In downtown San Antonio, archaeologists excavated an 11-acre site to uncover artifacts from the 1836 battle at the

Alamo between the Mexican Army and the colonial Texas defenders. Since much of the area around the Alamo had never been seriously examined, as complete a survey as possible was undertaken. Metal detectors were among the tools used by the archaeologists. Coins, musket balls, buttons, weapon fragments and many other metal historical relics were located.

Mel Fisher, Robert Marx and Bert Weber, men well-known for their discovery of sunken Spanish galleons, use underwater metal detectors in their quest for treasure and priceless artifacts these ships carried to their watery graves. Marx, perhaps the world's most knowledgeable and experienced underwater archaeologist, has used metal detection equipment all over the world at countless underwater historical sites. His discoveries could fill dozens of museums.

Doctor Richard Fales has carried out archaeological work both in the United States and the Holy Land. He deploys metal detectors in his work and has located many valuable metal artifacts.

In Israel, where thousands of sites have been worked and where probably 10 times as many await the hands of the archaeologists, metal detectors are being used on an

These two Bronze Age Mycenaean daggers, from approximately 1500 B.C. and found with a Garrett instrument, are believed to be the oldest relics ever discovered with a metal detector.

341

increasing scale. Metal detectors being used not only at digs but at sites for ground-level surveys will aid archaeologists and historians in their future planning and surveys. For instance, metal weapons and armor found at a site might be conclusive evidence the location is the precise battle site where archaeologists want to excavate.

Kent Ubil, an amateur archaeologist, made a name for himself when his curiosity got the best of him. For many years he and his wife, Becky, walked over and explored what apparently was the site of an old ranch or farm house in North Texas. They had seen old construction bricks and relics lying about that indicated the area had once been a place of residence and/or work for some unknown persons. Kent decided to do a little investigating, not only by digging an exploratory trench or two, but by using a metal detector to see what he could find.

With his metal detector he found horse shoes, cartridges, weapons, axe heads, stove and other appliance pieces, weapon fragments, kitchen utensils, thimbles, square nails, harness buckles, hinges, single-tree and wagon parts, scissors, garment buckles and numerous other items in had been use during the 1880s and 1890s. During his work, he proved the value of metal detectors to investigate historical sites. Of course, he spent many hard hours excavating various parts of the area, cleaning and preserving finds, drawing maps and sketches and recording every detail of his discoveries. The metal detec-

Facing

Metal detectors such as that shown being used by the Author in Egypt have proved to be an asset to archaeologists all over the world.

Over

These weaponry relics found in the attic of an old house included a powderhorn upon which was inscribed a drawing of the Alamo, famed shrine where Texas patriots died.

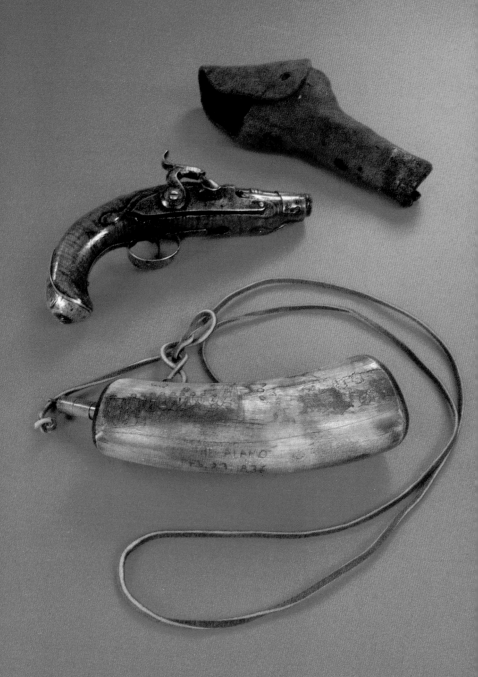

tor was, simply, an important tool that he used, quite successfully, in his work. Kent's research site was assigned Texas State Site Number 41PP307.

Several years ago I made a metal detector survey of an Indian site. The ground was covered with arrowhead flint chips. Many holes had been pounded into the flat rocks. Corn had been ground here over the years...time after time, slowly but surely making the holes deeper. I was curious about the age of the site. I scanned the area for three hours. Not one piece of metal did I find. Obviously, the site was very old.

In West Texas there are many adobe ruins. The settlers who lived in the area were constantly fighting with Indians. One day I scanned the inside walls of what was apparently the main building or the home where settlers lived. I found only one metal object in the walls...a pre-Civil War lead projectile. The projectile was in the wall immediately across the room from the door. Assuming that the bullet was fired from a gun outside the building, I stood near the wall and sighted through the door. Approximately 35 yards away was the corner of a crumbled wall that was probably a storage or work area. It seemed logical to me, that someone, perhaps an Indian, had fired his gun while standing within the protection of the out building. That particular bullet traveled through a window in the door, or through an open door, and embedded itself in the wall on the opposite side of the room. This was a very small bit

Facing

Diver at top searches floor of the Red Sea; below is the famed Emerald Cross and other jewelry recovered off Bermuda from a 16th-century Spanish shipwreck.

Over

French metal detector enthusiast displays golden coins and other relics discovered beneath the Mediterranean Sea with a Garrett underwater instrument.

of discovered historical evidence, no doubt, but, nevertheless, a moment of history brought into the future.

I received the following letter, the contents of which are self-explanatory, from Jim Paquette of Negaunee, MI.

"Dear Mr. Garrett,

"I am writing this letter to inform you of an exciting and important discovery I made. While involved in an archaeological survey in search of possible habitation sites of the ancient 'Old Copper' culture Indians, I hit a 'needle in a haystack' and discovered an extremely rare habitation/quarry/workshop area. The site, which shows evidence of extreme antiquity, has thus far produced an archaeological sampling of copper, quartzite, and flint artifacts. Although I am keeping the location of this site under wraps pending further extensive excavations, I have informed some university archaeologists here in Michigan of this discovery, and needless to say, it has caused quite a stir. Currently, I am awaiting word from the State Archaeologist, John Halsey, on the identification of some of the artifacts.

"The reason I am writing to you about this discovery is that the site was uncovered through the use of my Garrett Electronics Deepseeker. The site is located in a wooded area which made it extremely difficult, if not impossible, to locate any signs of prehistoric habitation areas using traditional surface inspection survey methods. However, with the detector, I was able to "see" through the forest floor cover, and, consequently, I discovered this most important site.

"My initial discovery was a buried cache of copper artifacts which has been buried eons ago by ancient Indians. This initial find led to further discoveries of more copper artifacts, including projectile points, awls and numerous worked pieces. Sample excavations of the area produced an assemblage of quartzite artifacts which may prove to be among the oldest ever uncovered in this region of the Great Lakes area. The finding of these quartzite weapons and tools lead to the additional discovery of nearby surface deposits of high-grade quartzite from which the material for the manufacture of the artifacts was quarried.

"Preliminary indications are that this site may be one of the most important archaeological discoveries ever made in the state of Michigan. You can be proud, Mr. Garrett, that this discovery was made with one of your detectors. I will keep you posted on further developments."

Thank you, Mr. Paquette, for sharing this remarkable find with our readers. Certainly, your work and discovery is an inspiration for all of us to work with archaeological groups in their quest to learn more of our great history. We look forward to reading more about your future work.

Metal Detector Applications

Archaeological and historical researchers can justify the metal detector as an important tool because of the many ways metal detectors can aid them in their work. An initial survey of a given land or underwater site can help locate all metal items to depths of several feet. This pin-pointing of metal objects can help the archaeologist in determining the scope, layout and occupancy charac-teristics of the site.

The metal detector when used to survey structural foundations can help develop the dimensions of buildings and by discovering window and door hinges and other construction items that were made of metal. As mud walls "melt" into the ground, metal items also fall to the ground, thus, marking the location of building features for the archaeologist.

A site can be scanned for metal artifacts of all types or just non-ferrous metal items with high conductivity, such as items made of copper, brass, aluminum, silver and gold. Since these non-ferrous metals do not corrode, they may bear a visible manufacturer's name, date or other valuable research information.

A complete detector scan of an area, with flags placed at each target location, helps in determining the areas most likely to be productive.

Quick dating of a site can be made from coins found with metal detectors. I found numerous coins, Circa 400 B.C., at a site in southern Europe. Metal detectors can be the "last" tool used by archaeologists at dig sites. When "ground zero" has been reached, the metal detector will sniff out buried caches, relics and other metal objects that were buried there.

Metal detectors can help determine when true "ground zero" has been reached. A scan can be made of the ground and from a study of metal objects found, the location of an original ground level can be roughly determined.

A quick metal detector survey of a "suspect" area can "prove" that the site is one historical field researchers wish to investigate, and the same investigation can prove the site is NOT one worth investigating.

In all communities, past and present, the patterns of refuse disposal can be determined. In prior years occupants tended to discard their refuse near the back door, the front door or in any nearby depression, preferably to fill natural erosion areas. The great attraction for archaeologists to these areas is that these sites are the deliberate depository for relics and artifacts of the day. Dating can be very precise since these depositories often filled quickly.

The metal detector is the perfect tool to use in locating such veritable "time capsules." Often, metal of all kinds wound up in these dumps. Because of the vast quantity of metal, the dumps can be located to great depths. The two-box Depth Multiplier attachment is the perfect accessory to use in locating these sites. About all that is necessary is for the archaeologist to walk, at a moderate speed, over the ground in a grid fashion. The metal detector will search deeply and will perfectly outline the shape of the depository.

As important as refuse depositories are, their importance can be overshadowed by the results that can come from excavation of ancient outhouses or privies. Many times, outhouses prove to be storehouses of valuable artifacts. The majority of the artifacts will be non-metallic, but considerable metal trash is sometimes mixed in with everything else. Since a metal detector "sees" all metal items within the detector's detection pattern, a few small items can look like one large target to the metal detector. Consequently, outhouse refuse pits can be detected quite deeply. The same scanning techniques used when locating refuse dumps should be used when scanning for outhouse pits.

Rescue Archaeology

Rescue archaeology, sometimes called "Salvage Archaeology," is a technique archaeologists use during emergency situations when a site is soon to be covered by the rising waters of a new lake or by the construction of buildings, highways and railroads. This technique is also used at canal excavation sites.

In such situations, archaeologists realize that only a small fraction of the historical relics can be saved, but, even a small part is better than none at all. Thus, compromises are made to recover, as quickly as possible, relics from the site. The metal detector is just the tool to help the archaeologist in his plight. The metal detector will quickly locate all buried metal objects. A marker is placed at each location and a team of people can come behind the detector operators to recover the detected items. One metal detector can keep numerous "recovery" teams busy.

Using Rescue Archaeology, much knowledge of the history of a site can be obtained that, otherwise, would be forever lost. A community can be rewarded with the knowledge of a portion of the history of their ancestors. Educational museums can be established for the townspeople.

351

Detector Recommendations

The most versatile and deep seeking of all modern detectors, a computerized Grand Master Hunter CX model, with its full range of accessories, is the recommended metal detection equipment for the archaeologist. The ground balanced All Metal mode is the primary mode and the most useful for the archaeologist. Often, every single metallic item, regardless of its size and metallic content, is to be recovered...sometimes to great depths.

Discrimination is sometimes specified only because the more important non-ferrous metals are to be located and recovered.

Searchcoils of various sizes are often required. The four-inch diameter size is important because of its selective nature in high trash areas, especially when only non-ferrous metals are wanted. Elliptical coils with their excellent reception of signals in areas where junk metal abounds are often preferred by archaeologists. The general purpose size, the eight-to-nine-inch-diameter searchcoils, will be used most often. Larger diameter searchcoils are often needed when more deeply buried objects are searched for such as money caches below ground level.

The two-box Depth Multiplier is an important accessory because sites are often covered with many feet of soil, and archaeologists need all the detection depth they can get to recover large objects.

Underwater searchcoils are required when the work involves underwater scanning. As an example, at Civil War battlefield sites, relics are often found in water. In Louisiana I have found cannon balls in wet creek beds. A large quantity of 20-pound Parrott shells were discovered where soldiers had either dumped them in a creek or a supply wagon had fallen in the water, spilling its ammunition cargo.

Normal scanning procedures as used in coin, cache and relic hunting will give the greatest efficiency. Use of plastic, nonmetal marker flags are recommended to mark discoveries so that they will not interfere with nearby metal detector operation or give false signals that could confuse the recovery team's detection (pinpointing) efforts.

Recovery teams can follow immediately behind the deep seeking metal detectors, or they can come later as time permits the retrieval of objects. Recovery teams will be the most efficient if they have their own metal detectors. Since it is of the utmost importance that objects not be damaged in the recovery process, a detector must sometimes be used in the process of precisely relocating, pinpointing and recovering targets. A pocket scanner type metal detector such as the Pocket Probe is recommended because of its portable and maneuverable size. These instruments do an excellent job of pinpointing objects. While the main, deeper seeking instruments are used when scanning the ground on the initial search, the recovery teams can be digging targets more quickly and carefully with the small hand-held detectors providing the signals needed for careful retrieval.

Hobbyists using metal detectors assist professional historians to recover valuable artifacts from excavations at the location where Tampa, FL, was founded as Fort Brooke in the 1820s.

Archaeologist vs. Treasure Hunter

The subject of metal detectors has long been hotly debated. Some archaeologists steadfastly refuse to acknowledge the detector as a viable tool and even seek to brand users of detectors as mere artifact collectors. But, through the efforts of many archaeologists, the value of the metal detector in research is being realized.

I am on the side of *both* the archaeologist and the treasure hunter. In my writing as well as my work in the field I would never encourage or instruct any "treasure hunter" to remove even a single artifact from a valuable historical site. I place historical knowledge far above any monetary value to be gained from artifacts. The treasure hunter should never encroach upon an established or defined historical site. Neither should an archaeologist, as an archaeologist, encroach upon potential treasure sites by imposing general restrictions on locations that represent no value to archaeology.

There are tens of thousands of places where relics and treasures from the past can be found in varying amounts. But, never in ten thousand years can archaeologists locate and excavate them all. Nor, would they desire to! For the archaeologist and historian to attempt to keep the treasure hunter from all such sites is wrong. Not only will all the "historical" sites never be discovered, the passage of time will continue to destroy them along with their artifacts and treasure. Why not let the treasure hunter search for and recover treasure from sites that archaeologists know *realistically* they will *never* work?

On the other hand, historically important sites should not be touched by the treasure hunter. To remove even a single item is the loss of great knowledge about that site and the customs of the people who lived there. Archaeologists are like Sherlock Holmes, veritable detectives of science and history. They doggedly investigate our heritage to provide valuable knowledge about our past. It's remarkable how their investigation and

354

analysis reveals the finest details of life as it took place thousands of years ago. Work is very demanding and thorough. Consequently, they don't need anyone to come along and destroy even a single shred of evidence. They need all the help they can get.

Why can't the archaeologist and treasure hunter work together? It's been proposed and discussed many times. Some critics of treasure hunters strongly oppose any such coalition. To do so, they believe, would confer an unwarranted respectability on the treasure hunter. Instead of recognition, the treasure hunter is often deplored and likened unto looters and thieves. Granted, there are some treasure "hunters" who, without regard to the law or the value of ancient sites, willfully vandalize and destroy as they remove artifacts and treasure. But, are all archaeologists really *clean?* Are there no misplaced artifacts or treasures concealed in home closets and cellars? Never are all members of a profession or calling perfect. Has there never been some minister, banker, law officer, archaeologist or treasure hunter who hasn't "gone astray?"

And what about the thousands of cultural areas that are never discovered before they are destroyed by erosion? What about bulldozers and earth-moving equipment of developers and builders? Don't they mutilate and completely eliminate countless sites every day?

Well, neither side can win 'em all. Nor, should either expect to! What both the archaeologist and the treasure hunter should try to do, however, is to see the other's point of view and realize that we should work together...at least, not hinder each other. Certainly, working together makes the most sense. It has worked before as proven at numerous sites including the Custer battle site.

A start would be for each side to learn the true nature of the other's complaints. What are the real objections of archaeologists? And, what is the treasure hunter's gripe? Again I ask...*why won't the two groups work together?* Certainly, each can learn a lot from the other. I believe that if most treasure hunters knew how to recognize a valuable historical site when they found one, they would stay away from it and would direct the archaeologist to the location. It has happened many times. Also, if the treasure hunters knew what was historically important, they would be careful in their recovery work and would supply important site and artifact data to the proper people. Many metal detector hobbyists would gladly, without charge, work with archaeological groups. The archaeologists could achieve many objectives simply by educating treasure hunters on the basics of archaeology and the importance of certain objects.

Since the metal detector *is* an important tool of discovery, archaeologists should benefit from knowing how to use it. Few are the metal detector users who don't welcome the opportunity to instruct others in the use of their .equipment. Metal detector manufacturers would offer free training for archaeologists. I would. I have written three times to a Texas state archaeologist and offered such training at no expense to the scientists. Furthermore, I have offered my skills with a metal detector to be used at historical sites anywhere in Texas...free of charge. I am still waiting, after several years, for an answer, yes or no.

What can you, the treasure hunter, do to protect historically important sites and help close the gap between the treasure hunter and the archaeologist? You can start by trying to understand the point of view of the archaeologist. You can become an amateur archaeologist and try to learn a little about archaeological methods and techniques. You can acquaint yourself with the background and aims of archaeology. Try to form a partnership with your local archaeological community, with historical societies, museums and universities. Reach out to them. Offer to work as a site volunteer using your metal detector when and where it would be useful.

Stay alert to the possibility that you may someday discover an important archaeological site. For instance, should you be working a beach or surf area and locate a bronze axe, contact your local or state archaeologist. You may have discovered the site of a ten-thousand-year-old prehistoric settlement.

Learn the nature of the responsibilities of your state's archaeologist. Ask your State Senator or Representative for such information. Obtain a copy of your state's antiquities law and learn what it says. Read it carefully to determine your rights, provisions for licenses or permits and which agency or individual has the authority to issue such documents.

Encourage local archaeological groups, museums and historical societies to establish a central clearing house where you and other amateur archaeologists and historians can turn for information on identifying and preserving important locations and finds. When you make such discoveries, contact this group and report them. Ask if they are interested in the site and joining you in your work. Make your contacts first by telephone or a personal visit, and then by letter. Certainly, you would want proof that you disclosed the location of an important site. Be businesslike, serious and ready to propose a plan. Offer to continue working the site using archaeological knowledge and methods you have learned, and to report data about finds. Welcome the opportunity of having an archaeologist monitor your work. Each time there is a successful encounter between professional archaeologists and treasure hunters, a closer bond is cemented. I know of many persons who have shared their finds with historical groups and federal, state or local authorities. In almost every case, they were made welcome and encouraged to continue working. Also, such contacts resulted in their being granted permits to work in areas otherwise restricted to the metal detector operator.

To sum up, do not trespass in restricted areas and on known archaeological sites. A British author points out that doing so is stupid, inconsiderate and, of paramount

357

importance, is against the law. This author further compels us "to remember that each time we go out with a metal detector, we are an ambassador for an activity that is rewarding in very many ways. We must face up to our responsibilities as both treasure hunters and citizens. The reputation and future of ourselves and others who enjoy treasure hunting will be secure."

It is my sincere hope that we metal detector hobbyists can develop a rapport with archaeologists and learn from them. There are actions that all of us can take to facilitate this joining of interests. We can become knowledgeable about applicable laws and take an active part in writing and passing good new legislation. We can always remain ready to teach others about treasure hunting and metal detecting.

Most important of all, however, we should attempt at all times to live up to the Metal Detector Operators Code of Ethics. It is the duty of all metal detector hobbyists to remain ever responsible to insure conservation and proper management of the archaeological resources of our nation and the world.

Detectors Are Vital

As the threat of terrorism has increased worldwide, law enforcement and security agencies at all levels have turned more and more to the metal detector as the first line of defense. Of course, the use of metal detector by law enforcement and security personnel is nothing new. In fact, such use had become a matter of routine to the Federal Bureau of Investigation and such other governmental agencies as the Post Office department, the Internal Revenue Service, and the Bureau of Alcohol Tobacco and Firearms; various state and local agencies including prisons, correctional institutions, fish and wildlife departments, and local police and sheriffs.

Garrett Electronics personnel have been working with law enforcement professionals for years now in developing specialized metal detection instruments, assisting them in conducting metal detection training seminars, and teaching men and women one more skill to use in crime prevention and crime scene management. Law enforcement personnel have been eager to learn, and have quickly grasped metal detection concepts relating to their specialized work.

The law enforcement community has been aware of the utility of metal detection in crime scene management for many years. In many instances, however, this investigative tool has been shunned or ignored as a credible tool for the crime scene investigator. It may be that many agencies view metal detectors as toys, used only by coin and treasure hunters, and, as such, unworthy of their consideration. More and more law enforcement agencies, however, have begun adding metal detecting devices to their arsenal of crime scene management equipment. As this trend began, many of the instruments were obsolete, some of World War II vintage, and others of extremely poor quality, purchased on a low-bid basis.

During the 1970s when terrorism showed a marked rise, a greater need for specialty metal detection equipment and expertise became apparent. Some agents of the FBI became specialists in this field and have developed exhaustive metal detection training seminars.

There are many areas in the field of law enforcement, such as security and crime scene management, where valuable strides are being made in the use of metal detectors. Superior equipment is being developed, and certainly the metal detector has come to the forefront as a recognized and valuable law enforcement and security investigative tool.

Metal Detector Sizes & Types

In the fields of law enforcement and security the requirements for metal detection are many and varied. One day an officer may need to search in a roadside snowbank to recover a pistol that was discarded by a fleeing bank robber. On another occasion the same officer may be called on to search the cold, swiftly flowing waters of a river where stolen goods or other metal evidence has been discarded. The officer may also be required to scan a bookcase for hidden contraband, or a wooded area for a buried jewelry cache. Searching a wall for a spent .22 caliber projectile or a lake for a stolen safe may now be undertaken by the officer trained in metal detection.

Design Features: The design features of law enforcement and security detectors must include dependability, reliability, ruggedness and simplicity of operation. All controls must be minimized and simplified. Simplified controls are important since numerous officers in a department may be required to use any specific detector which may sit on a shelf for an extended period of time until its services are needed. Officers should not be required to master the operation of complicated detectors. Detection instruments must be operated regularly, however, to insure continued officer proficiency. For these reasons, it is necessary, even mandatory, that detectors be simple to operate.

It is not necessary that every conceivable detector capability, circuit, accessory, knob, etc. be installed on law enforcement instruments. Detection features that coin and gold hunters use are sometimes of little value to law enforcement personnel.

The *law enforcement detector* needed for most investigative purposes should be of modern design with computerized circuitry. Models similar to Garrett's CX detectors with their All Metal mode capabilities are slightly preferred over the automatic adjusting (motion type) detectors. The law enforcement detector must have a wide range of submersible searchcoils. The detector should have ground balancing capability, maximum detection depth and stability. Protective cases and headphones are also desirable. The detector must be capable of operating under environmental extremes.

Searchcoils as small as three-and-one-half inches in diameter and as large as 12 to 14 inches in diameter should be available. Optional searchcoils, capable of operating in water to depths of about 50 feet, should also be provided. Optional equipment such as extension handles and weighted searchcoils with a minimum of nine feet of cable should be available for shallow water searching.

Deepseeking attachments which can multiply detection depth should be available to the investigator. For instance, officers regularly locate automobile engines buried at depths of 10 feet. The engines, removed from stolen automobiles, are considered "too hot" to sell and are buried. The Bloodhound Depth Multiplier attachment is used to locate this important evidence.

361

Often, departmental budgets are limited; consequently, it is desirable that a detector be versatile enough for body scanning. This can be accomplished by employing a hipmount accessory kit. The control housing is carried on the belt (or on a waist strap) with a searchcoil attached to a short handle. The operator may use the searchcoil handle arrangement to scan parcels, mail, prisoners, suspects, etc. This arrangement is much more satisfactory than scanning a person with a standard configuration land type metal detector.

The *underwater metal detector* is another widely used crime scene management tool. While some underwater searches will be done at shallow depths and along embankments the detector must be capable of operating to great depths. The detector also should be capable of operating in extreme temperatures. Convertible detectors are available that may be used on land and in water.

Underwater detectors must be rugged, easy to adjust and operate and be equipped with headphones. Metal diving tanks and associated gear worn by scuba divers should not interfere with the detector's operation. Rechargeable batteries are recommended, and battery chargers capable of plugging into automobile 12Volt cigarette lighter sockets and 110V/60c outlets, should be available. Adaptors for recharging batteries at various other voltage and frequency levels are desirable if overseas work is anticipated.

Compact hand-held scanners are used in body and wall searches, as well as in other evidence collection endeavors. A device widely used for scanning is the miniature pocket detector with its simplicity of operation,

Walk-through detectors such as this Magnascanner CS 5000 with microprocessor controls are newest security weapons; note Super Scanner in man's hand at left.

stability, automatic tuning and durability. In using a metal detector for body scanning, the officer must be able to scan a person for all types of metal evidence concealed in clothing, hair and body cavities.

The world's most popular detector for this purpose is Garrett's Super Scanner which is rugged, compact and sensitive, as well as simple to operate...with only a single on/off switch. Dozens, and perhaps hundreds of security guards may use any one given detector at an airport security check station. Consequently, the instrument must be easy to operate. This detector, with its long handle, allows a more impersonal search of a suspect; the operator's hand is kept further away from the person being scanned.

Body scanning detectors should be sensitive enough to detect the smallest weapon, such as razor blades, hat pins, knives and miniature guns. These small weapons are often concealed in the hair and body cavities.

A larger, more powerful portable detector is also needed by law enforcement. With more power and a larger searchcoil it can cover an area quicker and can scan more deeply into trees and brush for weapons and bullets. It can scan deeper into mail sacks and large parcels to detect bombs and can reach deeper into walls to detect weapons, hidden jewelry, etc. Worn on the belt, it frees one of the operator's hands.

Specialty types of detectors are needed in law enforcement and security, such as the walk-through unit to be discussed in the following section.

Metal detectors are often used to protect cultural relics such as these Magnascanners which guarded a touring exhibition of artifacts from the time of Ramses the Great.

Certainly any manufacturer who produces detection equipment for law enforcement, security and crime scene personnel should produce only the very best, most reliable instrument. Limited capability and inferior equipment has no place in law enforcement. Quality built, sensitive, rugged, environmentally tested and field proven detectors are the only type equipment that should be used by law enforcement and security personnel; lives depend on it.

Walk-Through Scanning

Because of its growing widespread usage the walk-through metal detector has become the most obvious evidence of metal detection in security and law enforcement. Once seen by the general public only at airports, walk-through metal detectors are now literally everywhere...schools, public and private office buildings, sports arenas...anywhere that terrorism might be suspected.

Persons passing through a walk-through archway are scanned for all types of metal objects in the search for weapons, bombs and devices related to terrorism. This type detector must be capable of detecting all metal, and must be adjustable in order that various sizes of targets can be detected or eliminated as required. The entire walk-through area must be uniform in detection, and free of "dead spots." These detectors must be simple to assemble and operate, and must be foolproof. Advanced design walk-throughs can be programmed not only for various levels of sensitivity but also to "ignore" certain jewelry and other metal items. Walk-through detectors should be equipped with audible or silent detection signals, and must be capable of working properly when placed on metal floors or situated near x-ray equipment and other walk detectors. Special circuitry and construction to prevent tampering and detection inhibiting must be incorporated in them.

No metal can be concealed from the invisible electromagnetic field of the latest, state-of-the-art designs of walk-through detectors. Some people hold the belief that they can "fool" a walk-through unit by covering a large belt buckle with their hands. This is a misconception; it has no effect on the operation or detection properties of the unit. When a quality metal detector's sensitivity level is appropriately set, all metal items, regardless of orientation, will be detected.

Walk-through detectors offer various operating settings. A maximum sensitivity mode will detect all metals, regardless of their mass. A less sensitive setting (or a "discrimination" setting) allows the detection of guns and knives, etc. while ignoring certain jewelry items such as a wristwatch. The mode selection and sensitivity setting of walk-throughs should be made based upon the requirements of the person responsible for security.

Only one person can ever be allowed to pass through the archway at a time, and the person being scanned should proceed through the center of the archway without turning his body in any direction. The arms should be held at the sides in a normal walking posture. Walk-through speed should be a normal pace, free of stopping, skipping or running. In the event the walk-through sounds an alarm the person should be processed with a hand-held weapons detector. The person may also be requested to pass through the detector a second time, following removal of all metal objects from his person and clothing.

Any items detected by the hand-held scanners, such as pocket items and cigarette packages, should be visually checked.

Some persons who have metal surgical devices implanted in their bodies will trigger a response from the walk-through detector. Most implants may be verified with hand scanners.

All detector signals must be resolved prior to the subject being allowed to pass into secure areas.

This discussion on metal detector scanning is by no means exhaustive. Basic techniques of scanning have been presented and discussed in general terms. Persons using metal detectors in law enforcement and security settings must learn the full capabilities and limitations of this equipment, as well as the legal aspects relating to their application. Further information on the use of metal detectors in security is available in *Effective Security Scanning*, published by Ram.

A second and more comprehensive book, *Metal Detection Screening*, authored by retired FBI agent David Loveless and Charles Garrett describes metal detectors as the "first line of defense in terrorist and security management." This book which covers all aspects of security metal detection is also designed as a text book to be used by security and law enforcement schools.

Prison and Jail Search

Walk-through detectors have become popular tools of security at penal institutions all across the nation. Garrett manufactures a special heavy duty instrument, with sides reinforced by heavy gauge metal for such usage. These detectors are used to inspect both inmates and visitors alike.

At other times an officer will have occasion to search a jail cell for contraband, weapons, or other items of evidence. The metal detector will find any metal contraband.

Body Searches

There are many different situations that call for an electronic search of an individual. A patrolman may scan an individual just arrested to determine if that person has a concealed weapon. An employee may be scanned to determine if he or she is removing company property from the premises. An individual may be scanned in an airport security checkpoint setting. A party-goer may be scanned prior to gaining entrance to a night club.

In law enforcement settings it is often necessary to conduct a search incidental to an arrest. Metallic weapons may be concealed in a subject's hair or within body cavities. Criminals often display great creativity in concealing weapons and contraband.

The search is best started at the back. The suspect should hold his or her arms straight out from the sides. The arms should not be bent. Hats must be removed and scanned with the metal detector. Make circular motions over the head and hair. Bring the detector horizontally across the neck and make several scans over the back working down to the crotch area. Pay particular attention to the small of the back and the crotch. Then scan up one side, under the armpit, and proceed along the underside of the arm to the hand. Continue along the outer arm, across the shoulders passing over the full length of the other arm, and returning by way of the inner arm to the armpit. Scan down the side following the outside of the leg to floor level. Pass the metal detector around the ankle and up the inside of the leg to the crotch. Proceed down the inside of the opposite leg, across the ankle, and up the

Metal detectors regularly guard notables at public events such as these 11 Garrett walk-throughs at the 1984 Republican National Convention when President Ronald Reagan was renominated.

369

outside of the leg. The person conducting the search should now move to the front of the subject and pass the detector under the chin. Several horizontal scans must be made over the torso, paying particular attention to the breast, waist and crotch areas.

The purpose of the frontal scan is to locate small metallic objects which may be concealed in the mouth (metal teeth fillings will also be detected), and items concealed in brassieres or suspended around the neck and hidden behind the belt.

It is important that the individual being searched know that the metal detector is operational. This may be accomplished by scanning the person's arm and calling attention to the signal produced by a wristwatch or ring. It is suggested that in body scanning, two additional techniques be employed. The first is to occasionally touch the body in areas such as the shoulders, arms, legs, below the knees and the back with the metal detector to make the subject more aware of the progress of the search. The second technique is for the person conducting the search to use his hands in connection with the metal detection scanning process. Prison officers agree that all of the senses should be used in body searches.

The searcher's hands should be used whenever possible. For example, as the search proceeds along a sleeved arm, the hand should be passed over the area indicating to the subject that a thorough review of his person is being conducted. The hands may detect items attached to the body, as well as confirm metal detection signals resulting from the presence of metal. This creates additional stress on the person and improves the search. It should be noted that certain search situations may not permit a "pat down" in conjunction with a metal detection scan.

During the course of a search, always request the person to tilt out large belt buckles enabling the searcher to determine if hidden weapons are present. A light touch behind the buckle will disclose if items are concealed behind clothing. Belt buckles are made with built-in weapons, and small guns which may be concealed behind large buckles. These body scan techniques require approximately 30 seconds to complete if no suspect items are detected.

Detector Search Techniques

Search methods employed by the investigator may be compared to a farmer's plowing methods. The farmer utilizes the methods best suited to his particular terrain. The crime scene investigator should do no less. Crimes may occur along a roadside, necessitating a strip type search. In an open field an investigator might conduct a grid or zone search to best address the uniqueness of the situation. A metal detection search should be conducted much as a field is plowed...attention must be paid to systematically covering every inch of the crime scene area.

Land and House Searches

This book was conceived and written for all persons interested in metal detection. Most of my career as the president of Garrett Electronics has revolved around working with treasure and coin hunters, prospectors and law enforcement personnel who spend much time during their lives attempting to locate metallic objects that have been lost or hidden. One close personal friend, the late L.L. "Abe" Lincoln of Rogers, AR, remarked that people conceal valuables in the same locations today that they did 200 years ago. People are creatures of habit; they tend to hide their possessions where they can frequently and easily observe the hiding place. Years ago, people who did not trust banks would hide valuables in places easily seen from the bedroom window. They used a corner of the house, a well, a tree or some other landmark as reference points when burying their possessions.

Thus, set up your lines of search to correspond with prominent physical objects. The chances of finding what you are looking for will be increased a hundredfold.

371

Treasure hunters know that valuables have been concealed under manure piles. Recently, an arson squad in a Midwestern town solicited assistance from Garrett Electronics regarding the search of a farm. The arson officers were advised to scan manure piles. They subsequently informed us that they had been successful...a search of a manure pile inside a barn resulted in locating five fire bombs.

When attempting to locate hidden items, try to put yourself in the position of the person doing the hiding. A person might conceal items beneath a stairway, on top of a cupboard, under a drawer bottom or in the attic. Just use good common sense. Make inquiries of your fellow officers and friends and determine where they might hide items of value under different conditions.

Water Search and Recovery

Numerous cases have been solved with the recovery of evidence once thought forever lost in the murky depths of rivers, lakes and oceans. Once a permanent depository for instruments of crime, these waterways can now be forced to give up their secrets. Equipment of progressive law enforcement departments now include new types of sonar and modern metal detectors. Submersible metal detectors and searchcoils will detect ferrous and non-ferrous metals. Detectors can locate metals concealed by murky water, aquatic growth or bottom soil. Large metal masses, such as aircraft, boats, automobiles, and even safes, can be detected at surprising distances from the searchcoil. Yet in dark water searches mere inches can make a big difference in the search.

Sonar equipment should not be overlooked by those responsible for conducting underwater search and recovery programs. Sonar sends electronic signals through the water. Upon striking a submerged object, the signal rebounds to the sonar receiver where it is analyzed and recorded on a screen or heat sensitive paper.

372

There are two basic types of sonar devices: sub-bottom profilers and side scan. Sub-bottom profiling sonar generally transmits electronic signals straight down from a surface-mounted transducer, producing cross-sectional images of targets.

Side-scan sonar, a substantially more expensive piece of equipment, emits its electronic signal from transducers mounted in a "fish," a torpedo-shaped device submerged and towed slightly above the bottom. It emits signals both to the right and left. Signals bouncing off objects protruding above the bottom are analyzed and recorded, and images appear as having height and depth.

Side-scan sonar is recommended for large search areas with relatively flat bottoms. Sub-bottom profilers are used in waterways with rugged bottom contours and are most effective as pinpointing devices.

Another instrument that has proved invaluable to search and recovery specialists is the electronic ranging system. The type most widely used by law enforcement personnel utilizes two primary sources of distance ranging: satellite and fixed base. Signals are transmitted and received. Time intervals are measured, and very accurate calculations are made automatically. Positioning accuracy on the water's surface of plus or minus one meter can be maintained.

These systems can be combined to organize, operate and successfully complete two kinds of underwater search and recoveries.

When locating a weapon or small metal object discarded in a water area of one-quarter square mile or less, an organized diver search team should be used. A dive plan has to be established, and all divers familiarized with bottom times, signals, and search techniques. The search area is marked off at all four corners, using magnetic headings to establish marker positions. The reason for using magnetic headings is to keep search diver patterns parallel to the grid through the use of wrist compasses.

Divers are staggered, every other diver maintaining sufficient distance behind lead divers to eliminate electronic metal detector "cross talk." A six-foot distance should be adequate for most detectors.

Guidelines can be used to maintain underwater sequencing. Lines must be of sufficient diameter and of non-floating construction to eliminate hazardous entanglements with divers. Generally, a large diameter tightly-wound rope will not entangle divers and can be easily grasped and lifted off equipment. A small cord easily becomes entangled with diving gear and is difficult to remove.

A sharp knife is always recommended as part of any diver's equipment. Line anchors should be substantial to maintain their position, even through severe storms. A three-foot diameter marker can easily move a car engine block anchor in moderate waves.

When the object of the search is located, mark the spot where it was found. Mentally record all surrounding terrain and unusual items. Photograph the entire area if possible. Remove the object, using proper techniques. Remember that a loaded gun, even under water, can discharge.

In searching large areas or in locating targets such as boats, aircraft or automobiles, a combination of metal detectors, sonar and ranging equipment must be used. A search program similar to the one used by Cross International, Orem, UT, in locating a United States Air Force F-16 fighter which crashed into Utah's Great Salt Lake shows how this equipment can be applied.

During the wintry month of January an F-16 disappeared from the radar screens of Hill Air Force Base, located in Ogden, some 90 miles away. Violent storms kept search aircraft from the area for approximately 13 hours while debris vanished. Heavy snow, and temperatures with wind chill factors of 40 degrees below zero, made the problem of searching over 1,700 square miles of water more difficult. In testing equipment to be used in this particular search, it was learned that the 29% salt content of the Great Salt Lake rendered most metal detection equipment useless. After extensive testing, the search team chose Garrett Sea Hunter metal detectors because they could cancel out the heavy mineral concentration and still detect the metal used in the F-16.

After studying wind directions and currents during the previous twenty-four hour period, Cross International selected a probable search area of approximately fifty kilometers. Fixed-base ranging stations were established at strategic points around the lake, and specialized surface craft were put on the water.

Ranging equipment and side scan sonar was installed on one barge. Diving equipment, and special helmets and suits were made ready on another. The search began.

Perimeter coordinates were established and four-kilometer sweeps that covered paths 60 meters wide were

The metal detector required for most investigative purposes is a VLF motion type instrument with discrimination and which can utilize a wide range of different size searchcoils.

375

begun. After 13 days and searching over almost 50 square miles sonar revealed wreckage, scattered over an area one-and-one-half kilometers long and three-quarter kilometers wide. Each sonar target was plotted and marked. Metal detection searchcoils were lowered from the barge to verify that the targets were metal. To conserve the divers' energy, bogus targets such as boulders had to be identified.

The pilot's body and 95% of the weight of the aircraft were recovered. Submersible metal detectors greatly improved the search and recovery aspects of the work since murky conditions sharply limited visibility. Extremely small metal pieces, as well as gigantic ones, were readily detected. A good percentage of the aircraft pieces could not have been recovered without the metal detectors, as they were buried in mud. An extremely difficult job came to a successful ending by using the new eyes and ears of search and recovery electronics.

Snow Search

Obviously, fallen snow of almost any depth can conceal weapons discarded by persons fleeing from the scene of a crime. These weapons must be located as quickly as possible. What is seemingly an impossible task, that of locating a gun in a large, snow covered field, is in reality simply one of carefully analyzing the area and conducting a systematic search, since snow does not inhibit operation of a metal detector. Without the use of detectors in snow searches, evidence may be overlooked and suspects never brought to trial.

Poaching Investigations

All types and sizes of projectiles, including metal arrow points, can be located in animals. The scanning process is complicated by the fact that salt, present in animal tissue, becomes conductive as the carcass decomposes. Body fluids, combined with salt, produce saline solutions which most metal detectors will detect, thus, masking, somewhat, the detection of projectiles. This masking process begins on about the second day following death and continues until most of the animal's fluids have dried or the meaty tissues have decomposed.

Iron minerals in the ground must also be considered since the detector, as it penetrates the carcass, will react to the iron minerals, further adding to the masking effect described.

Any ground balanced modern detector can be used with more or less success, depending upon the degree of salinity of body fluids. These fluids will be detected, but many game wardens have learned to "ignore" these effects, while carefully listening for projectile indications. Smaller searchcoils are preferred.

Psychological Aspects of Searches

There are psychological factors relating to the search of an individual with a hand-held and/or walk-through metal detector, which should be considered since the officer involved can use these factors to his advantage. Few individuals who permit themselves to be searched with a metal detector are free from some form of apprehension. This is particularly true with a criminal who would intentionally hide a weapon on his person with the thought of injuring someone. The psychological effect builds when the criminal is faced with pieces of unknown electronic equipment that have different sizes, shapes and colors.

During the 1984 Olympics, Garrett Electronics established an unprecedented trend by introducing five different types of searchcoils to scan individuals, mail, food and supplies.

And, during the 1984 Republican Convention this same equipment was used. Some prisons throughout the United States are currently following this trend. The different searchcoils have kept the criminal element off guard. Whether the criminal is about to board an airplane or is in jail, he is left to wonder WHEN he will be searched, WHAT type of equipment will be used, WHERE he will be searched and HOW he will be searched.

I am reminded of a sign on a fencepost of some private property, "No Trespassing! Trigger-happy gunman and man-eating dog patrol these premises four days a week! YOU guess the days!" I do not feel we owe the criminal any consideration. Let him guess the type of equipment that will be used, when it will be used, how it will be used and where it will be used.

Fish and Game Applications

A number of fish and game departments use metal detectors routinely during their investigations of game violations. The Utah Wildlife Resources Department has developed perhaps the most advanced metal detection program of its kind in the world. Through the use of metal detectors, Utah game wardens have recovered metallic evidence from illegally killed animals, resulting in numerous successful prosecutions.

Law enforcement officers historically have used creativity and innovation in solving complicated cases using metal detectors. A case in point was related by a Texas game warden. The officer became aware of fish being poached with gill nets. Upon locating the nets, he placed his calling card inside a small metallic vial which he then forced into the stomach of one of the poached fish. He and several other game warden subsequently waited for the poacher to clear his nets and depart with his illegal catch. The violator was stopped shortly after his departure from the scene of the crime. While the official examined the suspect's fish, the poacher alleged they were caught legitimately and were not taken with gill nets.

The officer scanned the fish in question with a metal detector, immediately located the metallic vial, and retrieved his personal business card. No alibi could refute this small piece of compelling evidence.

378

Crimes of Violence

In all crimes of violence, the detector can be an important investigation tool. In one investigation spent bullets from a murder weapon were sought. The detector not only located the desired slugs, but also a mark made by one of the bullets on a nearby fence which established the trajectory of the projectile. This information established important aspects of the crime, leading to the successful prosecution of the offender.

An officer, using a metal detector, located fragments of an automobile grill that had fallen from a hit-and-run vehicle. This evidence was used to convict the subject who, subsequent to the hit and run, staged an automobile accident in an attempt to cover his crime.

The Medical Examiner

In crimes involving homicide, metal detectors should be used to scan the body to locate valuable metallic evidence. Medical examiners are discovering a new application for metal detection devices relating to examination of the body at the time of autopsy. Bodies are

Investigator uses underwater-type detector in a search for metallic evidence that was discarded months before in the cold and swiftly flowing waters of this stream.

routinely x-rayed as part of this procedure. Metal detection instruments, however, can be used to locate metal fragments inside the body without requiring expensive x-ray equipment. Medical examiners are frequently required to assist in the processing of a body at crime scenes. A hand-held metal detector can prove an invaluable resource in locating and protecting metal evidence found in the body of victims.

Medical examiners will frequently examine the victim's clothing. The metal detector can also prove valuable in these searches.

Olympic Security

The largest single security event in the history of the United States was the 1984 Los Angeles Olympics.

Olympic Security is discussed several times in this book because an understanding of the complete use of metal detectors at an Olympic setting is also an understanding of the metal detector's use in almost any other type of security situation. Metal detectors were utilized in virtually every aspect of the Olympic games in an effort to provide security and safety for all participants. When it becomes necessary to scan small or large numbers of people, whether it be in a convention or industrial setting, corporate or hospital, or for any other type of security, the application and operation of walk-through metal detectors is similar.

The role of metal detectors in security settings has taken on new dimensions because of their proven capabilities during the 1984 Olympics. Similar security measures were used during the 1984 Republican National

In recent years more and more schools have begun using such equipment as Garrett's Magnascanner walk-through and Enforcer G-2 hand-held detectors.

Convention held in Dallas. Metal detection played a more significant role at that time than in any other political convention in history.

Court Security

Metal detectors play an important part in the protection of our elected and appointed officials and judges, jurors, prosecutors, and defendants. We continually find the need for greater security in our nation's capitol, the White House, our embassies and other significant government installations. It is imperative that only the finest metal detectors be produced to perform with the degree of excellence which would insure the safety of all people they are deployed to protect. It's unfortunate, but a fact, that security extends into all of our lives. Metal detectors protect us and help to insure that we have a safer existence.

Search and Rescue Electronics

There has been a sudden interest in the use of metal detectors in avalanche search and rescue. A research program revealed that more than 50% of the victims of an avalanche, are within 36 inches of the surface. When you consider the amount of metal items an average skier wears, the odds of finding them have significantly increased. It was demonstrated, that often avalanche victims leave a "trail" of various items including skis, poles, glasses, and other metal objects that could lead a metal detector operator to the victim.

In another situation, search and rescue personnel sought the body of a murdered woman reportedly buried in a certain area. The area was gridded and searched with metal detectors. A metal detector detected a ring on the victim's hand, which was six inches below the surface.

The Super Scanner, world's most popular and effective hand-scanning metal detector, is used by guards in countless security and loss prevention environments.

383

In recent years numerous mudslides have occurred in the Rocky Mountains. On one such occasion, a Volkswagen, believed to contain four small children, was swept away and buried beneath tons of mud. Search and rescue personnel, using a Garrett Deepseeker detector with a Depth Multiplier attachment, located the vehicle.

During a snowstorm, a vehicle containing two females skidded off a road and was quickly buried. A motorist who saw the accident, notified the Sheriff's department. Metal detectors were quickly brought into use. The vehicle was located within a relatively short period of time. It contained two very cold, but very much alive young ladies.

Another success story is worthy of Ripley's *Believe It or Not*. A young man was ice skating and fell through the ice. A member of a search and rescue team resided near the lake. According to the officer, he was getting ready for a trip to a warmer climate, where he planned to do some metal detecting. He was checking his detector when an excited skater informed him of the accident. As he ran to the lake, he remembers looking in his hand to find he was still holding his metal detector. As he began a visual search, he also began scanning the ice with his detector, hoping that the skater might be wearing something metal.

Apparently, the skater had presence of mind to remain in an air space between the ice and water. He was attempting to break through the ice with a skate, when the officer detected the skate with his metal detector...believe it or not!

Crime Scene Investigation

Before processing a crime scene, factors which significantly affect police response and effectiveness of the investigating team include: the fixed responsibilities for a specific task at the crime scene; handling of liaison with the media; training of emergency medical personnel; involvement with the medical examiner's office; in-service training for personnel involved; involvement of the prosecutor at the crime scene; training of hospital personnel in handling of evidence relating to crime scenes; development of programs to enhance the liaison between investigative, forensic, and prosecutive branches of law enforcement and police community relations.

Two of these factors involve metal detection. Departments need to plan and budget for the appropriation of metal detectors and other specialized equipment that will facilitate the management of the crime scene. Officers should be specifically assigned the task of metal detection, and metal detector training should be an ongoing part of in-service programs.

Garrett's Letterscanner detector is specifically designed to protect against dangerous devices enclosed in envelopes and small parcels by sounding an alarm whenever metal is contained in them.

Metal Detector Use

The following procedures should be adhered to by law enforcement agencies in their selection and deployment of metal detection devices:

— Select only quality equipment. A metal detector for use in crime scene management should be selected with the same strict criteria as a crime scene photographer would select a camera. Care should be taken to purchase only state-of-the-art, field-proven equipment.

— Insist that all metal detector operators use metal detection equipment in off-duty hours in hobby pursuits to gain experience and develop techniques in metal detector use. Even though a number of law enforcement agencies own quality metal detection devices, in many cases the instruments have been abandoned because of a lack of trained operators. Proficiency in the use of metal detectors can be easily obtained through a minimum of instruction accompanied by many hours of practical field use. An officer who can locate coins in the earth can just as easily find small items of evidence like shell casings and lead slugs. The value of metal detection in crime scene management is directly proportional to the experience and understanding of the operator.

— In crime scene applications, gather as much information as possible before using metal detection instruments. This process should include interviewing primary witnesses and cooperative subjects for detailed information regarding the area to be searched with the metal detectors to narrow and limit that area. Information indicating that a weapon was thrown from a moving vehicle between locations several miles apart is far too general to make a metal detection search practical. Likewise, information regarding a weapon reportedly thrown into a river or other type of waterway provides little detail of value to the investigator.

This procedure should be adhered to wherever possible...The investigator should interview primary witnesses and cooperative subjects before the search. The metal detection expert should never rely on information obtained by a third party since such information is often non-specific and fails to provide details of import to the person conducting the metal detection search.

As an example of a detailed interview, let's consider a case where a weapon was thrown from a moving vehicle. The interviewer must determine the speed and lane of traffic of the vehicle at the time of the disposal of the weapon, the location in the vehicle of the person discarding the evidence, whether the person is right-handed or left-handed and which hand was used in throwing the weapon, whether the weapon was thrown over the top of the car or from the window, whether it was thrown overhand or sideways, what force was used in the throw, and the exact size and shape of the object. Identifying markers and points of reference along the highway will narrow the search area. Where practical, cooperating witnesses or subjects should be returned to the search area to provide their best opinion on where the evidence was discarded.

These procedures can greatly limit the primary search area and may save the investigator countless hours of fruitless search. It should be remembered that no matter how advanced the investigator's search techniques may be, and regardless of the quality of the detection instrument, if the item of evidence being sought is not in the area of his search, it will not be recovered.

— Prior to every search metal detector tests must be conducted on an object of similar weight, size, shape and composition as the object being sought. This similar weapon or object should be tested to determine the sensitivity (response) of the detector and to determine the characteristics of detector response. The item being sought should be compared with other metal items buried in the general area of the crime scene. These items might include cans, pulltabs and possibly larger pieces of ferrous metal. These tests will perhaps allow the investigator to use discrimination circuitry and techniques that might speed up target detection and recovery.

— Conduct tests to determine the probable extent of the search area where the items of evidence may be located. This series of tests, in the case of a weapon thrown from a moving vehicle, require the investigator to obtain an object of similar size, shape and weight as the object of the search and simulate all conditions at the time the actual weapon or other evidence was thrown from the vehicle by conducting tests to determine the distance these items can be thrown under similar conditions. The investigator must pay strict attention to every detail obtained from interviews with primary witnesses. The test vehicle should be traveling in the same lane of traffic and at the same rate of speed, and the weapon should be thrown using the identical methods employed by the subject in the original case. This test should be conducted a minimum of three times to determine flight parameters of the object being sought. In cases involving disposal of evidence in waterways, a light-weight, strong cord should be attached to the test object so that it can be readily recovered from the water.

Following these evidence recovery rules will greatly increase the investigator's likelihood of locating evidence with a metal detector. It has been proven time and again that important items of evidence can be located by the deployment of state-of-the-art metal detection devices. It is hoped that all law enforcement agencies will recognize that the metal detector is, indeed, a dependable and invaluable investigative tool.

Locators & Tracers

There are two major types of instruments used in industry to find metallic objects: the metal *locator* and the pipe/cable *tracer.*

As its name denotes, the "locator" is designed to locate or detect metallic objects in the conventional metal detection manner. A manhole cover with its large, flat surface area, for example, buried several feet deep must be located using conventional deep seeking-type metal detectors. But, since conventional metal detectors are surface area detectors, and are not efficient in locating rounded objects, deeply buried pipe, cable, conduit and other elongated metal objects must be "traced" with suitable instruments.

Modern Equipment

The photograph on the following page shows the three main configurations of a twin-circuit metal locator/pipe and cable tracing instrument. Depending upon the searchcoil attached, the instrument can...

— Locate manhole covers, valve boxes, sprinkler heads and other buried and concealed metal objects,

— Trace pipe, cable and conduit,

— Measure depth and locate breaks in objects being traced.

Locator Configurations

To use this instrument as a *locator,* attach the 12-inch diameter searchcoil supplied as standard equipment. The circuits automatically switch to the locator mode, and the detector is then used in the same manner as a conventional

389

metal detector. Large objects such as manhole covers can be located to depths of more than six feet.

The Bloodhound Depth Multiplier, an optional accessory, can be easily attached to the control housing to locate large objects to depths of about 15 to 20 feet.

Tracing Configurations

To use as a *tracing* instrument attach the probe and circuits automatically switch to the tracing mode. Pipe, cable, and conduit can be traced, its depth measured, and locations of any breaks determined. In the tracing mode an energizing signal must be coupled into the pipe, cable, or conduit. This can be accomplished with either conductive or inductive coupling, as shown in the drawing on the facing page. An electromagnetic source is supplied to generate the energizing signal.

To make a direct connection one wire leads is attached to the pipe, cable or conduit, with the other clipped to a

Three main configurations of the LT-2000 tracer/locator are shown, with the optional two-box Depth Multiplier at left, tracing probe in the center and 12-inch locator searchcoil at right.

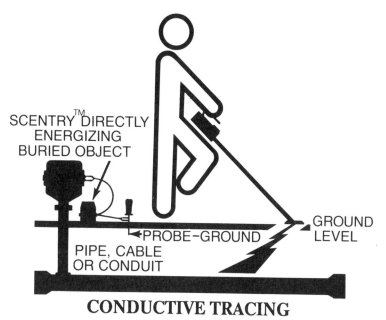

SCENTRY™ DIRECTLY
ENERGIZING
BURIED OBJECT

GROUND
LEVEL

◄—PROBE-GROUND

PIPE, CABLE
OR CONDUIT

CONDUCTIVE TRACING

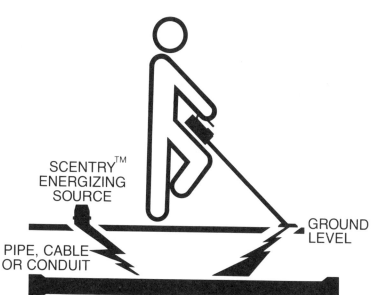

SCENTRY™
ENERGIZING
SOURCE

GROUND
LEVEL

PIPE, CABLE
OR CONDUIT

INDUCTIVE TRACING

391

rod, or plate that is in electrical contact with the soil. A grounding plate (standard equipment) may be used if direct contact with the soil is impossible. When the grounding plate is used, a rock or other heavy metal object should be placed on it to facilitate better ground connection. Direct connection provides the best means of tracing because the signals from the object to be traced are generally stronger than those generated by the induction method.

To trace inductively the energizing source is placed at a point on the ground directly above where the pipe (cable or conduit) is believed to be buried, and a powerful electromagnetic field penetrates the ground. Electromagnetic energy is then induced into the object to be traced.

The electromagnetic energy travels along the object, creating a secondary signal which radiates upward through the ground and into the air. With the tracer probe connected to the instrument, the operator simply walks along scanning side-to-side as in normal detection. The tracer probe detects the secondary or field, alerting the operator to the presence of the pipe. The pipe location and underground route is determined as the operator marks the locations where the strongest signals are detected.

When the electromagnetic energy flowing along a conductor reaches a break, a junction, or a direction change, the characteristics of the energy field are altered, a condition which the tracing probe senses. This principle enables breaks and changes in direction of concealed pipe, cable and conduit to be located easily with modern metal detection equipment. Operating instructions are included with pipe and cable tracers explaining the various discontinuity situations so that they may be easily analyzed.

Measuring Depth

To measure the depth of underground pipe, cable and conduit the tracer probe must be attached to the tracing instrument. The operator must determine the point (strongest signal) on the ground which is directly above the buried pipe or object whose depth is to be measured and rotate the probe 90 degrees at that point while standing at right angles to the pipe. The depth measuring edge of the probe is placed flat (squarely) upon the ground. The instrument is then pushed away from the pipe with the measuring edge of the probe sliding along parallel with the ground. The signal will begin to decrease in loudness. At the point where a null (minimum sound) is reached, a marker should be placed. The distance between the marker and the point directly above where the object is buried, is equal to its depth. Accuracy of this measurement is determined by how carefully the operator holds the edge of the probe parallel to the ground and how carefully he locates the object and the null point. With only a small amount of experience, an operator can become quite efficient measuring depth.

Because their use can save both time and money, industrial locators and tracers are invaluable tools for utility and construction companies who must probe, drill or excavate.

Efficiency and Economy

Industrial locators and tracers are invaluable tools for utility and construction companies who must probe, drill or excavate. These instruments permit significant savings in all areas of operation. Construction crews, for example, once ripped through underground artery telephone lines that supplied telephone service to two large communities just north of Dallas. For more than 24 hours, a half-million people were without telephone service. When the cost and inconvenience caused by those severed cables is analyzed, the true value of an industrial locator/tracer employed ahead of earth moving equipment can be quickly determined.

Wiring and Plumbing

These same techniques can be used to trace wiring and metal plumbing in buildings of all sizes. Plastic pipe that contains a metal tracing wire can also be traced.

Miniature pocket detectors can aid the plumber, electrician, telephone repairman and others who must locate any type of metal object concealed in building walls, ceilings and floors.

Maintenance

Sooner or later a detector being used in the field may fail to perform as it should. If that ever happens, don't despair! The chances are about 50-50 that your problem can be discovered and remedied at once.

As simple and plain as it seems to be, the most likely "problem" you'll encounter is dead batteries. Treasure hunting trips are called off, people go into a state of near shock, and detectors are actually shipped back to the factory or service centers for repair...when all they need is fresh batteries.

One lady at a treasure hunt in Oklahoma City brought her detector to me and said, "This detector you made won't work and now my whole trip is ruined!" I discovered that the batteries in her detector were the same ones that had been installed at the Garrett factory when the detector was built four years earlier! New batteries "corrected" her problem!

So, if your detector fails, *check your batteries!* Always carry along a fresh set every time you take your detector out. Any time your detector fails to work properly, install the new batteries and see if the problem is corrected. Some batteries will, on rare occasions, show a good state of charge yet not be capable of delivering current. A high internal battery impedance can develop that prevents the battery from delivering power.

Some battery-check circuits test all batteries. Some only check the batteries that power detection circuits. If your detector has no means of checking the battery that powers its audio function, simply continue using the detector until the audio drops to an unacceptable level. Then change batteries.

Always make sure you insert new batteries correctly and that they test satisfactorily. Also give your detector an extremely thorough visual inspection. Check battery terminals for tightness. Carefully examine the detector by looking through any doors and portals. Observe every component for damage. Look for damaged wires that may have been pinched when you last changed batteries. When panels are replaced hastily or carelessly, detector wires are sometimes pinched, setting up a potential problem that can result in failure in the field. If your detector is factory sealed, *never* open it. At best, you accept the risk of having your warranty voided. And, worse things can happen!

Battery Characteristics

These are the features of the four types of batteries you can use in your metal detector:

Carbon Zinc cost the least and deliver current the shortest length of time. They operate most efficiently at temperatures from 32 to above 100 degrees Fahrenheit. They are more prone to leak corrosive acid than alkaline and NiCads. Their performance during their active life is satisfactory.

Heavy Duty (zinc chloride) are generally more expensive than carbon zinc but will give additional life. They are more prone to leak corrosive acid than alkaline and Ni-Cads. Their performance during their active life is satisfactory.

Alkaline (alkaline manganese) cost more than carbon zinc and heavy duty types and give considerably more current for a much longer period of time. They last longer in storage and are less susceptible to leakage. Their performance is better in extreme temperatures. Their use is probably cheaper in the long run than carbon zinc and heavy duty types. Their performance during their active life is satisfactory.

NiCad Rechargeable (nickel cadmium) can be recharged and used over and over hundreds of times. Manufacturers claim they can be recharged 1,000 times. They are more expensive than the above three types. Longer life and best performance can be obtained if they are used often and recharged immediately at room temperature. They will take a "set" if repeatedly used the same length of time. For example, if repeatedly used one hour per day, and then recharged, the NiCads will "set" themselves for this length of time, and one hour is the maximum length they will deliver current. It's good to let the batteries occasionally run down completely before recharging them. At least once every three months com-

Because many detector owners believe that using NiCad rechargeable batteries saves them money, Garrett offers various types of rechargers for these batteries.

397

pletely discharge and recharge NiCads to restore a full charge and extend their life. NiCads will power a given circuit only 40% to 50% as long as carbon zinc. For example, if carbon zinc batteries power your detector 20 hours, NiCads will power it for eight to ten hours. Since NiCad operating voltage is less than carbon zinc, NiCads will test lower on a detector's battery check system. Their performance during their active life is satisfactory.

Speaker Contamination

Contamination such as dirt, black magnetic sand, small metal shavings and other things can fall into a searchcoil's cover or a detector's speaker. This can cause erratic sounds that are very annoying and give the appearance of a faulty detector. It is easy to clean out a searchcoil cover but if magnetic particles are sticking to the speaker cone, turn the detector upside down so that the particles can fall out of the detector. Turn on the detector and adjust it to make a sound. Sometimes, the vibrating effect of the speaker tone can loosen particles that have become magnetically attached to the speaker cone. A small magnet may pull the particles out.

Cable Connector Inspection

To investigate further if you hear erratic sounds when you lightly twist the searchcoil cable where it goes into the cable connector remove the connector cable clamp screws and visually inspect the wiring. Rotate the wire slightly, if necessary, to test for broken connections. These broken connections can be repaired there on the spot if you can use a small soldering iron. Of course, you'll want a reputable repair technician to examine your field repairs.

As a snowstorm threatens on this Colorado mountain, Charles Garrett puts the Grand Master Hunter through its paces and compares it with competitive models.

Testing Searchcoils and Cables

Erratic operations and no audio can be the fault of the searchcoil and/or cable. If you suspect this, pick up the detector, turn it on, grasp the searchcoil and gently twist it back and forth. Gently pull on the cable where it goes into the searchcoil. Sometimes wiring breaks loose at this point. Should this occur, you may find that you can press the searchcoil cable down or tape the cable in a certain way that will cause the detector to operate. With care you can continue scanning. Of course, you must eventually make permanent repairs.

Also, test your detector with another searchcoil. If the instrument works, you will know you have a faulty coil.

Intermittent Sounds

If these occur, check the battery connections. In fact, it's a good idea to check these connections occasionally just to make sure they are tight. With an eraser or some similar tool, carefully push the female connector clips toward center so that male connectors mate up in a good connection. Take care not to short out the battery. Make sure that none of your batteries are corroded. Batteries may sometimes leak a small amount of battery acid, creating a small amount of corrosion on the contacts. Visual examination will reveal corrosion. Immediately discard such batteries and clean detector battery mating terminals with a soda/water solution sparingly applied with a brush.

Non-Detection

If a coin, lying on the ground, produces no detection, make sure your detector is correctly ground balanced. If you are operating in the Discriminate mode, make certain you have not dialed in too much discrimination.

The simple *joy of discovery* has brought the author, Monty Moncrief, Bill Fulleton and Roy Lagal (from left) into the field where they find pleasure, profit and camaraderie.

Audio Threshold Drift

This was once a problem even on quality detectors, but no longer! Modern circuitry has essentially solved this problem. Still, if your detector audio threshold won't remain where you set it and slowly drifts up or down, check your batteries. At certain atmospheric and temperature conditions some detectors will require warmup time. Make sure you have allowed at least five to ten minutes adequate warmup time.

Removing your detector from an air conditioned car and then operating it in direct, hot sunlight can cause components to heat, necessitating a few minutes warmup time.

Submerged Searchcoil

If a manufacturer guarantees that searchcoils are submersible, it's all right to submerge them to the cable connector. Still, searchcoils have been known to leak. Sometimes the cable covering has been punctured, either by careless handling or by thorns when the detector was brushed up against bushes, barbed wire or other sharp object. Underwater detector searchcoil cables can be punctured by sharp coral. Water can seep into punctures and down through the cable into the searchcoil. Also, searchcoil leakage has been known to happen when a detector, after having been stored in a hot trunk, was removed and the searchcoil suddenly plunged into cold water. When hot and expanded air inside the searchcoil cooled, a vacuum formed, pulling water in through a punctured cable or at the point where the cable connector goes into the searchcoil plastic.

Whenever you suspect your detector has failed because of water seeping into the searchcoil, let it dry for several days in a warm place. Do not place it in a hot oven which can permanently damage the searchcoil. If you can locate the place where the water seeped into the coil, use silicone material which can be purchased in tubes at most hardware stores. Apply generously to the location of the leak and let it dry thoroughly before using.

After hunting in the water, do not elevate the searchcoil above the level of the control housing. Any water that is trapped in the stem may flow back into the housing. It may be necessary to remove the lower stem to remove accumulated water. Searchcoil covers are highly recommended, as they provide excellent protection for your searchcoil.

Audio and Threshold Disturbances

These probably are caused by operating the detector near high voltage power lines, televisions, TV transmission lines, airports or another metal detector. Nearby CB radios have been known to cause this problem. The solution is to get away from these electromagnetic interference sources.

When using a modern detector such as Garrett's CX models which offer more than one operating frequency, you can change frequencies. This should definitely eliminate audible disturbance if it is being caused by another detector and might overcome other types of disturbance.

If your detector appears to fail, unplug your headphones! A broken headphone wire will cause erratic operation or the detector may quit working completely. If this happens, you can continue your search using the speaker or a spare set of headphones.

Short Battery Life

If this occurs and you use NiCad rechargeable batteries, read the battery section in this chapter. If it occurs with regular batteries, place a fresh set into the detector and keep careful track of the amount of hours the new batteries give you. You may find that your faulty batteries were actually not fresh to begin with. Use headphones instead of the speaker. Your detection efficiency will improve, and you'll extend battery life because headphones use less power than a speaker.

403

No Detection Depth

If your detector achieves threshold sound and your batteries are strong, in all probability the problem lies with you and not the detector. Since searchcoils have been known to fail, test your instrument with another coil. If the detector is still giving poor depth detection, reread your Owner's Manual and carefully follow its instructions. With a test plot as described in an earlier chapter you can regularly check your detector's performance.

Check-Point Tests

Many of the previous problems and a few more, have been compiled into the following check-point test. If your detector fails to operate correctly, check the particular points below:

No operation

Battery checks zero:
Check battery holder and battery cable connector.

No Operation

Battery checks normal, power on:
Check for disconnected connectors.

Operation Normal

Battery checks zero:
Check for cold solder joints at battery check switch and other wiring points.

Sound Normal

No meter operation nor battery check:
Check for disconnected wire to meter.
Check for defective meter.
Check for cold solder joints at battery check switch.

No Sound

Meter operation normal:
Check for disconnected speaker connector.
Check for loose wires at speaker.
Check for a damaged headphone jack or plug.
Jack springs can "spring" open.

Constant Sound
Substitute a good coil.
Check touchpads, control switches and related cables.
Clean connector pins. (Use pencil eraser.)
Meter operation low or complete failure
Check for a pinched wire.
Cannot set threshold
Substitute a good coil.
Check touchpads, switches and associated cables.
Clean connector pins. (Use pencil eraser)
Intermittent operation
Check for loose terminals on the battery holder or batteries.
Check tarnish on coil connector pins.
Battery pack difficult to install
Look for restricting wiring.
Use flat file (six inch or eight inch) on battery holder or tray to smooth out nicks in runners, etc.
Check for bent or misaligned battery tray and mating connector pins.
Modes reversed
Control switch connected backwards.
Wires reversed in control switch cable connector.
Erratic operation
Substitute a good coil.
Check for excessive stem movement.
Clean coil cable connector pins.
Check for loose connector and housing screws.

Additional Tips

Your detector is a sensitive electronic instrument. Although it is built to be rugged, care in transporting and handling will extend its life.

Do not store in sunlight or subject detector to high temperatures such as those in an automobile's trunk.

Keep detector clean. Wipe housing and wash coil after use. Protect from dust and sand as much as possible.

Disassemble stem and clean after use in sandy areas, especially after working in or near salt water.

For storage periods longer than one month, remove batteries from detector and/or battery tray.

Never use any petroleum product on or in your detector. Never use any kind of spray cleaner or lubricant on the printed circuit board or controls. Such materials leave harmful residues.

And, again, don't forget to check the headphones. Headphones have been known to fail, especially the connecting wires where they are soldered to the earphone plug. With the detector turned on and operating, wiggle the headphone wires. Pull on them slightly where they enter the headphones and where the wires enter the plug. Detectors have been returned to repair stations when the only problem was the headphones.

If all of the above procedures fail and your detector still will not operate, factory or service center repairs are necessary. If you are on an extended trip, you can perhaps find a local dealer who can examine your detector. Many dealers are highly qualified and are factory trained and can make minor repairs. Some may charge a small service fee. Don't overlook this possibility as one way of getting back into the field rather than going home.

If the detector must be shipped to a service center, be sure to pack the detector very carefully and use a lot of packing material. It is not necessary, in most cases, to return stems, headphones, etc. Definitely do not include any digging tools, etc., which would add only weight and increase shipping costs. Be sure to enclose a letter with your name and address and a *brief,* yet complete, description of the problem, when and how often it occurs and any special conditions relating to the problem.

Let's hope your detector never fails in the field, but don't baby it to protect it. *Use it!* Quality detectors are built to stand up in the field even during many years of hard use.

Glossary

Chapters 7 through 16 contain additional metal detector terminology and provide more information concerning most of the terms described in this chapter. Italicized words within a definition refer to another defined term.

Air Test — A method to determine the *Sensitivity* of a metal detector; i.e., how deeply it can detect. So called, because the test is performed with nothing but air between the detector's searchcoil and the object being detected. Depending primarily on soil/mineral and atmospheric conditions but also on the detector itself, depth performance in the field can (and, usually does) vary widely from that of an air test.

Alarm — The *Signal* either audible or visual, given by a security metal detector when it detects metal on an individual being inspected. The source of every such alarm must be discovered before that individual can enter (or leave) a *Screened Area.*

All Metal Mode — The *Non-Motion Detector* mode of operation in which *all* metal targets are detected. Precise *Ground Balancing* is essential in this mode to eliminate or minimize the effects of mineralization in the soil. This mode of detector operation should be used for effective *Electronic Prospecting* or hunting for deep caches. It is also preferred by those operators who insist on "digging all targets." (See *Discriminate Mode*.)

Ampere — A unit of electrical current which measures rate of flow of electrons in a conductor.

Amplifier — An electrical circuit that draws its power from a source other than the input signal and which

407

produces an output voltage/current that is an enlarged reproduction of the essential features of the input signal.

Antenna — The component of a transmitter or receiver that actually radiates or receives the electromagnetic energy. (See *Searchcoil.*)

Archway — The name sometimes used to specify the top frame of a *Walk-through Detector.*

Audio Adjust — The control used to adjust the sound produced by a metal detector to the desired audio *Threshold* level or *Silent Audio* setting. (See *Tuning* and *Volume.*)

Automated Detector — One of the most popular types of instruments generally used today, especially for hunting coins and searching beaches. Featuring *Automatic Ground Balance*, this type of instrument is generally referred to as a *Motion Detector* since it can respond to a target only while the searchcoil is being moved over that target.

Automatic (Audio) Tuning — A circuit incorporated in most modern detectors that keeps the *Audio* level at a predetermined setting by automatically compensating for *Drift* and changing environmental conditions that often affected audio adjustment in older model *(Non-Motion)* instruments. Do not confuse with *Automatic Ground Balancing.*

Automatic Ground Balancing — A type of metal detector circuit featured on most modern instruments. With this circuit no manual adjustments are required to cancel out the detrimental effects of iron earth and salt mineralization. Some circuits on *Non-Motion Detectors* continually analyze soil beneath the detector's searchcoil and automatically adjust the detector circuitry to "ignore" minerals. This is a vitally important circuit. Do not confuse it with *Automatic Tuning,* also an integral part of most modern detectors.

Bar Graph — A series of lights that serves as a gauge to indicate the level of metal detection activity currently taking place, usually within a *Walk-through Detector.*

BFO Detector—A type of metal detector utilizing Beat Frequency Oscillator (BFO) circuitry. Such detectors were popular in the 1960s and 1970s and are important in the history of metal detector development. Although some older hobbyists continue to use such models, they must be considered obsolete. Results possible with them are totally unsuitable when compared with the capabilities of modern instruments.

Black Sand—See *Magnetic Black Sand*.

Body Mount—A somewhat uncommon detector configuration in which the control housing is strapped to the front of the upper body for use by surf hunters. (See *Hip Mount*.)

Calibration—A term that generally refers to factory adjustment of a detector to specific operating performance. For instance, accurate ore-sampling requires that a detector be set at a factory-calibrated point at which the distinction between metal and mineral is clearly recognizable. Most quality treasure hunting models are permanently calibrated and require no adjustment. Accurate calibration of walk-through security detectors is also important.

Canceling—Obsolete and imprecise terminology that is sometimes used to refer to *Ground Balancing* or *Discrimination*.

Circuitry—An electrical or electronic network providing one or more closed electrical paths. More specifically, it is a grouping of components and wiring in devices designed to perform some particular function or group of functions. Examples of circuits within a metal detector are transmitter circuit, receiver circuit, antenna circuit and audio amplifier circuit. (See *Microprocessor*.)

Circuit Board—The thin sheet of material upon which electronic components are mounted If the circuit board is completely self-contained, it is usually referred to as a "module." Circuit boards may be hand-wired or have the interconnectors printed electrochemically upon them.

Such modules are then designated PCB (printed circuit board). (See *Surface-mount PCB*.)

Classification, Audio—An audible method (or methods) for classifying detected targets into conductivity classes or categories. (See *Coin Alert*.)

Classification, Visual—A visual (metered or light) method (or methods) for classifying detected targets into conductivity classes or categories. (See *Meter* and *Graphic Target Analyzer*.)

Coil—See *Searchcoil*.

Coin Alert™—An audible method of producing a special tone only when coins (or high conductivity silver and gold items) are detected. All other detected targets produce normal accept/reject signals. A Garrett trademark.

Component—In a metal detector this term generally refers to an essential part of a circuit; i.e., resistor, capacitor, coil, tube, transistor, etc. The term can also refer to complete functional units of a system; i.e., transmitter, receiver, searchcoil, etc.

Conductance—The ability of an element, component or device to permit the passage of an electrical current; i.e, *Eddy Currents*. It is the reciprocal function of resistance.

Conductor—A wire, bar or metal mass (coin, gold nugget, ship's hull, etc.) capable of conducting electrical current.

Control Housing—The container in which is placed all or most of the electronic assembly and batteries of a metal detector. Those on older model detectors are usually bulky and awkward-looking metal boxes. Newer models use high strength engineering polymers for compact, stylish housings. On most detectors this control housing *must* be protected from water.

Depth Detection—A term usually used to describe the ability of an instrument to detect metal objects to specific depths. (See *Sensitivity*.)

Depth Penetration — Applied to electronic metal detectors, the term is used to define the specific distance into a particular medium (soil, water, air, etc.) that the electromagnetic field of a metal detector is capable of satisfactorily penetrating. This affects the *Depth Detection* abilities of an instrument.

Depth Scale — The markings (or LCD indicators) on a *Meter* or *Graphic Target Analyzer* that report the depth of coin-sized targets.

Detection Pattern — See *Searchcoil Detection Pattern.*

Detuning — A term with older model detectors that was required to describe the "down tuning" necessary to enable precise *Pinpointing.* Modern electronic circuitry with *Automatic Tuning* and *Electronic Pinpointing* have virtually eliminated any need for detuning.

Discriminate Mode — The mode of operation of a metal detector in which metallic targets are specifically designated by the operator to be eliminated from detection. (See *Discrimination.*) Many modern detectors, particularly *Motion Detectors* (see *Automated Detector*) can be operated only in the Discriminate mode. (See *All Metal Mode.*)

Discrimination — The ability of specific circuits within a detector to eliminate from detection certain undesirable metallic objects. Using a detector in its Discriminate mode, a detector operator chooses which types of targets are to be eliminated through proper manipulation of discrimination control(s). This function is sometimes described as *Elimination.* (See *Notch Discrimination.*)

Drift — A term used, primarily with older model detectors, to describe the inclination of an instrument's tuning to vary from its setting because of temperature, battery condition, faulty components, poor design, etc. Drift is seldom a problem with modern detectors,

Eddy Currents — Also called Foucalt currents, they are induced in a conductive mass by the variations of electromagnetic energy radiated from the detector and tend to flow in the surfacer layers of the target mass. Flow is directly proportional to frequency, the density of the electromagnetic field and the conductivity of the metal. Eddy currents flowing in a target produce the same effect as that of a shorted-turn secondary and are a primary electrical phenomenon that produces metal detection signals in all metal detectors.

Earplug — Metal detector accessory that converts electrical energy waves into audible waves of identical form. Used with security hand-held detectors in installations or environments where no audible alarm is desired. (See *Headphones*.)

Electromagnetic Field — An invisible field that surrounds the transmitter winding; generated by the alternating radio frequency current that circulates in the transmitter antenna windings.

Electromagnetic Induction — See *Induced Current*.

Electronic Circuit — A circuit wherein current flows through wires, resistors, inductors, capacitors, transistors and other components.

Electronic Pinpointing — A detector mode that causes a "sharpening" of detector signals when objects are detected. An electronic aid to precise target location.

Electronic Prospecting — The use of a metal detector to search for gold, silver or other precious metals in any form. Most common electronic prospecting is the search for gold nuggets with a detector that offers manual ground balancing capability.

Elimination — Terminology that is sometimes used to explain characteristics more accurately described as *Ground Balancing* or *Discrimination*.

Elliptical Searchcoil — A specially designed oval-shaped searchcoil with length approximately twice its width. Intended initially for use by electronic prospectors in tight, rocky spaces, their design has now been enhanced to provide "knife- edge" scanning that isolates good targets in areas with quantities of trash metal. (See *Searchcoil*.)

412

False Detection—Responses to objects or anomalies other than sought metallic targets.

Faraday Shield—The conductive covering surrounding the searchcoil antenna wires (and other components) of a metal detector. Its purpose is to provide electrostatic shielding and reduce *False Detection* signals caused by ground and wet grass capacitance effects.

Fast Track™—A type of detector circuitry, requiring computerized microprocessor controls, that automatically *Ground Balances* a detector's *All Metal* (non-motion) circuitry. A Garrett trademark. (See *Ground Balance* and *Ground Track*.)

Ferrous—Pertains to iron and iron compounds, such as nails, bottlecaps, cannons or ships hulls.

Firmware—Computer programs stored permanently as memory in the microprocessors(s) of a computerized detector.

Frequency—Applied to alternating current or voltage, the term describes the number of periodic recurrences of a complete alternation or cycle zero, plus-maximum, zero, negative-maximum, zero, current or voltage levels that occur within one second.

Frequency Designations

Very Low	VLF	3-30 kHz (cycles or 1,000 Hertz)
Low	LF	30-300 kHz
Medium	MF	300-3000 kHz
High	HF	3-30 mHz (cycles/10,000 Hertz)
Very High	VHF	30-300 mHz
Ultra High	UHF	300-3,000 mHz
Super High	SHF	3,000-30,000 mHz

Gain—An increase in voltage, current or power with respect to a previous quantity or a standard reference. Gain occurs in vacuum tubes, transistors, transformers, etc. as gain per component, gain per stage and gain per assembly. Such gain can be measured in terms of voltage, current, power or decibels.

Graphic Target Analyzer™ — That device on a metal detector that reports continuously and visually on an *LCD* such information as depth and type of target, audio and tone levels, sensitivity, battery condition, etc. A Garrett trademark.

Ground Balancing — The ability of a metal detector to eliminate (ignore or cancel) the detection effect of iron minerals or wetted salt. (See *Automatic* and *Manual Ground Balancing, Fast Track* and *Ground Track.*)

Ground Track™ — A type of detector circuitry, requiring computerized microprocessor controls, that automatically *Ground Balances* a detector's *All Metal* (non-motion) circuitry and continually maintains proper ground balance while the detector is being *Scanned.* A Garrett trademark. (See *Fast Track* and *Ground Balance.*)

Hand-held Detector — A metal detector that can be held in the hand of an operator. These are generally used in security environments for bodily inspection of individuals. They are used separately or as part of a screening system to support *Walk-through Detectors.* Treasure hunters use hand-held detectors to scan behind walls, inside boxes or in other areas where conventional searchcoils will not reach.

Headphones — Metal detector accessory that converts electrical energy waves into audible waves of identical form. Used by treasure hunters in place of detector loudspeakers, especially in noisy or windy locations. Because they present the audible signals more effectively than a loudspeaker, headphones are recommended for use any time possible with a metal detector. They are less susceptible to damage by rain and utilize less battery power than a speaker. (See *Earplug.*)

Hertz — Unit of frequency equal to one cycle per second.

Hip Mount — A common detector configuration used in many types of treasure hunting in which the control housing is strapped to the hip. This is a popular configuration for surf hunters since a control housing on the hip can be easier to manage than one on a stem. (See *Hip Mount.*)

Hot Rock — A mineralized rock that produces a positive signal in a metal detector.

Induced Current — The current that flows in a conductor or conductive mass when a varying electromagnetic field is present. Except for eddy currents, induced or secondary currents flow only where there is a complete circuit or closed loop. *Eddy Currents* are, in themselves, closed loops.

LCD — A constantly operating visual display, such as the letters and numbers on the *Graphic Target Analyzer* of the Garrett Ultra detectors. The letters LCD literally stand for liquid crystal display.

Magnetic Black Sand — Magnetite, a magnetic oxide of iron and, in a lesser degree, hematite; may also contain titanium and other rare-earth minerals but serves mainly as an indicator of the possible presence of *Placer* gold.

Magnetometer — Not a metal detector, even though the term is sometimes used improperly when metal detectors are discussed. Rather, this is an instrument for measuring magnetic intensity, especially the earth's magnetic field. Treasure hunters searching for large masses of metal such as a ship often use a magnetometer to locate the increased magnetic field density caused by the hull.

Manual Ground Balance — The type of metal detector circuit that first offered instrumentation to permit canceling (ignoring or eliminating) the detrimental effects of iron earth and salt mineralization. Not required or included on *Automated Detectors.* On some modern instruments this circuit presents an important option to *Automatic Ground Balance* when extremely precise ground balancing is required, especially in *Electronic Prospecting.* Manual Ground Balance is a feature of the *Non-Motion Detector.*

Manual Inspection — The physical inspection and searching of hand-held items with a security metal detector.

For a screening system to be effective all hand-held items must be searched either manually or by x-ray before they can be taken into a *Screened Area.*

Matrix—The entire area below a searchcoil that is "illuminated" by the transmitted *Electromagnetic Field* transmitted from the antenna in the *Searchcoil.* A matrix may wholly, partially or intermittently contain conductive and/or non-conductive targets which may be of either ferrous or non-ferrous materials. The matrix may contain moisture, sulfides, metallic ores, etc. The *Detection Pattern* is only a portion of the matrix.

Metal Detector—An electronic instrument or device, usually battery-powered, capable sensing the presence of conductive objects lying underground, underneath water, hidden on an individual or otherwise out of sight; then, providing its operator with an audible and/or visual indication of that presence.

Metal/Mineral—Refers primarily to that "Zero" *Discrimination* point on a properly calibrated detector at which time any signal given by the detector will indicate that a target is metal, not mineral.

Meter—That device on a metal detector that reports information visually concerning depth and type of target, battery condition, ground conditions, etc.

Microprocessor—An integrated circuit that contains the necessary elements of a small digital computer. These circuits are now being used in the most advanced detectors. The "memory" of a microprocessor is preprogrammed to permit a detector to automatically perform numerous functions that even the most knowledgeable operator would normally have to carry out manually. In addition, microprocessor-controlled *Circuitry* performs these functions instantly and simultaneously as well as automatically.

Mode—The manner in which a detector operates, usually controlled by the operator. Modern detectors generally offer two modes, *All Metal* and *Discriminate.*

Motion Detector – See *Automated Detector.*

Narrow Scan – A scan width less than full searchcoil diameter. In earlier days, TR detector searchcoils scanned an effective area equivalent only to about 30-40% of the diameter of the searchcoil being used.

Non-Ferrous – Pertains to non-iron metals and compounds, such as brass, silver, gold, lead, aluminum, etc.

Non-Motion Detector – A type of instrument that permits the searchcoil to be hovered directly above a target for any length of time while detecting it. Such instruments generally require *Manual Ground Balance* and are used when maximum depth is required; i.e., for *Electronic Prospecting* and cache hunting.

Notch Discrimination – A special type of circuitry, requiring computerized microprocessor controls, that enables a detector to easily eliminate from detection specific undesirable metallic objects. Using an instrument with *Notch Discrimination*, a detector operator can be highly selective in choosing just which targets are to be sought and which are to be avoided. (See *Discrimination.*)

Null – A tuning or audio adjustment condition that results in "quiet" or zero audio operation.

Optical Monitor – Important component of a quality *Walk-through* (security) metal detector that enables it to detect more effectively by neutralizing the environment. Because instruments with this feature detect only when individuals and/or objects are passing through them, they can ignore all other influences. Also counts individuals passing through.

Oscillator – The variation of an observable or otherwise detectable quantity of motion about a mean value.

Overshoot – A "false signal" characteristic once common but essentially eliminated by modern circuitry.

PCB – Printed circuit board. (See *Circuit Board* and *Surface-mount PC Board.*)

Penetration – The ability of a detector to penetrate earth material, air, wood, rock, water, etc. to locate metal targets. Penetration is a function of detector design and type of detector, as well as the material being penetrated.

Performance — The ability of a detector to carry out the functions of which the manufacturer has claimed this instrument is capable.

Permeability — The measure of how a material performs as a path for magnetic lines of force as measured against the permeability standard, air. Air is rated as 1 on the permeability scale; diamagnetic materials, less than 1; paramagnetic materials, slightly more than 1; and ferromagnetic materials, much more than 1.

Phase — The angular (mathematical or time concept) relationship that exists between current and voltage in all AC circuits, regardless of type. When both voltage and current cycles rise and fall in exact unison, voltage and current are said to be in phase. When the rise of current flow lags behind the rise of voltage, the circuit is said to be inductive. Conversely, when the rise of current leads the rise of voltage, the circuit is said to be capacitive.

Phase Angle — The number of angular (mathematical concept) degrees that AC current and voltage peaks are out of phase — or out of step with each other.

Pinpointing — The ability of a detector operator to determine exactly where a detected target is located. (See *Electronic Pinpointing.*)

Placer — Pronounced like "plaster" without the "t," the term describes an accumulation of gold, black magnetic sand and other elements of specific gravity higher than sand, rock, etc. found in the same area.

Portal Metal Detector — Term sometimes used to describe a *Walk-through Detector.*

Pulse Induction — A metal detection technique that employs the phenomenon (characteristic) of electromagnetic decay to sense the presence of a conductive material (metal). The system operates by delivering short bursts of energy to the antenna followed by a passive period when the antenna can sense the decaying electromagnetic field induced in a target. Sea Hunter underwater detectors and Magnascanner *Walk-through Detectors* utilize the pulse induction method of detection.

Push-button — A type of mechanical control used in some, generally older, types of metal detectors. Distinctly different from the more modern electronic *Touchpads.*

Receiver — That portion of the circuitry of a metal detector that receives information created by the presence of targets, acts upon that information and processes it according to intentions indicated by instrument design or actions of the THer; then activates the readout system in proportion to the nature of the received data.

Receiver Gain — The amplification of input signals to whatever extent required.

Response Time — Time delay in audio performance of a metal detector between detection of a target and the report of this detection by the instrument's audio and/or visual indicators. Once a critical factor, response time is virtually instantaneous on modern instruments.

Retuning — Important on older instruments, this act of restoring the audio threshold of a detector to a predetermined level is performed automatically on modern instruments. Manual retuning is offered as an option on some more expensive detectors because of its occasional importance in areas with large amounts of metallic junk or in electronic prospecting with *Manual Ground Balance.*

Scanning — The actual movement of a searchcoil over the ground or other area being searched; also describes the physical search of an individual with a hand-held instrument.

Screening — A system of guarding and protecting whereby electronic devices and *Manual Inspection* are employed to prevent forbidden items from entering or being taken out of a *Screened Area.*

Screened Area — The secured area designated for protection by an effective security system. Absolutely no person is to be permitted within this area unless that person has been properly inspected. Access to a secure area must be rigidly controlled by barriers and/or locked doors.

Searchcoil—The component of a metal detector that houses the transmitter and receiver antennas. The searchcoil is usually attached to the control housing by way of an adjustable connecting stem. The searchcoil is scanned over the ground, or other area being searched.

Searchcoil Detection Pattern—That portion of the *Electromagnetic Field* in which metal detection takes place. It is located out from and along the axis of the searchcoil generally, starting at full searchcoil width and tapering to a point at some distance from the searchcoil. Its actual width and depth depend upon the type and strength of signals being transmitted by the detector as well as the size and nature of any given target.

Sensitivity—The ability of a detector to sense conductivity changes within the detection pattern. Sensitivity of a detector increases inversely with the size of a metallic target that is detectable. One of the most important operational characteristics of an electronic metal detector, sensitivity determines the actual size of targets that an instrument will detect and the depth to which they can be detected. Although sensitivity is ultimately determined by design characteristics of a detector, a control on most instruments permits some regulation by the operator.

Signal—Generally describes the electromagnetic data received by the detector from a target and the audio and/or visual response generated by it. (See *Alarm*.)

Silent Audio—The tuning of the audio level of a detector in the "silent" (just below *Threshold*) zone. When operating in this fashion, the operator hears no sound at all until a target is detected.

Splashproof—A designation of environmental protection that indicates that minor wetting of detector's housing and/or searchcoil (light mist, dew, etc.) will not affect its operation.

Stability — Ability of metal detector circuits to remain tuned to predetermined operating points. Once a critical aspect of detector operation, now a standard operating feature of any quality detector.

Submersible — A designation of environmental protection that indicates that complete submersion of a detector's housing and/or search will not affect its operation. Always note depth to which submersibility is permitted. All Garrett searchcoils can be submerged to the connector. The Sea Hunter detector can be submerged to 200 feet, the Beach Hunter to six feet.

Super Sniper™ — A Garrett trademark used to describe its 4 1/2-inch searchcoil and the method for using it to enhance individual target detection in specialized situations. This type of treasure hunting is especially effective for hunting in areas with large amounts of metal "junk" or near metallic objects such as fences, posts, buildings, etc.

Surface Area — That dimension of a target lying parallel to the plane of the detector searchcoil; in other words, that part of the target that is "looking at" the underside of the searchcoil. This is the area through which the electromagnetic field lines pass and on which eddy currents are generated.

Surface-mount PC Board — Describes the modern method of manufacturing printed circuit boards (PCBs) in which miniaturized components are all mounted on the board's surface for increased design efficiency, production economy and more reliable performance. (See *Circuit Board.*)

Sweeping — See *Scanning.*

TH — An abbreviation for Treasure Hunt, used in THer, THing, etc.

Threshold — Adjustable level of audio sound at which a metal detector is operated when searching for treasure.

Touchpad — A type of electronic control popular on modern detectors because of its effectiveness and dependability.

TR Detector — The type of metal detector that first utilized the Transmitter-Receiver circuit, which is essentially the circuitry of all modern *VLF* instruments. When first introduced, TR Detectors represented a distinct improvement over existing *BFO* models, offering *Discrimination* and other features. As such, these instruments are important in the history of metal detector development. Although some older hobbyists continue to use TR detectors, they must be considered obsolete. Results possible with them are totally unsuitable when compared with the capabilities of modern instruments, even with the similarities in circuitry.

TR Disc — A non-motion mode of metal detector operation in which discrimination can be achieved with *Manual Ground Balance*. Used almost exclusively in *Electronic Prospecting.*

Tuning — That adjustment an operator makes to bring the detector's audio level to a previously designated *Threshold* level. While quite important, this adjustment is no longer of particular concern to THers since it is accomplished automatically by the circuitry of modern detectors.

Universal Capabilities — Describes a metal detector that can effectively accomplish most THing tasks...coin hunting, beach and surf hunting, ghost towning, electronic prospecting, cache hunting, etc. (See *Versatility*.)

Versatility — A measure of the applications in which a detector can be used effectively. In other words, for how many different kinds of hunting can a particular detector be used? (See *Universal Capabilities*.)

Visual Indicator — Generally means *Meter* on a THing detector, although some more modern instruments utilize an *LCD*. Some security devices use other visual indicators (*Bar Graphs* and lights) not related to either an LCD or a pointer-type meter. (See *Graphic Target Analyzer*.)

VLF Detector — The initials stand for Very Low *Frequency*, a segment of the RF spectrum that includes frequencies from 3 kHz to 30 kHz. All modern instruments (except Pulse Induction-types) can be designated as VLF detectors.

Volume Control — A control, generally resistance, used to limit voltage and/or current in an audio amplifier and, thereby, control volume of sound or "loudness" when a target is encountered. Do not confuse with the audio adjustments involved with establishing a *Threshold* setting. This term also denotes the control that regulates the level of sound produced by the *Alarm* of a security detector.

Walk-through Detector — Resembling the frame of a door, this style of security metal detector is designed to determine whether metallic objects are being carried on the body or in the clothing of an individual passing through it. When such items are detected, the instrument signals their detection with an audible and/or visual alarm(s). The *Sensitivity* of such a detector can be regulated to determine what items (amount) of metal will be detected.

Waterproof — A designation of environmental protection that indicates that heavy rainfall or splashing surf on a detector's *Control Housing* and/or *Searchcoil* (light mist, dew, etc.) will not affect its operation. It does not mean that the housing and/or coil is *Submersible*.

Wetted Salt — The most prevalent mineral encountered in beach and ocean hunting; is ignored by *Pulse Induction* and *VLF detectors* with *Ground Balancing* capabilities, either automatic or manual.

Wide Scan — Generally implies that the scanning width (detection pattern) of a detector, as the searchcoil passes over the ground, is equal to the full width (or wider) of the diameter of the searchcoil being used. This term is particularly appropriate to *Elliptical Searchcoils,* which can effectively scan an area full length toe to heel.

Ram Books

Coin hunting...beach and surf hunting...cache hunting...electronic prospecting! All of these subjects--and much more--are covered in detail in the *Treasure Hunting Texts* available from Garrett dealers. Written by experienced hobbyists and treasure hunters, these books combine stories of adventure and discovery with practical, down-to-earth advice.

True Treasure Tales are fictionalized accounts of real treasure hunts. Share the thrill of discovery with a new metal detecting hero, Gar Starrett.

In the *Garrett Guide* series a single aspect of treasure hunting is presented in each convenient, pocket-sized booklet designed to be taken into the field and used for on-the-spot help.

Treasure Hunting Texts

The New Successful Coin Hunting
The world's most authoritative guide to finding valuable coins, totally rewritten to include instructions for modern computerized detectors, No. 1501500.

$10.95

Modern Treasure Hunting
The practical guidebook to today's metal detectors; a "how-to" manual that carefully explains the "why" of today's detector performance, No. 1506600

$12.95

Modern Metal Detectors
Advanced handbook for field, home and classroom study to increase expertise and understanding of any kind of metal detector; rewritten for the 1990s, No. 1501700.
$14.95

Treasure Recovery from Sand and Sea
Precise instructions for reaching the "blanket of wealth" beneath sands nearby and under the world's waters, totally rewritten for the 1990's, No. 1505700.
$14.95

Sunken Treasure: How to Find it
One of the world's foremost underwater salvors shares a lifetime's experience in locating and recovering treasures from deep beneath the sea, No. 1507500.
$14.95

Treasure from British Waters
Noted British hobbyist reveals his secrets (with maps) for finding treasure on the beaches and in the surf of his native island as well as the Balearics, No. 1507600.
$7.95

Buried Treasure of the United States
Complete field guide for finding treasure; includes state-by-state listing of thousands of sites where treasure is believed to exist, No. 1505500.
$10.95

Modern Electronic Prospecting
  Explains how to use a modern detector to find gold nuggets and veins of precious metal; includes illustrated instructions for panning, dredging, No. 1506700.

$9.95

Weekend Prospecting
  Offers simple "how-to" instructions for enjoying holidays in the great outdoors profitably by locating and recovering gold, No. 1505000.

$3.95

Gold Panning is Easy
  This excellent field guide shows the beginner exactly how to find and pan gold; follow these instructions and perform like a professional, No. 1505400.

$6.95

True Treasure Tales **-- Gar Starrett Adventures**
Each $2.95

The Secret of John Murrell's Vault
  Join THers in their effort to recover an outlaw's fabulous treasure cached in a Louisiana cemetery more than 150 years ago, No. 1506900.

The Missing Nez Perce Gold
  An Idaho couple seek Gar Starrett's help in finding the cache of gold coins left behind when Chief Joseph and the Nez Perce tribe fled to Canada, No. 1507200.

Garrett Guides -- **Pocket-size Field Guides**
Each $1.00

An Introduction to Metal Detectors
Find More Treasure With the Right Metal Detectors
Metal Detectors Can Help You Find Coins
Money Caches Are Waiting to be Found
Find an Ounce of Gold a Day
Find Wealth on the Beach
Find Wealth in the Surf
Avoid Detector Problems
Use the Super Sniper

A convenient order form for these RAM books can be found on the last page of this book.

For additional information call (214) 278-6151.

Garrett Video Library

Outdoor Family Entertainment and Instructional Programs. Available in VHS video cassette.

Each Video $19.95

Sand & Sea Treasures

Two slide/videos that take the viewer treasure hunting in recreational areas and a castle are available on a single VHS video tape. No. 1670300.

Treasure Recovery from Sand & Sea--No matter what you know about treasure hunting with a metal detector on land or what you think you know about hunting in the water, this slide show video will provide valuable "how-to" tips about discovering lost wealth. A companion to this book. 25 minutes, color.

Treasures of the Indian Ocean--Robert Marx, internationally known American underwater archaeologist and treasure salvor, leads a team of professionals on a search for the 18th century wreck site of the French merchant ship, the *St. Geran*, wrecked in 1744 off Madagascar. This color/sound film of historical interest shows many different methods of recovery, as well as touching on research and archaeological procedures. 25 minutes, color.

Southwestern Treasures

Two colorful Southwestern treasure tales are available in a single VHS video tape. No. 1670100.

Treasures of Mexico--Host Charles Garrett invites fellow treasure hunters to accompany the Garrett field team on an outing to the fabulous Cobre Canyon, near Batopilas, Mexico. The team searches a beautiful old city, silver-laden rivers, and finally, an old mine. The video makes vividly clear how productive electronic prospecting was in these areas. 25 minutes, color.

Gold and Treasure Adventures--Charles Garrett describes a competition treasure hunt in the California desert and a treasure hunting trip to Europe. While in the desert, Charles and a field team hunt an old mining area where many good recoveries are made. Actor John Quade is featured and narrates part of the film. 25 minutes, color.

Treasure Adventures

These two treasure adventures filmed on both sides of the globe are available in a VHS video tape. No. 16702000.

The Silent Past--An old prospector, killed by hostile Indians after he discovers a silver mine, is transformed into a ghost whose destiny is to roam the Big Bend area of West Texas until one of his descendants comes to the area. His great-great-grandson and parents travel to the area and discover many artifacts buried during the passage of time. 25 minutes, color.

Tracking Outlaw Treasure--This beautiful production in vivid color tells an exciting tale of a modern-day search for the cache hidden after a stagecoach robbery more than a century ago. The use of advanced electronic detectors and research techniques is carefully explained by Charles Garrett and his companions as they seek the treasure. 21 minutes, color.

Gold Panning is Easy

The program illustrates methods of using the *gravity trap* and other pans in both wet and dry panning for gold and other materials of high specific gravity. Tells where and how to locate gold. Techniques of Roy Lagal from the book of the same name are demonstrated in Arizona by Virgil Hutton and introduced by Charles Garrett. No. 1670400, 25 minutes, color.

Weekend Prospecting

This production was filmed while Charles Garrett, Roy Lagal, Tommie T. Long and Virgil Hutton were actually hunting gold in the Northwestern United States. Thus, the hobby of "weekend prospecting " is accurately depicted, showing techniques for locating and recovering gold that all family members can put to productive use during vacations and weekend trips to gold country. Electronic prospecting with metal detectors, and both wet and dry gold panning and recovery techniques are fully illustrated. Informative, instructional and interesting with gorgeous Northwest United States scenery. Roy Lagal's book of the same name (see Page 427) is a companion piece that covers in greater detail everything presented in this video production, which is introduced by Charles Garrett. No. 1670600, 50 minutes, color.

Instruction Videos

An "Illustrated Instruction Manuals" best describes each of this series of videos demonstrating the use of Garrett detectors. In addition to explaining visually all that is in the Owner's Manual for each detector, these videos illustrate various types of treasure hunting with the detector.

Grand Master Hunter CX II, No. 1671000
(Also applicable for Master Hunter CX)
Ultra GTA 1000, No. 1671200
Ultra GTA 500, No. 1671400
Freedom 2 Plus, No. 1671500

A convenient order form for these Garrett Videos can be found at the end of this book.

For additional information call (214) 278-6151.

LETTERS, CERTIFICATES AND AWARDS RECEIVED BY GARRETT ELECTRONICS AND THE AUTHOR

To Charles Garrett
With my personal best wishes and appreciation to you for
a job well done in supplying metal detection equipment
and security training at the 1984 Republican National
Convention held in Dallas, Texas.

Ronald Reagan

J.Walter Coughlin & Associates
6907 Kings Hollow Drive · Dallas, Texas 75248 · (214) 744-7082

September 4, 1984

Mr. Charles Garrett
President
Garrett Electronics, Inc.
2814 National Drive
Garland, Texas 75041

Dear Charles,

Thank you for making the 1984 Republican National Convention such a great success.

You and your professional staff, as well as your excellent equipment, are what allowed all of the security aspects of the convention to work perfectly.

All of us involved in security with the Republican National Committee owe you and your company a great deal of gratitude.

Thank you.

Sincerely,

J. Walter Coughlin
Director of Security
Republican National Convention

JWC:tg

Security Consultants

Charles L. Garrett

IN RECOGNITION AND
APPRECIATION FOR
YOUR CONTRIBUTION TO
THE SUCCESS OF THE
GAMES OF THE XXIII OLYMPIAD
LOS ANGELES, 1984

LOS ANGELES
OLYMPIC
ORGANIZING
COMMITTEE

© 1980 L.A. Olympic Committee   TM

PAUL ZIFFREN, CHAIRMAN

PETER V. UEBERROTH, PRESIDENT

HARRY L. USHER, EXECUTIVE VICE PRESIDENT
AND GENERAL MANAGER

Garrett Metal Detectors

IN RECOGNITION AND
APPRECIATION FOR
YOUR CONTRIBUTION TO
THE SUCCESS OF THE
GAMES OF THE XXIII OLYMPIAD
LOS ANGELES, 1984

LOS ANGELES
OLYMPIC
ORGANIZING
COMMITTEE

© 1980 L.A. Olympic Committee ™

PAUL ZIFFREN, CHAIRMAN

PETER V. UEBERROTH, PRESIDENT

HARRY L. USHER, EXECUTIVE VICE PRESIDENT
AND GENERAL MANAGER

FROM THE COUNTESS OF STRATHMORE, GLAMIS CASTLE, ANGUS, SCOTLAND
GLAMIS 244

4 June 1986

Charles Garrett Esq.,
President
Garrett Metal Detectors
Garrett Electronics Inc.,
2814 National Drive
Garland
Texas 75401
U.S.A.

Dear Mr. Garrett,

It was such a pleasure to meet you here at Glamis at the Metal Detectors Rally and what a wonderful surprise I got when you presented me with your wonderful Garrett Detector! I was really delighted to be given it and feel very proud to own such a beautiful detector. All my family are equally thrilled with it and have been trying it out. It was enormously kind of you to give it to me and I do thank you so very much indeed for it.

I do so hope you will be able to return to Glamis one day and spend a bit more time here, and I certainly hope I can see you on my next visit to Dallas. As I told you there is just the slightest possibility that I might visit Austin, Texas, during the International Gathering of the Clans between the 8th and 16th November this year.

Again, may I say what a pleasure it was to meet you and your two colleagues.

With my most grateful and appreciative thanks for such a wonderful gift, and with warmest good wishes.

Yours sincerely.

Mary Strathmore

 **SEOUL1988**

SEOUL OLYMPIC ORGANIZING COMMITTEE

Olympic Center, Kangdong-gu, Seoul, Korea
Telex: K21988/Cable Address: SLOOC/C.P.O. Box 1988
Telephone:

Our Ref: SECURITY

Date: Feb. 26, 1988

TO WHOM IT MAY CONCERN :

After careful evaluation of security equipment on the world market, Garrett Security Systems, 2814 National Drive, Garland, Texas 75041 USA, was selected to provide electronic security equipment for the 1986 Asian Games held in Seoul.

We have again evaluated security equipment on the world market and have, for the second time, selected Garrett Security Systems equipment for the 1988 Olympic Games.

In addition to the outstanding performance of Garrett Security Systems' equipment we have been pleased with their company's assistance in setting up the equipment, providing operator training and their overall program that has been beneficial in our total security effort.

We are very pleased to recommend Garrett Security Systems for your security program.

Sung Dae Suh
Security Administrator
Security Department

DEFENSE LOGISTICS AGENCY
HEADQUARTERS
CAMERON STATION
ALEXANDRIA, VIRGINIA 22304-6100   1 8 JAN 1991

ACCEPTANCE OF A GIFT IN SUPPORT OF
OPERATION DESERT SHIELD

Mr. Charles Garrett
Garrett Security Systems
2814 National Drive
Garland, TX 75041-2397

DESCRIPTION OF GIFT: Security Screening Equipment

ESTIMATED VALUE: $17,995.00

Dear Mr. Garrett:

Thank you for your recent donation to the Department of
Defense in support of Operation Desert Shield.

Your gift will be used to further our mission in response
to recent events in the Middle East. Your generosity does
more than save the taxpayers money -- it lets our fighting
forces and the whole world know that the American people
are concerned about the welfare of our troops.

Please accept our sincere thanks. Your generous offer is a
wonderful show of concern and support for those serving our
country overseas.

Sincerely,

JOHN R. MARSHALL, JR.
Colonel, USAF
Senior Military Assistant
to the Assistant Director,
Policy & Plans

Thank you for your generous efforts in behalf
of the United States Armed Forces serving in
the Persian Gulf. The overwhelming support
of the American people, expressed time and
again through selfless actions like yours,
has contributed not only to the personal
well-being and morale of our troops but also
to the success of our mission. You have my
heartfelt appreciation. God bless you.

Department of Defense

Certificate of Appreciation
in support of
Operations in the Persian Gulf

To all who shall see this greeting,
this is to certify that

Charles Garrett
Garrett Security Systems

has earned grateful appreciation for an unselfish and
generous contribution to the men and women of the
United States Armed Forces serving in the Persian Gulf

APR 1991
_____
Date

Secretary of Defense

In Special Recognition and Appreciation

of

Garrett Electronics

for

their continued support of the nation's sheriffs
and the advancement of law enforcement capabilities and services
through participation as an exhibitor

at

The National Sheriffs' Association

Annual Informative Conference

1984

COMMONWEALTH OF KENTUCKY

WALLACE G. WILKINSON

GOVERNOR

To all to Whom These Presents Shall Come, Greeting:

Know Ye, That HONORABLE CHARLES GARRETT, GARLAND, TEXAS

Is Commissioned A

KENTUCKY COLONEL

I hereby confer this honor with all the rights, privileges and responsibilities thereunto appertaining.

In testimony whereof, I have caused these letters to be made patent, and the seal of the Commonwealth to be hereunto affixed. Done at Frankfort, the 24TH day of JULY in the year of our Lord, one thousand and nine hundred and 89 and in the one hundred and 98TH year of the Commonwealth.

By the Governor

Secretary of State

By

Assistant Secretary of State

Garrett Videos

Please send the following videos:

$19.95 Each

☐ Southwestern Treasures
   Treasure of Mexico
   Gold and Treasure Adventure

☐ Treasure Adventures
   Silent Past
   Tracking Outlaw Treasure

☐ Sand and Sea Treasures
   Treasure Recovery from Sand and Sea
   Treasures of the Indian Ocean

☐ Gold Panning is Easy
   Gold Panning Instruction Video

☐ Weekend Prospecting
   Gold Hunting Instruction Video

☐ Grand Master Hunter CX II
   Instruction Video
   (Also applicable for Master Hunter CX)

☐ Ultra GTA 1000
   Instruction Video

☐ Ultra GTA 500
   Instruction Video

☐ Freedom 2 Plus
   Instruction Video

Garrett Video Productions
2814 National Drive
Garland, TX 75041

Please add $1 for
each video ordered
(maximum of $3)
for handling charges.

Total for items $_____

8.25% Tax (Texas residents) $_____

Handling Charge $_____

TOTAL $_____

Enclosed check or money order

I prefer to order through

☐ MasterCard
☐ Visa

_____
Credit Card Number

_____
Expiration Date   **Phone Number (8 a.m. to 4 p.m.)**

_____
Signature (Credit Card orders must be signed.)

_____
NAME

_____
ADDRESS (For Shipping)

_____
CITY, STATE, ZIP